THE UNTOLD STORY OF DETROIT'S
SECRET CONCEPT CAR BUILDER

LEON
DIXON

CREATIVE
INDUSTRIES OF DETROIT

CarTech®

CarTech®, Inc.
838 Lake Street South
Forest Lake, MN 55025
Phone: 651-277-1200 or 800-551-4754
Fax: 651-277-1203
www.cartechbooks.com

Edit by Wes Eisenschenk
Design Concept by Connie DeFlorin
Layout by Monica Seiberlich

ISBN 978-1-61325-213-0
Item No. CT544

Library of Congress Cataloging-in-Publication Data Available

Written, edited, and designed in the U.S.A.
Printed in China
10 9 8 7 6 5 4 3 2 1

Front Flap: *Famous entryway of Progressive Welder in late 1940s. Sign above was trimmed in neon, illuminated at night. Doorway later became main entry to Creative Industries headquarters. Note the multiple confusing addresses of 3050 and 3070. The address became 3080 when Creative occupied building.*

Title Page: *Photo replaces a thousand words. Dick Teague was not previously included in Packard concept pics, but is now shown seated at the wheel while Ed Macauley merely looks on with engineer Bill Graves. Photo taken on Concord Avenue outside of Packard Plant. Note "Gray Wolf II" lettering already made and installed here prior to forced name change to "Panther."*

Table of Contents: *With higher profile quad sealed-beam headlights, nose, and tail fins, this version looks more dated but nothing like 1950s or 1960s car. Quad headlights were considered very futuristic in 1950s. Tape measure indicated large model.*

Back Cover Photos

Top: *Spring 1955. David Margolis at the wheel of Rex Terry's newly restyled experimental Packard Panther concept car in front of Creative Industries' headquarters at 3080 East Outer Drive in Detroit. Note Creative's trademark offset "V" symbol on both the building and the rear of the Panther.*

Bottom Left: *Two Mach III Mustang concepts ready for show. (Photo Courtesy Richard Rinke)*

Bottom Right: *Model, wearing beige gloves and copper color shoes, pretended to drive XM-800 version number-1. Note tinted plexiglass sun visors, copper color upholstery, and gauge faces.*

Publisher's Note: In reporting history, the images required to tell the tale will vary greatly in quality, especially by modern photographic standards. While some images in this volume are not up to those digital standards, we have included them, as we feel they are an important element in telling the story.

DISTRIBUTION BY:

Europe
PGUK
63 Hatton Garden
London EC1N 8LE, England
Phone: 020 7061 1980 • Fax: 020 7242 3725
www.pguk.co.uk

Australia
Renniks Publications Ltd.
3/37-39 Green Street
Banksmeadow, NSW 2109, Australia
Phone: 2 9695 7055 • Fax: 2 9695 7355
www.renniks.com

TABLE OF CONTENTS

ACKNOWLEDGMENTS

It is one thing to retell a history that everyone knows. But it is quite another to write an automotive history for the first time. Likewise it is a daunting task to find photos, most of which have never been seen before. Double the difficulty if you are talking about persons, cars, and projects from the 1940s, 1950s, and 1960s. And triple the difficulty when factoring in items and faces nobody knew, along with years that have passed and the people who have likewise passed.

And then comes the factor that most automotive authors rarely have to include in their storytelling: secrecy. I don't mean the usual wait-till-next-year kind of secrecy, but rather the kind that remains that way in perpetuity. In this case, the history of Creative, a company that kept most of its activities so far off the radar that only the most obvious are known. Even people who worked there didn't know everything that was going on in the company and shops. And even what people thought they knew is often not really what happened. So like an enigma wrapped up inside of a riddle, the real core of information about Creative Industries is cloaked in mystery, virtually unknown, even among the most knowledgeable automotive historians today.

But peeling back the many layers of secrecy and assembling a reasonable and accurate history could never be accomplished without the input, kind cooperation, and encouragement of a number of people. While my own knowledge and collection, assembled since the 1960s, is substantial, many have provided invaluable assistance with photos, anecdotes, and important information, without which, this book would be a far lesser work. Hopefully I won't miss anyone here, but in case I do, it is purely unintentional. Although I cannot possibly list each and every name, please know that, listed or not, I thank you all for any input and assistance you may have provided. Among the many who contributed, there are some names I especially want to point out.

First and foremost, Robert J. Denton and Marilyn Johnson Smith, whose assistance on Fred Johnson is priceless. Likewise priceless was help from Pamela Terry Bonk and her daughter, Nicole, for amazing information and photos on Rex Terry.

I also want to thank the late David Margolis of Creative Industries who first planted the spark of enthusiasm back in the 1960s. Thanks also to the late Garriston (Gary) Hutchings (former Creative staff); Steve Koppin (former head of Special Cars Division); the late Rex Terry (Creative Industries president and general manager); Verne Koppin; the late Richard Leasia; Fred Minturn (CEO MSX); Beverly Olson; James Resztak; former Creative personnel, Janet Merzoian; Larry O'Dowd; Ron Pacella; Joe Ramsay; Lynn Griffin; Gary Smythe; Larry W. Short. Also, Richard Padovini (Wing King and Chrysler Gas Turbine expert); Gil Carlsen; Edge Leasia; Bill Collins (former De Lorean motors engineer); Ken Gazo; Marvin King; Tom Walsh (Detroit Free Press); Don R. Nemets (former Mitchell Museum Curator); Stuart R. Blond (Editor, *The Packard Cormorant*); Thomas W. McPherson; George L. Hamlin (The Packard Club and Professional Car Society); Tom Beaubien (former Packard Motor Car Company staff); Bill Robinson (former Briggs Auto Body designer); Al Bederka (GM Chevrolet Division); Dwight R. Heinmuller (The Packard Club); Leslie Kendall (Petersen Automotive Museum); Earl Rubenstein (Automotive Driving Museum); David W. Temple; Wes Eisenchek; Jo Davis; Taryn Greenman; the great Michael Lamm; and the late, great Dean Batchelor.

ABOUT THE AUTHOR

Leon Dixon knows and loves automobiles and has spent a successful career in the industry. He loves anything with wheels.

Although he has lived most of his adult life in California, Leon Dixon grew up in Detroit, Michigan, during the glory years of the automotive industry. He witnessed the heyday of Detroit's reign as the world's automotive capital. More important, Leon actually knew many of the people at Creative Industries. He wrote the only magazine history of the company in the 1970s.

Leon is an award-winning writer and automotive historian and collector. He's written about everything imaginable: owner's manuals, training programs, workshop manuals, historical pieces, magazine articles, newspaper articles, brochures, advertising copy, scripts, songs, and more.

Dixon has had a widely varied and challenging career, beginning in the music business at age nine. Leon appeared with major artists such as Frankie Lymon and Stevie Wonder and was contracted in his teens to recording labels. Leon is also a military veteran who survived combat in the jungles of Vietnam.

As an adult, Dixon worked in the automotive industry, in positions ranging from technical writer, product planner, project manager, lead engineer, and professional consultant. Leon proudly participated in the development of several vehicles, including the original famed Mazda Miata.

Leon is an expert on concept cars and Packard automobile history. He has owned several vintage Packards, as well as Italian sports cars, Corvettes, Mopar muscle cars, Lincolns, and Cadillacs.

Leon has also performed professional voice-over work and appeared in commercials. He studied for several years under famous actor Gordon Jump (*WKRP in Cincinnati*, the Maytag Man) in voice, live appearance, improv, public speaking, and more.

He has appeared on radio, television, and print media in magazines such as *Forbes, Sports Illustrated, Popular Mechanics, Hemmings Motor News, Car Classics, Antiques Roadshow Insider,* and more. He is a regular contributor to *The Packard Cormorant*, the glossy magazine of The Packard Club.

INTRODUCTION

General George S. Patton pointed to the right and yelled above the noise of the open, speeding vehicle. He was trying to get his driver to change directions. "It was over there! The battle took place right over there, dammit!" The men traveling with him were completely puzzled. Had Patton lost his marbles? They were already heading to the site of a very recent World War II clash and *that* should have been directly ahead of them. But Patton knew very well what he was saying and seeing.

In the movie, *Patton,* the general (George C. Scott) stops his Jeep driver and scrambles out of the vehicle to survey a barren countryside. Then the general stands silently, mysteriously scanning over a rolling piece of desolate landscape as the wind blows and echoing trumpets faintly sound. The rest of his entourage stand baffled, wondering what Patton is doing and talking about. Minutes pass. Finally Patton reveals that he is speaking of an ancient battle between Roman Legions and the Carthaginian people that indeed took place on this very spot, hundreds of years earlier. He muses aloud as if he had actually been there, witnessing the historic battle.

The real Patton claimed he could feel the energy of the past flowing beneath his feet. The enigmatic general firmly believed that he was a reincarnated man of history who had witnessed much in many past lifetimes.

Today in our 21st-century world, perhaps you, too, can get an inkling of this mysterious energy General Patton may have felt. But you don't need to reincarnate or travel to ancient battlefields. Just travel to Detroit and then go to the address of 3080 East Outer Drive near the intersection of Moenart Street.

If you stand on the curb at this very spot, look south, and close your eyes, you can almost feel the energy that once pulsed here. It somehow endures, hanging invisible yet heavy in the air. Your eyes may not see it, but if you clear your mind, your senses may feel it. Something important, almost spiritual, from Detroit's once-glorious manufacturing and automotive golden age indeed remains here.

Then look around. No, you won't see a battlefield. But you will see, and perhaps feel, what was once a place of struggle, creativity, ingenuity, and triumph of many years and many lives. A historic, almost sacred location where important industrial and automotive events took place. A place where people of immense talent and genius worked. That creative genius of men and women who invented, designed, and made things lingers here in the air, perhaps awaiting a rediscovery, or merely recognition.

But unless you remember the fire hydrant near the curb or the two weed-choked strips of concrete that mark an ancient sidewalk entry and a barely visible asphalt driveway, nothing else remains from the glorious past of this place. Not one easily identifiable clue survives. The buildings are all gone, and the people have gone with them.

But this seemingly unremarkable plot of vacant land now covered in weeds was once a cluster of companies known as Industrial City. And the exact yellow brick building that stood on this very address was first known as Progressive Welder Company, and then ultimately became known as Creative Industries of Detroit. It was a most remarkable enterprise. Yet, there is no marker, no monument, and no sign to commemorate this place. Just five acres of windswept weeds, overgrowth . . . and litter. To look at it today, how would anyone know?

Formerly, Progressive Welder Company, now Creative Industries of Detroit's headquarters office building at 3080 East Outer Drive as it looked in 1955. On the left, note one of the special lantern-style streetlights used on Outer Drive. On the far right (purposely cut off by the photographer) is an experimental Packard Caribbean, painted in colors the factory never used.

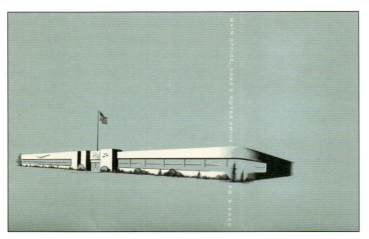

1956 rendering of Creative's headquarters building at 3080 East Outer Drive.

But even if you never knew the name of Creative Industries, or have forgotten it, the cars and technologies it spawned were indeed unforgettable, and very likely you *would* know them. The vehicles alone comprise an impressive roll call. A special Lincoln bubble-top parade limo used by President Eisenhower was engineered and rebuilt here. It was followed by what seemed like a never-ending string of amazing vehicles, many of them brilliant concept cars. There were dream cars such as Ford FX-Atmos, Mercury XM-800, Dodge Granada, Packard Balboa, Packard Panthers, Packard Request, Ford Mystere, Corvette Corvair, Plymouth XP-VIP, USS Innovari, and so many more. Ambulances, flower cars, flying cars, hovering cars, stainless steel cars, and electric cars were designed and even made here. And production vehicles were birthed here too. Ionia-bodied GM station wagons from the 1940s through 1960s were engineered here. The Dodge Charger 500 and the Daytona and Plymouth Superbird wing cars as well. And there were prototypes. Among them, Chevrolet Corvettes, the De Lorean, the Stutz Blackhawk, and Hummer prototypes all sprang from this company. Aircraft and even spacecraft were designed or engineered here. Rides for Dis-

ney attractions and people-mover designs and technologies had their beginnings with the company that once stood here.

There is also no mention of the genius that started it all. His name was Frederick H. Johnson and he single-handedly founded the incredible nine companies once known as Industrial City. His tireless innovation finally led Johnson to also found Progressive Welder Company. This amazing company provided some of the technology that revolutionized production welding and helped win World War II. Ultimately, Johnson also founded Creative Industries of Detroit, thus creating incredible automobiles and thousands of jobs that resulted from these enterprises.

Sadly, Frederick H. Johnson is no longer with us. Most of the creative geniuses he brought together, like the great Rex A. Terry and countless others have passed on, too. As I said, the companies, the buildings and the people are all gone.

But there is a way to recapture at least some of the magic of this company. I invite you to travel with me back to a magical era of automotive history and an amazing place. Walk with me now, past the art deco portico, through the double front doors to the receptionist's desk, and into the fascinating world of the company once known as Creative Industries of Detroit.

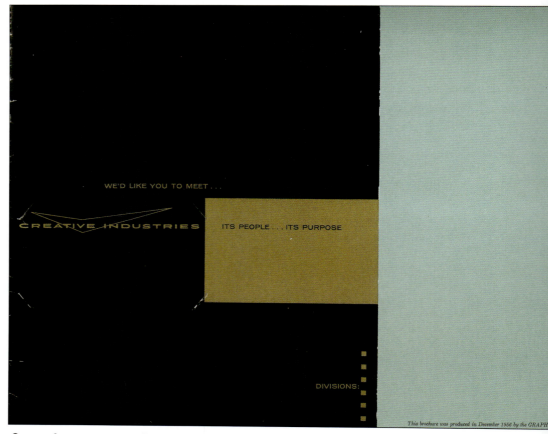

WE'D LIKE YOU TO MEET . . .

CREATIVE INDUSTRIES

ITS PEOPLE . . . . ITS PURPOSE

DIVISIONS:

This brochure was produced in December 1956 by the GRAPHI

Cover of very rare 1956 Creative prospectus brochure given only to select potential clientele in the automotive and aircraft industries.

CHAPTER ONE

THE TRADITION OF CAR BODY MAKERS

To fully understand the wondrous phenomenon of automobiles, one also needs to know the elusive notion of perspective; to see how all things relate, or don't. One also needs to understand the vital importance of how things change. And along with those changes go the fickle demands of the marketplace, particularly in America.

By "things" I don't just mean physical objects you can hold in your hands, but also the perception of those physical objects and how they fit into the world around you. Perception is, after all, everything.

One final and most important understanding is to also recognize that the thinking, the outlook of people, and public perceptions have indeed changed over time. Take Detroit, for instance. Today, people see Detroit one way; but when I was growing up, people saw it a vastly different way.

Having the rare ability to recognize a given perception at the right time and place and then being able to capitalize on it with product is pure genius. When it came to the auto industry, there were indeed a small number of people who had such talent, such incredible genius. And somehow, no matter where they came from, sooner or later, most of these people ended up in Detroit, Michigan.

It was here where the fruits of their talent and labor became real, beyond the wildest dreams of an average American. So to get a better perspective, let's take a look back at the early beginnings of the automobile. Only then will it become obvious how a company such as Creative Industries could have been born.

From the time that vehicles were first born, there was always some kind of rudimentary seating and eventually a body on each. But in the earliest days, that body was little more than utilitarian. Whatever might be looked upon as style was almost always inherited from (or based on) horse-drawn carriages that already existed.

Frankly, in many cases of the very first automobiles, the horse was simply removed, steering was installed, and then some kind of electric motor or internal combustion engine was positioned wherever there was room to fit it in. Thus the reference to early automobiles as "horseless carriages."

There were also bicycle- and tricycle-based machines such as the Benz Velo, which is officially claimed to be the first car. Few historians see the obvious today, but this Benz vehicle and S. H. Ropers' early car evolved out of what were then known as "sociable tricycles." And for a while, that was that.

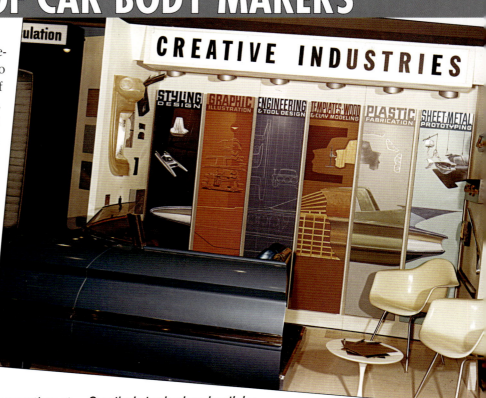

Creative's trade show booth by Creative's graphics division and plastics division. Notice chairs were fiberglass, which was considered very modern for that era.

As this was all taking place, consideration for the driver and passenger slowly began to emerge. Eventually as vehicles became enclosed conveyances, advancements regarding interiors began to take place. These were quickly followed by, or even accompanied by, comfort and convenience features. From here it was only a short time before influences from clientele of the upper crust began to spread. After all, anyone with the means to buy and operate a horseless carriage had ample finance, by definition.

Of course, horse-drawn carriages of the very wealthy always had some measures of comfort and style. But with the addition of an engine, a whole new level of refinement and luxury began to emerge. The people who owned and used these vehicles had higher expectations. They were accustomed to comfort, convenience, high style, and refinements. So to appeal to these buyers, details and style mattered more than ever before.

Now in the early days of super-refined carriages, so much was invested in building and refining custom carriage bodies that their owners naturally tended to want to save them. They didn't live in a mass-consumption throwaway world. Their world was one of the things that endured; a world of quality, craftsmanship, and art all bundled into products that made awestruck people marvel.

As chassis and engines evolved, there came a desire to simply transfer the precious carriage body, that enduring object d'art, onto the latest chassis and powerplant. After all, if you were a passenger on the Titanic, you marveled at the high art and sophistication that existed on the upper decks, not what went on in the dark bowels of the ship's coal room! The car chassis was pure machinery, something that nobody saw. But the auto body was expected to be a lasting thing of beauty, lined with velvet and leather.

Thus was born what became known as the coachbuilding industry. In those times, it was thought of simply as an upgrade, like installing a bigger hard drive in your laptop or downloading a new app for your smart phone. Essentially, the vehicle bodies were developed and even styled by one source, while the chassis and powertrain were engineered and developed by yet another source.

As automobiles transitioned from their roots in tricycles and wooden coaches to steel-bodied conveyances, there were still further developments. The ever-increasing demand for distinctive style and features that would attract, retain, and even endear customers, became paramount. As time went on, these sources of vehicle bodies quickly became the true masters of the high end of the fledgling automobile business. But then, the rest of the world changed, and so did the market.

Of course, as the industrial age took hold, there were increasing numbers of cars. Ironically, prices decreased with mass production and economies of scale. Before long, cars in general included style and design enhancements. And to be sure, the lower ends of the car business never remained stagnant. If anything, they rapidly grew and followed in the shadows of the high end. Likewise, aspects of cars that were once reserved to the upper echelon increasingly spread to the masses. The difference now was that most people bought whatever the carmaker offered in body and style. By the 1920s and 1930s, car companies had their own standard bodies and designs.

However, wealthy buyers could still order custom bodies from coachbuilders. These custom bodies could cost fortunes to build, and the idea of simply discarding them in a scrap heap would have been considered insane by some of the original owners back then. This notion was bolstered by the depression years that followed the stock market crash of 1929. But for those whose fortunes weren't wiped out, there were still automotive options. Well-heeled clientele still had the additional choice of buying a custom-designed, custom-built car body. In today's realm, think of it like either buying a suit off the rack at a store or having Sergio Armani design and make your suit personally.

In those days of separate rolling chassis sales, the mechanical parts of the car were either quickly outdated or worn out. So? The bodies were often simply swapped onto a new chassis and voila! This was considered a "new automobile."

Several names familiar to car buyers today originated with the old separate automotive body makers or "coachbuilders." Brunn, Dietrich, Hibbard & Darrin, Rollston, Fisher Brothers, Fleetwood, Henney, Le Baron, Brewster, and many more started as coachbuilders that came from this old tradition.

But by the post–World War II era in America, the glory of custom bodies and traditional coachbuilders had all but faded away with the Depression philosophies. And nobody was swapping bodies on chassis anymore. It was a new and different world, and prosperity had returned to America. The parking lots at factories in Detroit were now filled with employees' cars. The smokestacks smoked and the town hummed 24/7 with a revitalized industry. The paychecks were cashing and the bells on the cash registers at the stores were ringing. Americans finally, at long last, had money to spend again.

The beating heart of the automotive business pumped faster and harder. Things were moving far too quickly for all the old traditions now. Automotive styles were changing yearly. The chassis had become more integrated into the body styling and were not being sold separately. If your car was old or worn out, you simply scrapped it and moved on. Cars had adjusted to the thinking and the thinking adjusted even further to the cars. And so it was that an entirely new era was born in which the automobile had a built-in lifespan, not governed by the mechanical, but by the aesthetic. Mere use and technological advances were no longer the cause of obsolescence. The cause was now style.

The Morphing of the Coachbuilding Business

The coachbuilding business as it had once existed in the automotive industry may have *seemed* as if it were dead. But it just *seemed* that way. The era may have been dead, but it was merely the era that had died, not the business. It was mostly still there but morphed into an entirely new and more robust, highly flexible model. And this new business model took on new directions. Aside from rare instances such as the Dodge-powered Zeder Storm of the 1950s, there was no more talk of swapping of bodies on chassis by customer order. Things had been ratcheted up way past that old notion. The new directions were customizing and completely custom-built cars.

Little stand-alone and single-purpose shops could never generate the kinds of business required to make them financially viable. The new business model required an enterprise so complete and so flexible, so adaptable that it could respond to almost any automotive scenario. It also had to somehow meet both small or one-off productions, as well as economies of scale with larger productions. None of the old coachbuilders had this kind of flexibility, adaptability, and talent, not if they were going to meet a regular employee payroll. How could the new era in American automotive demands be feasible?

On the surface, the answer seemed complicated, yet for visionary men such as Fred Johnson and Rex Terry, the answer was simple: set up a company that could do it all. Something that could combine the output and talent of Johnson's old Industrial City and yet function as one ever-flexing entity. An agile, modern company had to be quickly adaptable to meet almost any demand from either the market or the industry.

A postwar shop had to be swift and agile on its feet. But able to swell and retract to meet the business, where the business lived. It had to have resources in staff and engineering not previously required. In the old days, coachbuilding firms had a successful period and grew to the point where they were so big they could no longer sustain themselves. That kind of inflexibility was passé.

And the *really* big money was now moving in a whole new direction: dream cars. "Dream car" meant a lot more than a bubble top and swoopy lines. The "dream" in dream car also meant that any company capable of what I've described, plus putting one-off concepts on car show turntables, would indeed be rich beyond their wildest dreams. Securing a contract, especially with any one of the Big Three automakers, could ensure success on a level all those old small operations of prewar years could never have imagined. And if you did a good job and the dream car was a success, it merely guaranteed more of the same!

Coachbuilding was back with a vengeance, just in a different format. This time, the truly successful model was based on Fred Johnson's partnering of companies, all evolved under one umbrella. And Rex Terry, fully steeped in the business of custom vehicle development and contracts, was the perfect man to captain this new ship on the automotive seas.

Johnson had shrewdly managed to hire another Chrysler alum, Verne Koppin. Koppin had worked doing body engineering for Rex Terry at Chrysler, and then went to work for Fred Johnson. Verne was steeped in the automotive business and had roots going well back. Verne's father, Alfred Otto Koppin, was chief body engineer of Hudson Motor Car Company and introduced Verne to Rex. As an irony that could only happen in the glory years of Detroit, Verne ultimately found himself right back working for Rex again.

The name of this new company was Creative Industries of Detroit. And although it eventually had imitators, defectors, rivals, spin-offs and more, Creative Industries became an amazing high-water mark on the American auto-

motive scene. It shone in other industries as well, such as aircraft. Whether engineering, design, or innovation, the industry could look to Creative to meet and solve nearly every issue that arose for decades to come. It offered Detroit's best technologies and engineering, along with the finest automotive people, to the world.

Creative's Early Beginnings

Fred was not only Creative's founder, but he also founded an amazing enterprise known as Progressive Welder Company in the 1930s. In the 1940s, Johnson also oversaw a conglomerate of cooperative businesses on Detroit's East Outer Drive, known as Industrial City. Fred's new Creative Industries company quickly occupied the newly vacated sections of the old Progressive complex, and that is how things began.

Creative Industries of Detroit was officially up and running as an entity by 1950. It basically took over as an umbrella company to continue where Frederick H. Johnson's Industrial City (see Chapter Two) left off at the end of the 1940s.

One person in the graphics department, who was a very longtime figure at Creative Industries, arrived as an employee in 1950. He put it this way: "The market was already exploding at the time with all of the pent-up demand for product and the changeover in the late 1940s back from World War II production to civilian production. During the war, everybody had been closed down. They were making airplanes and tanks and bombs for the military. But with the war over, they had to switch the entire industry back to commercial business. So they had to reconvert back over to making civilian items.

"When I arrived, Creative had a very up-and-coming technical illustration department. We worked together with

Sense of family and love of company was carried over from old Progressive Welder operation. Original members of Creative Industries Bowling League.

the engineers. Our department was under the leadership of a fellow named Casey Van Mourick. He had joined Creative Industries under Art Bradley. Art was the talented sales guru expert who had teamed up with Rex Terry. Rex had come in from Dodge. He was the business guy. Verne Koppin was hired as lead engineer, also in from Chrysler. And then Art Bradley was the guy who was out there bringing in the business. He was really very effective, and more than a sales guy. Art was really good. When Creative was formed, Art Bradley was in there, really, as his own company. And it was his connections combined with Rex's connections that really made Creative's business take off.

"You do know that Creative was also very strongly connected with the fiberglass company in Ionia. That relationship between Rex and Don Mitchell was one of the reasons Creative's business grew.

"I started off as an illustrator on the boards. I had come in straight from Cass Tech and later took a course in marketing at Michigan State and expanded my work into a department. We had a core group of about 10 illustrators.

"The Mt. Elliott location was just south of 7 Mile Road. In fact, when I started at Creative Industries, I worked in that building as a technical illustrator under Ray Campbell. Casey Van Mourick had his department in that building. We also had some engineering there.

"In the early days we had all kinds of weird ideas that came in the door. One that I recall was a fellow who had an idea for a traveling circus. But it was not by using trains and the typical circus, but all kinds of special vehicles. This guy had spent some time and did research and decided he could have these vehicles that could just drive up, do a few things, and then open up as a circus.

"This particular idea was so wild; I can remember this so clearly. The theme was to have the central circus tent be something you could just drive up in a truck, pull several switches and these things come up. He had these little illustrations, but when you put it into reality, it would have come out to 700 or 800 feet tall! I kept thinking, this is ridiculous to make it real. But they kept coming back in, trying to get us to do this. In order to get it across to them how improbable this was, we had to make a scale model layout. I contacted a guy who collected miniature circus items and we set up a circus display to demonstrate the reality or impossibility of making this all happen. That was when it finally died. There were a lot of other things like that.

"Another one that keeps coming back to mind was two young guys who came in during the 1950s. They brought a futuristic scale clay model with them that looked like the cars of today. They came to Creative and asked what we could do to approach this. These guys were saying that this was the way

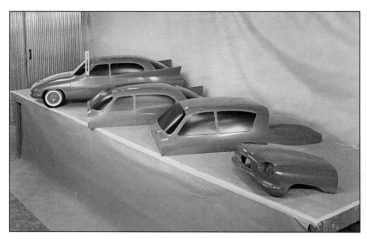

This 1950s scale model looks more like today's cars with exception of wide whitewalls and fins. Modular system allowed for several configurations on one basic vehicle. Note corrugated metal wall and door. Several of these private locked security areas were in shops behind Creative.

Two different noses, two different looks, same vehicle. Some U.S. laws mandated sealed beam headlights and higher front ends at this time. Vehicle could've met both requirements with same basic structure. Version on left was very 21st Century.

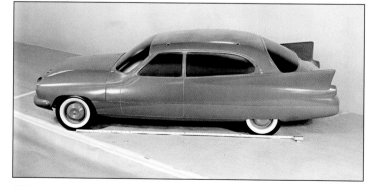

With higher profile quad sealed-beam headlights, nose, and tail fins, this version looks more dated but nothing like a 1950s or 1960s car. Quad headlights were considered very futuristic in the 1950s. Tape measure indicated a large model.

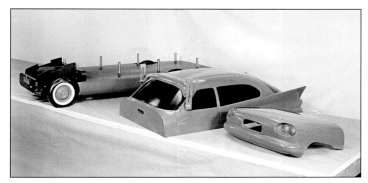

The modular system was worked out even down to engine packaging, which appears to be front-wheel drive. Very advanced for 1950s or 1960s! It's unclear what attachment above windshield was intended to do.

Creative had very strong aircraft knowledge its via ancestry of Progressive Welder Company, which did massive aircraft work during World War II.

that cars would be made in the future. But they were so far ahead, it was way too early to make money on it. To think what these guys had made was such an accurate prediction, but it was years away from making any money. It was the exact opposite of what cars out on the street in the 1950s were like.

"My department was the one that had to make illustrations of these concepts to decide how to proceed with them. You know, see what you can do with this, and then we'd have a meeting with Rex Terry and Verne Koppin and the team and go from there. Artists surrounded me, so a lot of those kinds of things started with us.

"This was back when we were also doing casket designs for a company in Indiana. There was a period of about seven or eight years where we did a lot of these front-end odd projects. Later, when I took some business courses, I realized that the core business I was actually in was not art, but rather it was training. And that was when my department began to expand."

As one Creative graphics person suggested, the very early beginnings of Creative Industries of Detroit may surprise you because sometimes they did not involve only automotive work. To get the company up and rolling meant getting contracts "in the door" as the saying went. Those contracts were honest work and generated decent revenues, but they were often outside of the auto industry.

The Aircraft Connection

Creative was never really intended to be just an automotive company and, in fact, usually referred to itself as an "engineering firm." Given the passions of both Fred Johnson and his friend Rex Terry, and the ancestry of Progressive Welder, it should come as no surprise that Creative was heavily involved in the aircraft business, even in the early years. By 1955, Creative counted several aircraft and aircraft-related firms among what they termed "subscribers." Among others, these included

Chase Aircraft Company, Republic Aircraft Company, and Boeing. And Creative engineers were loaned out to companies doing aircraft work. Even Chrysler Missile Operations was a client. In some ways, the aircraft connection also led back to cars. And Progressive Welder Company already had deep connections inside the aircraft business via its massive and often groundbreaking work during World War II.

Retired engineer Linder C. "Lynn" Griffin tells an interesting story about his beginnings at Creative Industries of Detroit in the early 1950s. His story also reveals more about how Creative's involvement with aircraft work took place. But most of all, Lynn's story reveals how Creative and the Mitchell-Bentley Company actually got linked in business. And how Creative quietly supplied a huge amount of the talent that ultimately went to Mitchell and other businesses. Most of it was done in stealth, so pay attention, otherwise it can get confusing!

Says Griffin, "I had never heard of Creative Industries. I was just a kid, about 22 years old. I left the Art Academy [Leighton Art Academy] in 1953, went to work for Prentiss-Weaver Products Company up in Rapids, Wisconsin, for a couple of years and did all of their product designs. Their apartment stoves, ranges, back rails, handles, doors. Then we had space heaters we made for four or five different companies. I designed all those.

"When I first heard about Creative, the last big job I had was in Niles, Michigan. I was working down there at Kawneer, a small company, laying out aircraft wings for Boeing.

"There were three engineers there on per diem from Creative and they said, 'Hey, with your talent, you've got to go to where we're from!' I asked them where that was and they replied it was Creative Industries of Detroit.

"I had a six-month contract to do the aircraft wings, but I finished it in six weeks! After that I went right over to Detroit to talk to Creative, and they hired me on the spot!

"I was only physically at Creative in Detroit for just a short time, maybe five months. The very first job I did there was designing caskets! I don't recall what company they were for, but they were funeral caskets. Then I moved over to designing schematics for heater controls and various numbers of other things in automobiles. Then of course came some design work on different cars, but I don't remember which ones."

Over the years, Creative continued to hire and lend out personnel to other companies, only you'd never know it. While the Creative staffers worked right alongside direct employees of other companies, everything appeared seamless. Sometimes even employees of those other companies had no idea that their coworker was actually employed and paid by Creative Industries of Detroit.

Involvement with Mitchell-Bentley

The interrelationship of Detroit automotive companies in those times was phenomenal, if not almost inescapable. The money, the work, and the talent all swirled around in one incredible bouillabaisse. Companies that appeared completely independent of one another were oftentimes very dependent upon each other. And when a company made a public claim of "we did it," the reality was often nowhere near as cut and dried as it may have seemed.

Creative Industries was absolutely, very definitely a major player behind the scenes. In most cases, Creative was steadfastly pledged via contract to secrecy. They played their role very well.

Over the years, some company in this mix might have taken credit for a vehicle or an automotive accomplishment, but the real truth often ran a lot deeper. In so many cases it was actually Creative that was supplying the talent, the engineering, the design expertise, and even the actual staff personnel. A good example of this situation is revealed in the connection between Creative and Mitchell-Bentley Corporation.

Don Mitchell, head of Mitchell-Bentley, knew Rex Terry of Creative very well. He also knew Fred Johnson well and wintered at Johnson's resort in Florida.

The first notation of a business meeting with Rex Terry is listed in Mitchell's business diaries on Wednesday, January 26, 1944. It reads "Chrysler Rex Terry." But it is likely the two men knew one another much further back in time.

At one point, Mitchell had an interest in a plastics company in rural Michigan. In those days in the automotive industry, "plastics" usually meant fiber-reinforced resin–FRP, more commonly known today as fiberglass. Even newspapers and magazines of the day referred to what we now call "fiberglass" simply as "plastic."

With both Fred Johnson's and Rex Terry's deep knowledge of the subject, it was a natural conclusion that Terry and Creative would become advisors to Mitchell. I mention the Japanese business concept of "keiretsu" elsewhere in this book, but it fits so well right here. Rex Terry ultimately sat on the board of directors for this plastics company.

For a designer or an automotive professional seeking to grow in the industry, it was hard to pass up the world's automotive capital in favor of moving to a small, anonymous country town. So it was difficult, even for a guy with the wonderful salesmanship abilities of Don Mitchell, to lure auto-engineering

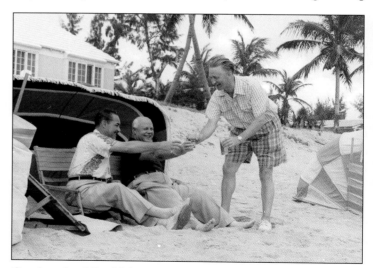

Left to right: Rex Terry, Don Mitchell, unidentified person, and Fred Johnson enjoy a sunny winter day at Fred's beautiful resort in Delray Beach, Florida. (Photo Courtesy Marilyn Johnson-Smith and Robert Denton)

Gracious host Fred Johnson serves guests (left to right) Rex Terry and Don Mitchell cool drinks on the beach as Michiganders enjoy a sunny winter day at Fred's resort in Delray Beach, Florida. (Photo Courtesy Marilyn Johnson-Smith and Robert Denton)

people out to small towns to work and live. This hurdle was tough enough. But there was also the expense and time needed to seek out qualified new recruits. Creative Industries of Detroit quickly resolved Don's dilemma. They did it by simply lending out personnel to other companies such as Mitchell-Bentley.

Lynn Griffin knew both Don and son, Bill Mitchell, very well. But in the early 1950s Griffin was unaware of the Mitchells and what they did in the car world. And he didn't know there was already a connection to Creative Industries.

Although Lynn had only spent a short time working on-site at Creative in their graphics and design division, he had already been steeped in Creative's drawing methods. By the early 1950s, Creative had developed and refined a revolutionary kind of 3-D drawing method that was intended to ease the tedium of reading and interpreting blueprints. Some of this method had probably first originated with Fisher Body Company, but Creative took it to new heights. The method was publicized in a November 1950 paper entitled, "A New Kind of Drawing." It was written by Creative's engineering and sales guru, Arthur L. Bradley, who some say was the early magnetic backbone of generating new business.

The paper, presented at the Annual Convention of the American Society of Body Engineers at Wayne State University, was simple, but pure genius. Engineering drawings were interpreted from a highly technical appearance down to what could be easily seen as x-ray view, sectional line drawings showing the true physical appearance of a component. The result was that any layman could then easily understand what formerly took an engineer or engineering draftsman to interpret. This knowledge, together with Griffin's background in industrial design and engineering, made him an ideal candidate to go to Mitchell's rescue.

Griffin states, "Here's how Creative got into all this. At the time, Mitchell-Bentley was located in rural areas such as Owosso and Ionia. When Don began getting so many contracts, he had to do something!

"Don was a *dynamic* salesman and got so many contracts that they kept hiring and hiring hundreds of local farm people. But because Owosso and Ionia were kind of out in the country [out there and back again] they couldn't recruit serious engineering and design people like those around the Detroit area. They didn't have anybody to hire around there in those

Taken at Mitchell-Bentley's Ionia Division, here is Creative's Lynn Griffin (far right) and his engineering group team at Mitchell-Bentley. Many of these people worked on the Packard Panther and presumably the Dodge Granada. Les Shoemaker was lured away from Packard Motor Car Company engineering. Note the full-size drawings on the wall in the background.

Front row (left to right): unidentified person, Gene Lemke, Cliff Hale (assistant engineer), Les Shoemaker (chief engineer), and Helge Fredine (assistant chief engineer)

Second row (far right next to Griffin): Gary Lasco (draftsman/illustrator), to his right with hand on hip and tie is Don Funky (layout engineer).

Back row (tallest person and glasses: Ted Hassler (draftsman). (Photo Courtesy Lynn Griffin)

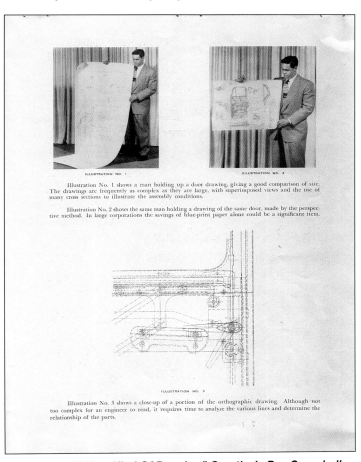

From 1950, "A New Kind Of Drawing," Creative's Ray Campbell holds X-ray type drawings that eliminate complexity in interpreting engineering blueprints.

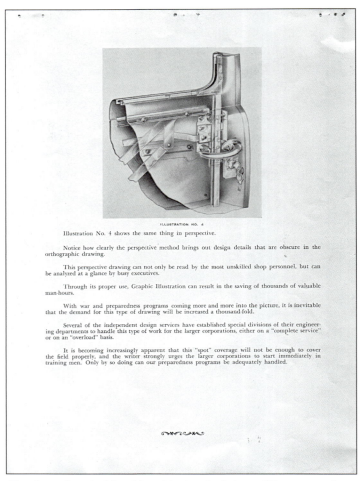

Also from the 1950 booklet, this detailed view of X-ray-type draw-ing eliminated complexity in interpreting engineering blueprints. Reference to war here was not World War II, but Korean War.

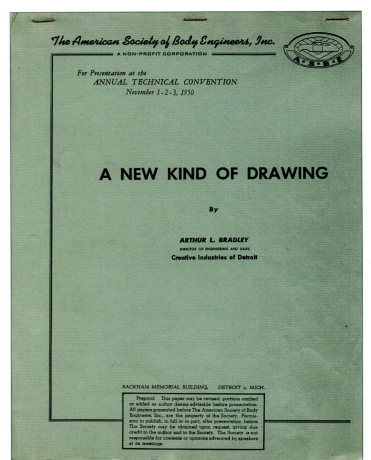

Creative Industries booklet, A New Kind Of Drawing, by engi-neering and sales guru Art Bradley, presented at Wayne State University to American Society of Body Engineers. Bradley later defected from Creative to form famous Aero Detroit Company.

country towns, except maybe draftsmen from the high schools. The only engineers they had were probably from some com-panies in Grand Rapids or Lansing [in fact, Lansing; we had several from there]. So Don had to go to some of these people he knew and find the right people to hire.

"He knew General Motors executives. He knew Ford and Chrysler, Studebaker, and Kaiser-Frazer, all of them. Alvan Macauley and Ed Macauley from Packard had interest and they knew Don."

But one of those people Don Mitchell knew well was Rex Terry at Creative Industries, and it wasn't long before Rex got the call.

Lynn Griffin continues. "At the time, I was the only one qualified with my background because I had been an industrial designer with other companies. So Creative sent me (to Mitchell-Bentley), but I didn't want to go because it [the assignment location] was a small town. You know, I was in Detroit and I loved Milwaukee and went to the art academy in Milwaukee and studied automotive design. So I

didn't want to go to a small town. But they put pressure on me, so I went.

"Creative sent us to Ionia on per diem. In all I think there were 10 of us at the time. I went to Mitchell-Bentley for two years on per diem and Mitchell-Bentley paid me a full wage too! So I was making like $600 a week back in the 1950s. That'd be like two grand or more now. And all my expenses were paid. My housing, everything. My food, everything for two years. I finally wound up in 1966, I think it was.

"Anyway, Creative furnished professional people for Don's factories in Owosso and Ionia to Mitchell-Bentley to help them fulfill their contracts. And that's how I got sent to Ionia to set up that department.

"When I got there they had no designers, no artists, and no graphics engineers, and that was my job. When I was sent there, I had to pull two fellows from Creative to work for me (and for Mitchell) there in Ionia. And then I had to hire and train three or four local draftsmen to get my depart-ment complete. I worked with the tooling department. And we interpreted pictorially, in a picture, where all the arc welds, gas welds, spot welds, and where everything went on the parts for those cars. This was late-1955.

"When I went up there we were taking in bodies of Buick and Oldsmobile and Mercury sedans and converting them into station wagons. We had to tear the roofs off. Then we had to cut the whole deck lid in the back. Then we made some side rails and the top. Then we made the lift gate and tailgate in the rear; we made those. Then we assembled all those pieces into the bodies we had cut open. For 1956 models, we were going to change the process and build the entire side assemblies on the Oldsmobiles, Mercurys, and Buick station wagons.

"I said to Helge Fredine, chief engineer [who was in charge of manufacturing at Mitchell], 'Well, what do you want of me?'

"He said, 'Well, these people can't interpret our engineering drawings. You gotta interpret these drawings in a picture form; you need to figure out a way to show them where the welds go and then get it to these people, the foreman, and the factory workers, so they can see what they are doing!'

"Helge Fredine said he wanted full scale drawings. He said to me, 'I want these in full scale.' I told him, well, Helge, that means some of the drawings would be 20 feet long! He said, 'I don't care! We want full scale!' So for a while, two or three of us drew full scale. Some of those prints were 18, 20 feet long!

"If you know how component parts are drawn up, they would lay out all the car parts out on a precision plate and draftsmen would come and take each part and draw it. Those drawings and parts had to be accurate to 1/64-inch clearance. Each had to be assembled and welded in a certain way and precise position.

"I invented parts manuals, assembly manuals, for our Ionia factory. And they were 18 inches by 12 inches. There was a little sketch of the three-quarter view of the body down in the lower corner and we would circle the area in that little body and blow that up full scale and it would show where the arc welds, spot welds, gas welds, or whatever we did went, and management just loved those! We made them for every car and everything we made after that. Yup. I contributed a lot to that company. I ended up being there for 16 years."

Remember, Lynn was working embedded at Mitchell-Bentley, but he was really an employee of Creative Industries of Detroit. Lynn Griffin became a direct employee of Mitchell-Bentley and remained there for many years; even

when new owners took over. Mitchell-Bentley and successive project overseers such as A.O. Smith and Dow-Smith became involved in manufacturing the magnificent Shelby Mustangs for Carroll Shelby in 1967 to 1970. Lynn continued contributing his technical advice and work to make these vehicles a success, all as offshoot from his original position at Creative Industries of Detroit.

So here was a clear case where Creative Industries had not only provided technical and design expertise, but also actual personnel to another company. And Creative did this kind of thing repeatedly, all over the automotive, aircraft, and aerospace industries. But Creative's mastery and influence didn't stop there. Creative was involved in countless other industries and manufacturing applications.

Creative was a treasure chest of technology and a place where almost anything could be done, especially if it rolled on wheels. It was an automotive Disneyland with a synergy of engineering, art, chemistry, plastics, wood, metals, sales genius, vision, fantasy, and people management. All these things came together to form a single company. From here, the formula, the recipe, and the people reached outward, spreading positive influence and genius on to others for the benefit of all.

Today, Hollywood has companies such as Industrial Light and Magic. But once upon a time, the automotive world of Detroit had Creative Industries. It was a company whose dawning could not have been timed more perfectly and whose existence could not have been more vital. It was also the ultimate dream of a lone young man who had left Europe decades earlier, bound for his destiny in America. We'll talk more about his incredible journey next.

Early version of Chrysler Parade Phaeton. Though not credited, Creative performed updates done in mid-1950s and possibly other work. This vehicle was photographed in front of Chrysler's Canadian headquarters.

BEGINNINGS, ENDINGS AND THE GENIUS OF FREDERICK H. JOHNSON

Michigan was a long, long way from his European origins. And American industry was a long, long way from his beginnings. Fred Johnson was an immigrant to the United States, but he had become a quiet force in American manufacturing and a major player in the automotive industry. So where else should his operations be located other than Detroit?

Funen Island, just offshore of central Denmark, is where it all really began. Also known as "Fyun" to the Danish, it was also where author Hans Christian Andersen was born and lived.

Frederick Hjalmar (pronounced "hyalmar") Johansen (later Americanized to "Johnson") was born to a farming family there in 1896. During his early years growing up on the farm, Fred quickly developed a serious work ethic. He even demonstrated a hint of some early inventive genius when he designed and built a little automatic door that closed behind the chickens entering the barn on the farm. But Fred envisioned so much more than just being a farm boy; Fred was also a dreamer.

Eventually his dreams led Fred off the farm and onto a ship bound for America. But the trip to the United States with his sister was not one Fred was sure he wanted to take, despite her urgings. After all, he had been told that Americans worked too hard and Fred thought he might not like a new life in this bustling country of factories.

There was also a language spoken in the United States that Fred didn't know. But as with all of the other obstacles he faced, Fred eagerly embraced the challenge. He began to teach himself English and eventually mastered the language well enough to communicate comfortably. This self-education eventually helped open the doors on many directions he pursued.

Fred must have been very confused when he arrived in America only to discover that it was difficult to get a job. Somehow he had always imagined this would be an easy thing to do, but employment reality was quite the contrary. After three months of searching, Fred's savings were exhausted and still no job. However, like most who ultimately succeed in life, Johnson refused to give up and was more determined than ever to find employment.

Ryan Navion Super 260 at Detroit City Airport with Fred's personal pilot. Fred Johnson had a bed built into this plane to sleep on extended trips. (Photo Courtesy Marilyn Johnson-Smith and Robert Denton)

In addition to not knowing English, up until this time Fred also had no knowledge of machinery. His era was not one of mechanized farms. As if to complicate things further, Fred had no experience in factory work or any kind of manufacturing. But eventually another Danish immigrant helped him get a position as a machinist. At long last, Fred was finally employed in America. Thus began a long series of jobs where Johnson continuously educated himself in the craft and the technology of the wondrous world of American manufacturing.

Despite a lack of formal education with machinery, Fred was eager to learn and quickly picked up the skills and techniques to make himself successful in the field. Soon he began traveling the country, tirelessly taking on challenging jobs that would advance his knowledge. Along the way, Fred noted shortcomings and shortcuts to better manufacturing processes. Johnson wisely began carefully documenting and cataloguing his own ideas to remedy the problems he observed. As word got around about the genius of this Danish immigrant, it wasn't long before Fred's vast imagination ultimately became highly valued by others.

By 1923, Fred found himself in the employ of the old Maxwell Automobile Company. His penchant for constant learning and problem solving put Fred in an ideal position when the

Fred Johnson's origin in Denmark. Funen is also known as "Fyn" by the Danish. Funen is situated between the two larger islands of Sjaelland and Jylland. Odense is the largest city and where author Hans Christian Anderson was born and lived. This comic was done by E. and I. Geller. (Photo Courtesy Marilyn Johnson-Smith and Robert Denton)

problems and solving them had clearly demonstrated he had capabilities and vision uncommon in the industry. But recognizing problems that needed to be remedied when others didn't created a new dilemma for Fred, or an opportunity.

All his life, Frederick Johnson had met every challenge and overcame every obstacle that presented itself. But Fred finally came to the realization that he was doing it all to make other people rich. Johnson realized that it was now time to step out on his own.

Armed with this knowledge and deep experience, Fred joined forces with a friend and invested $2,500 as partner in a resistance welding company in 1935. This new company was known as Progressive Welder Company and it was headquartered at 3050 East Outer Drive in Detroit.

At first, Fred held onto his position at Chrysler. But when the welder company initially struggled and lost a substantial amount of money in its first six months, Fred decided to go all in. But in

job at Maxwell ultimately led to a position in the new Chrysler Corporation as it was forming. There, Fred had a meteoric rise as an engineer and international trouble-shooter in Chrysler's manufacturing plants.

In this capacity it was Fred who invented the first multiple-point spot welders for use in auto production. This amazing development brought recognition directly from Walter P. Chrysler, establishing Fred as a top engineer not just at Chrysler, but also throughout the automotive industry.

Progressive Welder Company

Fred's success at Chrysler proved that Fred's ideas were not only great, but profitable as well. Fred's skill at identifying

Fred's mind, this was no gamble; it was a sure thing. He could see the future and he knew his company had to be a big part of things to come. So Fred left Chrysler and bought the remainder of Progressive. The rest is history. Within a relatively short time under Fred Johnson's shrewd leadership, Progressive became a runaway success.

At Progressive, Fred went on to invent and develop welding machines that performed near miracles. In a time when certain resistance welder machines could actually bring an electrical grid down with the raw power they consumed, Fred Johnson rewrote the book on this technology. He developed new resistance welders that used an advanced battery back-up system. This development seriously redefined the demands for power from the electrical grid and immediately took

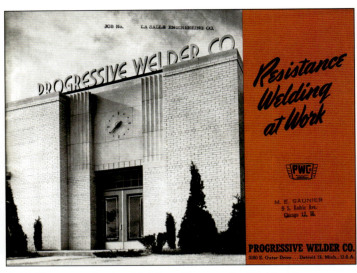

Famous entryway of Progressive Welder in the late 1940s. Sign above was trimmed in neon and illuminated at night. Doorway later became main entry to Creative Industries headquarters. Note the multiple confusing addresses of 3050 and 3070. Address became 3080 when Creative occupied the building.

A 1945 prospectus booklet from Progressive Welder Company. Building, address, clock, and front door on Detroit's East Outer Drive later became Creative Industries of Detroit headquarters.

Fixtures fabricated by Progressive Welder Company in the 1940s. Image at top was for a B-29 bomber aircraft wing and related parts. Car fans talk of "rotisserie restorations" today, but Progressive built such fixtures in the 1940s!

They don't come much bigger

Speeding the B-29 bomber program are high-precision giant fixtures such as this one, shown under construction recently at P.W.C. The company has long been known as a prime designer and builder of precision assembly, drilling, welding and checking fixtures of all types.

Shipping limitations made it necessary to build this 87-foot fixture in five sections. Leveling adjustments at each support permits the fixture proper to "float" on the frame independent of stresses caused by changes in temperature.

When assembly welding large sections, ease of handling can frequently be improved by mounting the fixture on swivel bearings to permit its being tilted in any direction for accessibility. Many such tilting fixtures are being produced at Progressive for both spot and arc welding.

· 58 ·

SCISSORS TYPE GUNS

Welding heavy truck frames with Progressive hydraulic pinch guns is practically effortless. There can be no chance of spot weld failure on truck frames—and there is none with these guns. The guns shown are mounted as a dual unit, two guns on one transformer.

High production spot welding of automobile and truck bodies is one of the largest uses for portable guns. Typical installations like the one shown below accelerate production line assembling to hitherto unknown speeds. Portable guns like those shown here can weld assemblies at the rate of 200 or more spots per minute. Progressive has installed as many as 500 gun units on one assembly line alone. Each gun in such cases is designed for only one or two of the hundreds of operations on the bodies.

SPOT WELDING

Welding Frames and Bodies

A 1945 novel scissors-type welding gun invented by Fred Johnson and Progressive Welder Company for welding vehicle bodies and chassis. They were also used for welding World War II aircraft.

production welding on a quantum leap ahead. Instead of drawing raw electrical power directly from an incoming line source, Fred's design simply diverted that power into batteries, stored it, then used it when most needed in the welding process.

This technology, combined with his other developments such as multi-point spot welding, streamlined production welding and hugely increased both the speed and capacity of welding machines. It also made geographic locations of such production welding possible outside of limited hardcore industrial areas.

This was an essential leap forward in World War II when immediate production was a necessity and manufacturing outside of traditional industrial areas had many positive wartime benefits aside from the massive boost to production. Among these benefits were that manufacturing could be located nearer to the workers and in actual areas where they lived, and manufacturing could be more easily hidden from the enemy.

Fred also devised welding machines of every imaginable size, type, and configuration. If an existing welder machine couldn't fit inside a wing, or reach a corner inside a truck body, Fred simply invented a machine that could! And he made certain that his salesmen in the field kept the company up-to-date on the latest production issues and bottlenecks. Fred never waited until a problem became unmanageable, but rather did his best to head it off and minimize any possible downtime or slowing

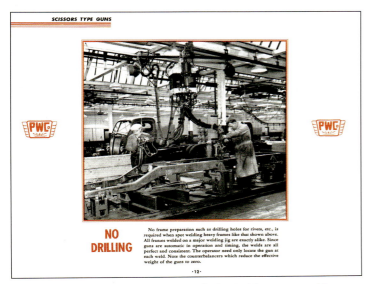

Progressive's amazing multi-spot welder machines were combination hybrid presses and fixtures. These designs and machinery sped up mass production by quantum leaps during World War II.

A Progressive motorized mobile battery welder from 1945 for spot welding aluminum revolutionized the industry.

Progressive's welding technology eliminated former need for drilling of holes to weld truck chassis.

A single order of revolutionary pedestal welders in 1940s represented tens of dollars in just one sale. These welding machines greatly increased both speed and accuracy in aircraft fabrication.

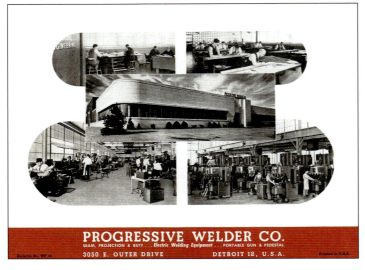

of production. This kind of genius was priceless during the war, and it rewarded Progressive with serious business contracts.

One single production order alone netted a sale of 500 complicated and expensive welding machines, a massive amount of technology but a massive amount of profit as well. The order was met and pictured within a company "pictorial," as they were called. These thick Progressive pictorials were essentially updates on resistance welding technology, listings of existing and new welding equipment, and factory fixtures also manufactured by Progressive. Each was jam-packed with photographs

Rear cover of 1944 Progressive Welder prospectus shows work area, offices, and building that would all later become Creative Industries. Note one department set aside for engineering. Windows faced Outer Drive.

Sense of family and love for the company shown as staff members of Progressive Welder, Industrial City, and their family members gather for a company photo and open house in the 1940s.

This view is looking toward Outer Drive (note no houses in background). Electrical company building would later occupy right up to edge of pavement where cars are parked on left. Note guard shack that was later moved to Moenart Street. Factory structure would be extended to center of pavement here in 1950s.

Open house festivities during 1940s included Progressive Spot Lite band composed of company employees. Band name was inspired by Progressive's welding machines that made quick, light, perfect spot welds as opposed to typical slow and heavy spot welds.

Family man and founder Fred Johnson holds daughter, Marilyn, while awarding trophy to Progressive's Junior Baseball Stars team. Members were sons of employees.

of the machinery at work and comparisons of quality regarding welding done by Progressive's advanced equipment, showing how much better it was against the industry standard.

Industrial City

A 1945 issue of *Modern Industry* described Fred Johnson's businesses and campus this way: "Johnson is interested in nine distinct companies. Seven of these are located on a five-acre tract known to Detroiters as Industrial City. These companies are loosely federated with Johnson as the connecting link. They supplement each other, that is, they serve each other; but in addition they work for all industry, hence the term 'City.' The nucleus of this City is Progressive Welder Company. It is the largest unit, employing some 400. Last year it produced over $3 million worth of welding equipment" (roughly $40.2 million in 2014 dollars).

"As the unit grew, Johnson organized new companies for specialized work instead of new departments. In such manner came the Detroit Sales Engineering Co. to furnish tool and product engineering and make perspective drawings. So, too, came the Hydro Manufacturing Co., which makes stampings. The Howe Pattern Works, which turns out wood patterns. The Industrial City Boring Co., which specializes in ultra precision work and runs an experimental machine shop; the Craftsman Tool & Die Co. producing small tools and dies. And Algoma Products, which goes in for bigger stuff: templates, fixtures, jigs, and dies. Elsewhere in Detroit, Johnson guides two other concerns: Champion Engineering Co. and Detroit Electronic Laboratories. The latter has two divisions; one repairs and rebuilds industrial tubes, while the other makes refrigerators and oil coolers.

"Johnson controls Progressive Welder. Key officials and foremen own the rest of it through stock holdings. The six affiliated concerns are all partnerships. The partners in each instance are former Johnson assistants or acquaintances in industry selected for their managerial ability."

His motto was always "Why Not?" It was coined in reaction to the many times when Fred was told some idea or technology he had was impossible, or for whatever reason couldn't be done. Yet time after time, Fred Johnson defied naysayers and succeeded in doing what supposedly couldn't be achieved.

One such project of particular pride was a steel-hulled cabin cruiser he had built in 1936. It was the ideal way to showcase Progressive Welder's prowess in both welding and nautical construction. Fred planned to entertain clients aboard while reminding them that Progressive had welded the hull.

The boat used Fred Johnson's motto as its name. Fred's *Why Not?* yacht was built in an era when such boats were normally made of wood. So why not make a cabin cruiser lakes yacht out of strong, durable steel? Conventional wisdom of the day said no for pleasure boats. Some nautical architects warned Fred that steel was too heavy and would sink or have other problems. But Johnson proved them all wrong. He had the triple-diesel inboard cabin cruiser built using Progressive's welding machines and used it successfully for many years along the Detroit River and Great Lakes. It was so modern that *Why Not?* was equipped with drive-by-wire type controls, as may be found today on modern aircraft, ships, and automobiles. Instead of rods and cables, electrical solenoids were used to remote-actuate mechanical movement aboard the boat.

Why Not? became a river cruiser and a full-bore lakes yacht that traveled all around the Great Lakes, promoting both the

Fred Johnson's Many Endeavors

- Progressive Welder Company (developed numerous welding machines and technologies, combined sheet metal presses with spot welding, famous for resistance welding machines and technology, and more)
- Industrial City (nine known companies, included die casting, sheet-metal prototyping/forming)
- Airline, Great Northern Skyways (operated out of Detroit City Airport and other airports in Michigan)
- Viking motor scooter and motorcycle
- Wood companies (actually under different names and locations, supplied hard wood for die models and clay model armatures)
- Upper Michigan (Canada) resort, Algoma Inn
- Delray Beach Florida resort, Holiday House
- Small refrigerator design, prototyping, and construction (some developed for aircraft)
- Folding rowboat design and prototyping (attached to pontoon aircraft for fishing)
- Nautical engineering, construction, including one of first steel-hull pleasure cruisers on Great Lakes
- Orphanage design and construction in Europe
- Aircraft components and welding machines development and production
- Employee profit-sharing business models developed in 1940s for his companies
- Developed company and techniques for refurbishing electronic components in 1940s to 1950s, especially electronic tubes (as for radio, TC, etc.)
- Operated janitorial service both for Industrial City and later for outside clients.
- Commercial food service and food preparation (had employee kitchen and cafeteria, later in Creative days operated by an outside contractor)

Fred Johnson (second from left) and other Industrial City managers look over laminated, sculptured hard wood pattern made for truck fender stamping die.

area and Fred's businesses. One of the main long-distance destinations was a fabulous vacation resort that Fred Johnson built on the Canadian side of Lake Huron. It was called "Algoma Inn" and featured everything from hotel-quality accommodations to swimming, fishing, boating, and more.

In the space of just a decade, Fred Johnson had built himself a far-flung empire of enterprises. Keep in mind that in addition to the multiple companies, Fred had scouted Canada and the upper peninsula of Michigan for sources of wood. Along the way he built at least two northern resorts and started his own airline! He owned a small airline that flew out of Detroit City Airport (DCA) out on Gratiot Avenue on Detroit's east side.

DCA really served as Detroit's main airport until Detroit Metropolitan Airport came into being many years hence. Based out of Detroit City Airport, Great Northern Skyways began offering flyaway vacations, hunting and fishing excursions, and more. At one point, Fred was rumored to have as many as twenty-five planes in his fleet. His personal Ryan Navion Super 260 actually had a bed that Fred had designed installed so that he could sleep in complete comfort on longer flights.

Some of the airline destinations were to resorts in the north that Fred had built. But for some destinations, the passengers changed over to pontoon planes based at a northern airport on the water. From there, travelers could continue on to remote locations that were paradise for hunters and fishers.

It was on one such outing that the great industrialist came face-to-face with his own mortality. This event took place in 1946 when flying in a pontoon airplane on a fishing trip. Onboard with Fred were three of his nephews, Stanley Hoeberg, 16; Gunnar, 25; and Ivan Johansen, 21. Fred's pilot, 23-year-old World War II veteran Douglas Bell, was at the controls when the amphibian aircraft took a hard chop and possibly caught debris when attempting a landing on a remote lake.

With the pontoon taking on water, flying back out again was not an option. The best the pilot could do was to struggle to get the craft ashore and radio for help. But despite the fact that the aircraft had only been purchased a couple of months earlier, batteries for the radio were nearly dead and help couldn't be contacted.

The temperature dipped to near freezing as food quickly ran out and the coatless travelers shivered in the cold and

MR. JOHNSON AND PARTY, JUST GOIN' PLACES, WHY NOT?

NOW .... WE INVITE YOU AND YOUR FAMILY TO VISIT US
AT OUR OWN LITTLE
ALGOMA INN
ON THE CANADIAN SHORES OF LAKE HURON

WHERE YOU CAN REALLY ENJOY YOUR SUMMER VACATION, FISHING, SWIMMING, BOATING,
DANCING, HIKING OR JUST REST AND RELAX IF YOU PREFER . . . COME ON, JOIN US.

Fred Johnson's steel-hulled yacht Why Not? in the Detroit River, 1936–1937 was used to entertain clients and friends. Although marine architects suggested wood and insisted steel was too heavy for a cabin cruiser, Fred defied them and built Why Not? completely of welded steel. It was powered by three diesel engines as would be imitated by World War II military P-T boats. Even though Fred had already launched his own company, newspapers were still referring to him as a "Chrysler engineer."

From the souvenir booklet again, Fred Johnson's fabulous Canadian Resort where Why Not? was put in to shore and where some of Johnson's pontoon-equipped aircraft and seaplanes visited.

Fred Johnson talks to new ticket buyers standing in line at beginning of his airline's operation at Detroit City Airport. (Photo Courtesy Marilyn Johnson-Smith and Robert Denton)

Fred Johnson's airline ticket depot at Detroit City Airport. (Photo Courtesy Marilyn Johnson-Smith and Robert Denton)

Fred in bed aboard his Ryan Navion Super 260. (Photo Courtesy Marilyn Johnson-Smith and Robert Denton)

Fred Johnson, wife, and pilots pose with one of his airplanes at Detroit City Airport. Large tank in background was painted with red-and-white checkerboard and was a landmark to old Detroiters in the 1930s through 1960s when air traffic moved to Detroit Metropolitan Airport, well out of town to the west of the city. (Photo Courtesy Marilyn Johnson-Smith and Robert Denton)

Onboard the same airplane with Fred in the co-pilot's seat. Johnson loved aircraft and was always ready to fly. (Photo Courtesy Marilyn Johnson-Smith and Robert Denton)

Businessmen and friends pose with one of Johnson's airplanes at DCA. (Photo Courtesy Marilyn Johnson-Smith and Robert Denton)

Another Johnson plane sits on the tarmac at Detroit City Airport. (Photo Courtesy Marilyn Johnson-Smith and Robert Denton)

Fishing junket to Northern Michigan in early 1950s with Detroit businessmen. Aircraft is Johnson's Seabee, very modern for its time and same type used decades later in the James Bond movie, Man With The Golden Gun. *Amazing folding boats in foreground were designed by Fred Johnson; they could be folded and transported on aircraft to remote fishing destinations. (Photo Courtesy Marilyn Johnson-Smith and Robert Denton)*

Another fishing expedition to remote Michigan, this time with another of Johnson's aircraft, and this one is equipped with pontoon floats. Note two folding boats designed by Johnson with trolling motors. (Photo Courtesy Marilyn Johnson-Smith and Robert Denton)

darkness. After all, they were only prepared for a day out fishing and never imagined spending the night on a remote lakeshore. As the cold became bitter and with no rescue in sight, Fred figured all they could do was hunker down, remain positive, and wait until help arrived. In the meantime, Fred decided to cannibalize the carpets and fabrics in the plane's cabin to create makeshift jackets for warmth.

It was two long nights and days later when a Canadian plane finally located the weary travelers and brought them back to safety. The only food they had eaten was one frog leg apiece, rationed from prey they had managed to capture on the lake shore. After this harrowing incident, Fred had his planes better outfitted for survival with such things as small refrigeration units and food.

Perhaps the earliest known photo mentioning Creative Industries on the doors of former Progressive Welder Company. Fred Johnson with two of his technicians. Note dream car artwork on wall. Fred holds a Christmas gift in the lobby around 1952. His young son, Ricky, is on left wearing overcoat and T-shirt. Engineer to far left was involved in the making of Creative's Viking motor scooter. Street outside is East Outer Drive.

Champagne toast launch of Creative Industries. Photo was taken in Fred Johnson's office. Rex Terry is standing third from right in front row.

The Birth of Creative Industries of Detroit

By 1950 Fred had resolved that yet another new direction was clearly needed in his enterprises. The war was long over and, while aircraft had provided lots of work in the 1940s, the most lucrative contracts that lay ahead were emerging from the auto industry. Fred and Progressive had built (and were continuing to build) a substantial portfolio of patents related to welding. But as Fred saw it, Progressive had reached its apex in the welding business and now the auto industry was beckoning in the postwar explosion of demand.

By the late 1940s, Fred could see the writing on the wall. He could see the auto industry was set to explode as returning GIs wanted cars and housing. He could also see via his airline and wartime experience with aircraft manufacturing that this business was likewise set to go supernova. Fred could see that in the upcoming peacetime years, travel in the airline industry was the coming trend. And there was no end in sight.

Wisely, Fred got busy hiring the best and the brightest engineers he could find and quickly either put them to work directly or contracted them out to other companies. It was a formula with unlimited growth potential.

As the 1940s were drawing to a close, it was obvious that much of the machinery in the war-weary United States was

Beautiful art deco waiting room outside of Fred Johnson's office. Fred's personal secretary sat at the desk on the right.

Fred Johnson's office. Although bare floors, especially of wood or fake wood, are considered upscale today, in those days wall-to-wall carpet was the ultimate in luxury!

either tired or worn out. With only minuscule exceptions, there had been no cars manufactured since the trickle that was made for a few months of the early 1942 model year. So people needed cars and the factories needed new machinery. The airlines needed airplanes. And Fred Johnson knew exactly how to supply them all. Johnson gathered all of the expertise from his own experiences in engineering and manufacturing. He poured all of the expertise of his amazing welder company on the fertile roots of his new company. Johnson combined this foundation with a mix of new talent to build an independent powerhouse unlike anything the automotive industry had ever seen before. Creative was not merely a coachbuilder. It was an engineering firm that could do it all, on the ground, in the air, and in many cases on the sea as well. There would be no stopping this new company of unlimited potential.

Just as Fred had envisioned, not just people, but companies got busy replacing worn-out machinery and products. The government was also busily replacing those things that needed replacing. But in one case, the government and the car business came together on the highest level.

Ford Motor Company decided that the limousine they had been providing to the president in Washington, D.C., was now hopelessly outdated. Even President Harry Truman needed a new vehicle. A Lincoln Cosmopolitan was now provided as the basis for an entirely new presidential limo. The engineering on this vehicle needed to be a serious jump beyond all that had ever been done previously for such vehicles. Safety, strength, power, occupant protection, and convenience all had to be major considerations. (I talk more about this fascinating limo later in Chapter Five.)

As a carryover gift from Progressive, the aircraft business with parts and engineering for companies such as Boeing was already humming along. The successful completion of the presidential Lincoln Cosmo, along with other dream cars for Ford, opened the floodgates. With Fred Johnson's connections and Progressive's amazing genius and winning reputation, contracts for special automotive work quickly came rushing in.

New contracts and alliances had only recently been made with Packard Motor Car Company and divisions of Chrysler. The contracts continued to flow and Creative's reputation for

Early employee Christmas celebration in the former Progressive Welder kitchen. Johnson's approach was to remain in the background and let whoever was in charge run the show. Here, Rex Terry (vest and tie in front of tree) is front and center, while Fred stands just behind him and to the right in this photo.

excellence had already become the latest buzz inside Detroit's car business. Most of this Creative work remains unknown to this day.

At the time of Fred's last letter to his son-in-law in 1954, two new cars (done jointly with Mitchell-Bentley Corporation) had already been completed. Suffice it to say that by the mid-1950s Creative was up and rolling at full speed. But to put it all in complete perspective, we need to return to the transition from Progressive to Creative.

The new company had its headquarters inside the same building and front door that was formerly used by Progressive Welder Company. Of course, the Progressive name up over the portico quickly disappeared. The sleek new logo, "Creative Industries of Detroit," with an offset "V" now appeared on the front of the building, which was now listed as 3080 East Outer Drive. Meanwhile, the complex of Industrial City behind the front building had changed immensely during the time of Fred's decline. The old alliances quickly became almost unrecognizable, although some were still holding. A few operations even moved away to other locations farther out of the city. Progressive Welder itself had not only expanded nationwide, but also into Canada. However, it was now largely a sales operation.

Most of Fred's businesses, for better or worse, involved partners. Some of those partners had their own agendas, which over time were sometimes wildly divergent from directions Fred had intended. Despite his legendary troubleshooting and problem-solving abilities, Fred could only do so much, even when it came to his own companies. Like any human being (no matter how skilled and intelligent), there were physical limits.

Although Fred had achieved great success in both business and working with people, inevitably there were those who envied that success. Some even wanted to cash in on it. Eventually, this greed and envy led to what seemed like endless courtroom battles, politics, and clashes with those determined to meddle in his businesses. In the end it all reached a point of critical mass. Fred could still envision what problems lay ahead and how to deal with them. But could one man manage it all? This was the question. Perhaps an overseeing company might just be the answer.

Creative Industries of Detroit, therefore, gathered the descendants of Industrial City and placed them all under one umbrella company. This allowed for a single formidable company that encompassed a cornucopia of skills and talent. It now offered all possible aspects, from engineering and design, to project management, to prototyping, to construction, and there was more to come. Good for the company, but Fred Johnson, the man, had reached a crossroads in his illustrious career.

It was now late-1954 and must have seemed as if the world was crashing in on him. Fred was tired and his health was failing. By his own admission, Johnson was now spending 80 percent of his time in bed. His wife was also ill and had just undergone a tonsillectomy. Then there remained the relentless daily pressures and headaches of business.

With everything partnered and to some extent interdependent, there were other business pressures, financial and legal. Somehow Fred had managed to hold onto his leadership. But after many years of holding it all together while relentlessly innovating, the sheer demands had become overwhelming for one man. His mind remained determined, but Fred's body could no longer persevere.

The Blond Dynamo, as some called Fred, had been a bundle of energy all of his life. He had created fabulous inventions, owned a small airline and numerous successful companies, and built an incredible vacation compound in Delray Beach, Florida. And he had a beautiful family that he adored.

The end finally came in November 1954 when the glue that held it all together finally relented. Fred died peacefully at home with relatives. He was only 58 years old. Memories are sometimes short in the fast and ever-changing pace of business that tends to look forward rather than back at what once was. Names of individuals behind the scenes can quickly disappear from the stage in the hustle and bustle of the now. Company names go on, but individuals behind the companies can quickly be forgotten.

Unfortunately, Fred was not immune to this sad phenomenon. So sometime in 1955, the portrait of Frederick H. Johnson was quietly, unceremoniously removed from the wall in the building he had originally constructed at 3080 East Outer Drive.

Marilyn Johnson-Smith poses in 2014 with a portrait of her father. She holds a rare bottle of Bush Pilot that commemorates Fred's airline and his brush with death after being marooned in the northern wilds of Canada when his aircraft was damaged.

CHAPTER THREE

REX A. TERRY AND THE BEGINNINGS OF CREATIVE INDUSTRIES OF DETROIT

*B*eing a man who was driven was a good beginning for someone who planned on going places in his life. But to be a successful engineer at Chrysler in the 1930s and 1940s, it almost seemed that one had to be named Fred. After all, there were several important engineers named Fred at Chrysler. Among them were Fred Zeder Sr. and Fred Johnson. It also didn't seem to hurt in this formula that one was Danish and had skills as a machinist.

Rex Augustus Terry had neither the first name nor the Danish ancestry. But he did have relentless drive, endless curiosity, great skill, great talent in diverse realms, and a way about him that fascinated people. He was an avid swimmer and lifeguard at River Rouge Park, a popular summer haunt for Detroiters. And Rex had a friend who was one of the Freds at Chrysler, namely Fred Johnson. Like his friend, Rex Terry was both an aircraft pilot and a renaissance man. He was also a survivor.

It was a beautiful August day in 1935 when Rex, the pilot, took to the skies and almost saw the end of both his aircraft and automotive careers. Rex lifted skyward off a runway from what was then known as "John R. Airport" at John R. Road and 16-Mile Road, just north of Detroit, Michigan. Rex and a passenger, John J. Gunter had only been airborne for about 10 minutes when disaster struck. For reasons that may never be known, the engine on their rented airplane sputtered and continued to falter.

Somewhere over the town of Big Beaver the plane lost forward momentum and thus, lift. It was a pilot's worst nightmare as the craft went into an agonizing, perilous stall.

Of course the small plane was fully loaded with two occupants and a full tank of fuel. So once the aircraft stalled in mid-air, gravity took over and they were on their way down. Somehow during all this, Rex succeeded in getting the engine restarted but getting into this kind of trouble at such a low altitude meant serious peril. Each second was an eternity. As the craft plummeted, Rex fought bravely to regain control, but try as he may, he just could not fully recover. In the end, the best Rex could do was to minimize the severity of the inevitable.

The Monocoupe clipped a roof and then careened into the front yard of a house owned by a Mrs. S. Spaulding.

Always the family man.
Creative Industries General Manager Rex Terry pauses for a Christmas visit with cake, a warm beverage, and Fred Johnson's daughter, Marilyn. Children often visited around the offices of Creative at Christmas. Time is around 1953. Street past the windows is East Outer Drive, now with houses. (Photo Courtesy Marilyn Johnson-Smith and Robert Denton)

After what must have seemed like forever, the smashed aircraft skidded to a violent halt, wedging itself between the adjacent house owned by a John Burg. Fortunately, no one was home in either house at the time.

When the dust finally settled, it was clear that both wings and the landing gear had been ripped off of the craft. Worse, now there was a whole new engine problem. Whatever caused the crash in the first place had obviously been resolved. But despite the plane being shattered in pieces on the ground, the engine now stubbornly continued to run! In the chaotic situation, Rex quickly regained his presence of mind and somehow managed to shut the engine down. Otherwise there surely would have been a fire, or worse.

Somehow, miraculously the fliers had survived after plummeting more than 300 feet, dead stick to the ground. Due to Rex's skill and quick thinking, they were alive. An alert bystander (reportedly with the interesting and almost prophetic name of Frank Vettes) struggled valiantly to pull Terry and Gunter out of the smashed aircraft. But the nightmare had only just begun.

Both occupants had been seriously injured. Gunter had severe facial cuts and a head injury. Rex also had severe cuts and scrapes, but worst of all, a back injury.

Rex A. Terry with biplane he flew. Terry was fascinated with flying and aircraft, an expert pilot; he was also a flight instructor and a member of a flying club. Rex eventually crashed in mid-1930s just north of Detroit. He recovered from serious injuries, became general manager, and ultimately president of Creative. (Photo Courtesy Pamela Terry Bonk)

Of course in the mid-1930s, EMTs and rapid transport to an emergency room was the stuff of science fiction. But even with the limitations of the day, the crash survivors were finally transported to Royal Oak private hospital where Rex was listed in serious but stable condition.

For a time it was feared that Rex Terry could end up paralyzed. He was in severe pain and at first, his lower extremities seemed slow to respond. This development alarmed the doctors and Terry underwent a series of X-rays performed on his back.

However, Terry was in top physical shape due to the fact that he was an expert swimmer and lifeguard at Detroit-area Rouge Park. His youth and skill as a pilot combined with his strong physical condition were factors that probably saved Rex Terry's life. These factors, bolstered by his positive mental attitude and strong will to survive, meant there was just no giving in to the pain.

So it wasn't long before Rex bounced back and was on his feet and fully functioning. He was twenty-four years of age and it soon became obvious that there wasn't much that could keep Rex down, even a plane crash. Soon Rex was back to flying again. He was just that kind of guy.

Here is how his daughter, Pamela, describes Rex today: "He was a bantamweight boxer, an equestrian, won diving medals, golfer, played couples bridge with mom, and lots of gin rummy with his buddies at the Detroit Athletic Club (D.A.C.). They had a club *within* the club called Room 634. He was meticulous about the outdoor aesthetics at home, at the Lake House (Crystal Lake in Michigan), and 3080 East Outer Drive, Creative Industries. Lots of flowers and freshly mowed grass. He actually had an engineering sensibility about everything. He was always saying, 'A place for everything and everything in its place!'"

Rex was always impeccably dressed and was a *very* Dapper Dan indeed. If ever you saw Rex Terry, especially behind the wheel of his beautiful

Terry and members of his Flying Falcons club review mechanic's manual for his biplane at Detroit City Airport in the early 1930s. Left to right are George Thurston, Rex Terry, Al Conklin, and Gene Crissman. The Flying Falcons met via lifeguard jobs at Detroit area River Rouge Park. (Photo Courtesy Pamela Terry Bonk)

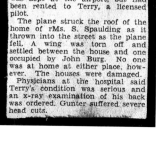

2 MEN INJURED IN PLANE CRASH

Monoplane Hits Roof, Tears Off Wing and Lands Between Houses.

ROYAL OAK, Mich., Aug. 6.—Two men were injured this afternoon when an airplane fell 300 feet and lodged between two houses in Big Beaver. The men were Rex A. Terry, 24 years old, 92 Arizona avenue west, Detroit, the pilot, and J. J. Gunter, 34, of 1129 Merrick street, Detroit. Both were taken to Royal Oak Private Hospital, Terry with serious back injuries.

Frank Vettes, og Big Beaver, who lifted the men from the wreckage, sai the motor was running with the plane hit the ground. Officials at the John R. airport, at John R. and the Sixteen Mile roads, however, said they believed a stalling engine caused the crash. The plane, a Monocoup, owner by William Warwin, 13498 Greeley avenue, Detroit, was kept at the airport, but had been rented to Terry, a licensed pilot.

The plane struck the roof of the home of rMs. S. Spaulding as it thrown into the street as the plane fell. A wing was torn off and settled between the house and one occupied by John Burg. No one was at home at either place, however. The houses were damaged.

Physicians at the hospital said Terry's condition was serious and an x-ray examination of his back was ordered. Gunter suffered severe head cuts.

Rex A. Terry plane crash. (Photo Courtesy Pamela Terry Bonk)

Dapper Detroit dressers and Chrysler connection. Fred H. Johnson (left), founder of Progressive Welder Company and Creative Industries, stands next to his luxurious 1951 Chrysler New Yorker convertible. Fred's Chrysler was done in a special copper color. Rex is on the right beaming.

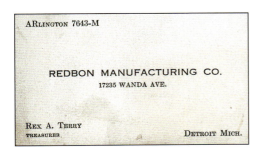

Rex's business card from his position at Redbon Manufacturing Company. (Photo Courtesy Pamela Terry Bonk)

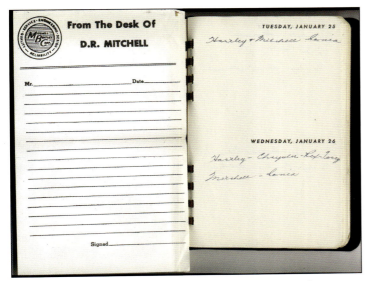

From Don Mitchell's 1944 business diary, which shows possibly the earliest meeting with Rex Terry as Wednesday, January 26, 1944. Notation states, "Hartley – Chrysler – Rex Terry."

Packard Panther driving around Detroit, it was a sight to remember in the 1950s. He was a serious businessman, but Rex knew how to live and with his movie star looks, he brought just a taste of Hollywood to Detroit.

And the elegance extended beyond dress in Rex's life. One of his favorite slogans was, "Always a gentleman, no matter how painful." Those weren't just words. As with the plane crash, Rex actually lived out his credo.

Now, Rex had become good friends with Fred Johnson via their years at Chrysler. Both were fascinated with and clearly understood machinery. Obviously, Fred and Rex both loved cars and making things. Both were meticulous problem solvers. Johnson and Terry were also pilots and loved flying. Both were shutterbugs and loved cameras and photography. Both were very devoted fathers and family men.

Like Fred, Rex had begun branching out early in his career, searching for ways to expand his knowledge and career. Rex developed skills at managing business money by serving for a time as treasurer to a Detroit company called Redbon Manufacturing. This was in addition to his other numerous activities.

During his time at Chrysler, Terry had risen to become assistant chief engineer of Commercial Vehicle Engineering. This position provided Rex with many key contacts that would later become invaluable in his position working for Fred Johnson. It also gave Rex much first-hand experience in knowing costs of engineering and parts, and his position at Chrysler allowed Terry to understand the best ways of interfacing with clients and how to appeal to them. Rex knew how to sell, but he wasn't a poser. He actually knew all of the technical aspects as well. These were things that anyone in the upper echelon of automotive engineering had to know in order to be successful. Of course, knowing your job was one thing, but gaining positive traction with clients was quite another.

Rex Terry also brought in a sales wiz named Arthur Bradley. Bradley was so skilled at landing clients that once he was teamed up with Terry, the combo was unbeatable. Art Bradley's services were considered so valuable in those days that he was not even listed as an employee, but rather as a separate company inside of Creative. At the beginning, it was Art Bradley who actually went out and made big presentations on behalf of Creative. Like Fred Johnson, Rex had a keen eye for talent.

It is unknown what title Rex held at the very beginning, but by 1952, Fred Johnson appointed Terry as general manager. Creative Industries of Detroit was now just two years old, but it already had a bright future in store.

The Mitchell-Bentley Company

In the case of Creative Industries, it was almost impossible for the circles of business, finance, and technology *not* to

Christmas party fun at Creative (this one believed to be 1953). Fred Johnson can just be seen standing in the rear on the right side of the doorway. A smiling Gary Hutchings (in glasses) is fourth to his right. Next row forward, at the far right, the tall fellow with dark hair (and Don Mitchell's son-in-law) is Treasurer Walter Taylor. Immediately to his left is David Margolis. The woman three people to his left is Rex's faithful secretary, Mary Jusco. Rex Terry sits in the front row in the dapper suit and French cuffs, on a secretary's lap, a traditional Christmas comic prank. Rex told jokes and thanked the crew for another good year.

Early company dinner honoring Rex on his appointment to general manager of Creative Industries. Founder Fred Johnson sits off to right of dinner table.

intersect. It was inevitable if whoever was in charge had vision. Fred Johnson's genius of operating and conceiving business seemed limitless and already set the stage for what seemed a never-ending chain of businesses interlinked, interdependent, and yet somehow self-generating. It worked, and no one in Detroit ever came up with a better model. But with Fred's passing in 1954, it would take someone with the panache, strength, vision, and style to hold it all together and focus on the job ahead. That person was Rex A. Terry. Terry had his own inimitable style, as well as a business network. Some of that network was in downtown Detroit where Rex often held court at the D.A.C.

Room 634 at the D.A.C. was a hotbed of wheeling and dealing Motor City style. The club was already a kind of corporate old boys' club. But Room 634 merely intensified and concentrated the mix of business and camaraderie. It was one of those very, very private melting pots where auto industry moguls rubbed shoulders over cigars, brandy, cognac, and games of gin rummy. While one might see a big exec from one of the companies elsewhere roaming the D.A.C., Room 634 was one of those places where friendships and the big deals *really* got cemented.

One of the regular visitors who began dropping by for socializing and card games was D.A.C. member Don Mitchell of Mitchell-Bentley Corporation. Mitchell-Bentley was particularly known for making station wagons, especially woodies, and was located in Owosso and Ionia Michigan.

Don and Rex became fast friends and their already successful businesses flourished even more as a result. According to Don Mitchell's personal business diaries, his first official meeting noted with Rex took place in January 1944. World War II was turning in favor of the allies and automotive men

THE STATION WAGON KING

Don Mitchell was a master dealmaker and salesman extraordinaire. He was known as the "Station Wagon King" due to his many contracts with the big three for converting sedans into station wagons going back to the 1940s. It is said that many of Mitchell's most lucrative contracts were either conceived or actually signed at the D.A.C. or at his vacation home in Northern Michigan, where he often flew auto execs in for posh vacations or weekend getaways. Mitchell was known for pulling rabbits out of a hat when it came to getting automotive contracts. At one time, Don had generated so much business, he had to hire entire staffs and acquire entire companies. He provided a huge amount of income for both the people who worked for him and the communities where his factories were located. He was a major player in the American car business who is barely known today.

MITCHELL-BENTLEY AND CREATIVE OWNERSHIP

Today there are rumors of Mitchell-Bentley or the Mitchells having owning 50 percent of the stock in Creative and even directing activities at Creative. But the facts do not agree with such a notion.

With Fred Johnson's family owning more than this amount and ultimately with Rex Terry acquiring 10 percent, the math just doesn't work. Whatever percentages the Mitchells may or may not have owned, it had to be far less than 50 percent. Either way, there was no control over Creative. And there was another financial connection to Mitchell-Bentley.

Don's daughter, Sue, became engaged to a young man from Rochester, Michigan. His name was Walter J. Taylor and he was (at least for a time) treasurer for none other than Creative Industries of Detroit. Taylor can be seen in several shots of Creative dinners and parties. But he eventually disappeared from the staff for unknown reasons and was never seen at Creative again.

on top of the business were beginning to seriously think about the coming boom of a postwar era.

Rex was working for Chrysler at the time. Only a few years later and because of Terry's deep knowledge of newly emerging fiberglass use in making car bodies, Don invited Rex to become a board member of a newly acquired subsidiary. The company, Mitchell Plastics, was renamed from Bolta-Carpart, Inc. of Owosso. Ownership was made possible by Mitchell spiriting stock away from General Tire & Rubber of Akron, Ohio.

By the early 1950s and with advice from Rex and Creative, Don Mitchell's Ionia Manufacturing Division of Mitchell-Bentley made a bold move of winning a contract with Packard Motor Car Company to build their fabulous Caribbean convertibles, starting in the 1953 model year.

Rex Terry did much to continue policies of Fred Johnson and continued to instill a feeling of family around the company. Creative employees of that period still considered themselves almost relatives and believed the company was as much a family and friendship as it was a job. As one staff member said, "No one would miss one of the parties, especially at Christmas. We worked very hard, but we always had great fun together."

While being a serious businessman, Rex also had a great sense of humor and could even laugh at himself. He was

Fred Johnson (far right) and Don Mitchell (second from left) relax at Holiday House. Rex stands behind. (Photo Courtesy Marilyn Johnson-Smith and Robert Denton)

Don "Station Wagon King" Mitchell stands next to 1956 Mercury just transformed into station wagon at his plant.

Creative's graphics division often produced humorous items for internal use that kept staff laughing in times of concern. Cartoon caricature was done during the oil crisis of the 1970s. Rex cracks a whip on the Creative upper management members dressed in slave garb, with names of each on the flaps. The occasion was the annual trek to Florida for winter vacation. Ever-smiling personal secretary, Mary Jusco, types away on the rear deck of the Cadillac Eldorado. Of course, I-75 was the main interstate highway route direct from Detroit to Florida. In those days it was a Michigander's version of a north-south Route 66. (Photo Courtesy Pamela Terry Bonk)

legendary for his joke-telling skills and was even occasionally caricatured in company cartoons.

Like Fred Johnson, Rex was also a devoted family man and always tried to find time to spend with his wife and daughter. In winters he vacationed with his family in Florida at the beautiful Holiday House resort compound that Fred Johnson had built in Delray Beach.

Rex's daughter Pamela put it this way: "Holiday House, I believe was owned by Fred Johnson. It was on Route A1A on the ocean, south of the town of Delray Beach. It was pink with a white roof. When you walked up from the circle drive where the Packard was photographed, there were two villas, one on the right and one on the left, freestanding. A Danish couple, friends of Fred's, rented the left one for the winter season I believe. She practiced oil painting. Straight ahead was a squared-off U-shaped building. The bottom of the "U" were two townhouses connected on the second story by a long hallway. The first floor was divided by an open archway that led to a courtyard. The other two arms of the "U" were efficiency apartments that were rented out. Straight ahead of the courtyard were the beach and the ocean. Fred and Josephine lived on one side in the townhouse, and Marilyn and Rick stayed in the connected townhouse on the other side with their governess, Mary.

"The Mitchells and the Terrys vacationed at Holiday House for a few weeks in the winter. I would bring my schoolbooks and attend Gerhart Day School in Delray with Marilyn and Rick. The school is no longer there."

Executives from the automotive world, politicians, and celebrities also stayed at Fred's Holiday House resort. One of these was Grover Whalen. He was the famous ambassador to New York, the fellow who ran the 1939 World's Fair and all of the ticker tape parades for dignitaries and celebrities for decades. Grover, Fred, Don, and Rex would pal around, go deep-sea fishing, and just relax beachside.

Sometimes Rex had his Packard Panther sent down from Detroit and it was used in the sunny climes for pure enjoyment. He referred to it as "Creative's Panther." Friends who came to visit took turns behind the wheel of the beautiful fiberglass Packard dream car.

Under Rex Terry's leadership, top automotive sales veteran Richard Leasia was brought onboard, and between the talents

Winter vacation in Florida at Fred Johnson's Holiday House resort. From left to right are Mrs. Metta Mitchell, Don Mitchell, and celebrity New York ambassador Grover Whalen. (Photo Courtesy Marilyn Johnson-Smith and Robert Denton)

Miriam and Verne Koppin at 45th wedding anniversary for Rex and Lois Terry. Verne became part owner of Creative upon Rex's retirement. (Photo Courtesy Pamela Terry Bonk)

Florence and Richard Leasia at 45th wedding anniversary for Rex and Lois Terry. Dick became part owner of Creative upon Rex's retirement. (Photo Courtesy Pamela Terry Bonk)

of Terry, Verne Koppin, and Dick Leasia, Creative Industries forged ahead to become a major powerhouse in Detroit's automotive industry, as well as in an amazing myriad of other industries including aircraft and aerospace.

Terry remained active for many years with Creative and took great delight in its continued success. But ultimately during the 1980s, he sold out his interest in Creative to his two key men, Richard Leasia and Verne Koppin. They became co-owners of Creative and took the company on to eventually become part of Masco Industries, whereupon it became known as "The Creative Group." But Rex Terry remained on the board of directors and continued to actively advise and promote Creative Industries long after he had sold his interests. He loved the business that much.

The 1962 U.S. Trade Fair in Tokyo, Japan. Rex Terry with hovercraft genius Dr. William Bertelsen. Terry prepares to give a presentation regarding Bertlesen's floating car constructed by Creative Industries.

Creative in Japan, about 1962. Rex meets with members of Mitsubishi Motors in Japan. It's customary in Japan even for very senior management to wear company shop jackets when working at corporate facilities. (Photo Courtesy Pamela Terry Bonk)

More Creative in Japan. Rex sits in front of large wall chart presentation outlining Creative's clay model and styling processes. (Photo Courtesy Pamela Terry Bonk)

In silk suit and tie, holding a gold Cross pen as a pointer, as he often did in demonstrations. Rex Terry gives perspective and analysis on advanced automotive design and engineering to team members at Mitsubishi Motors in Japan during the 1960s. (Photo Courtesy Pamela Terry Bonk)

Rex outlines fine styling points to Mitsubishi team members in Japan with customary gold Cross pen as pointer. Creative and Rex were pioneers in working with the Japanese auto industry, as far back as 1950s. (Photo Courtesy Pamela Terry Bonk)

It was late May 1987 and Rex had been having difficulties with chest pains and breathing for the previous two weeks at his Florida retreat. He was already aware that congestive heart disease had begun to wreak havoc on his body. However, there was some light at the end of what seemed to be a dark tunnel. An angioplasty procedure was scheduled for the following day at University of Michigan hospital in Ann Arbor. The procedure was envisioned as a countermeasure that would finally relieve Terry's condition. Once the angioplasty could be per-

formed, hopefully all would be well. But in the meantime, Rex's condition became so severe upon flying back to Michigan that he ended up at William Beaumont Hospital in Royal Oak.

Among the visitors to Beaumont hospital that day were Dick Leasia and Verne Koppin. The duo stopped by the hospital that evening to check on their former boss. Koppin says, "Rex was sitting up in bed and we had a nice chat, just like old times. It was just like the old Rex."

After Messrs. Koppin and Leasia left, Terry's longtime secretary, Mary Jusco, had decided to stop by on her way home after work. It was almost 8:00 p.m. and Mary walked in to find Rex sitting up in his hospital bed, combing his hair. Mrs. Jusco teased her boss about flirting with the nurses and invoked his old nickname of "Sexy Rexy." It was an affectionate name that girls called Rex in his youth because he looked so much like Hollywood movie star heartthrob Clark Gable. They had a good time chatting for a while and then said goodnight, promising to talk again the next day. But for Rex Terry, tomorrow never came.

Ironically Mary Jusco, his secretary who knew him best and for more years than anyone else at Creative, was probably the last person to see Rex alive. He died peacefully in his sleep that night at the hospital in Royal Oak. Rex Augustus Terry was 77 years old.

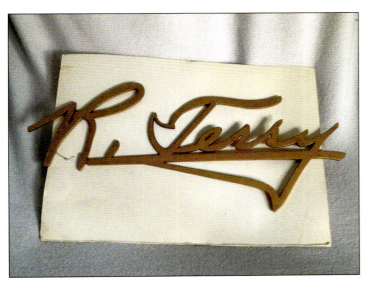

Rex Terry's signature in metal. Creative was a pioneer in computerized cuts of graphics in metal. (Photo Courtesy Pamela Terry Bonk)

Still stylishly attired in later years, Rex owned a Piper plane and had a personal pilot, Bill Rosenstenghal. (Photo Courtesy Pamela Terry Bonk)

Always with a sense of humor, Rex had this portrait done in a Napoleonic pose, with a grin and a wink! It now hangs in the home of his daughter, Pamela Terry Bonk, who is admiring her dad. (Photo Courtesy Pamela Terry Bonk)

CHAPTER FOUR

IT WASN'T ALL CARS: BIG AND SMALL THINGS YOU NEVER KNEW THEY DID

No matter which direction Creative may have ventured, you could always rest assured that the outcome would be intensely interesting. Here was a company with projects that could never be boring. And some projects may completely surprise you. Among them was one of Creative's very first projects. It overlapped with Fred Johnson's Progressive Welder Company and the beginning of Creative Industries (1949–1950). But this one wasn't an automobile.

Viking Motor Scooters

Fred Johnson was a man of ideas who was fascinated with machinery. Boats. Planes. Cars. He loved them all. Anyone who knew Fred was immediately aware of the fact that he was always looking for the next new direction to explore.

With the end of World War II, and the lack of automobiles in a world ravaged by war, not only the country, but the whole planet was hungry for transportation. The fighting was over and bombs were no longer falling. However, in most parts of the world, gasoline was tough to find and expensive to buy. Even in the United States and with restrictions lifted on buying gas, you still had to have a vehicle in which to use it.

Cars hadn't been manufactured since early 1942, yet the world needed to get back on wheels. The quickest, easiest vehicles to produce were motorized two-wheelers. So the 1940s and 1950s quickly became the era of the motorcycles, motor scooters, and motorized bicycles.

During the 1940s, salesmen from Fred Johnson's Progressive Welder were calling on manufacturing companies all along the West Coast. They had done major business in that area due to all of the war-related industries and aircraft manufacturing being done in California and Washington state. Progressive's salespeople knew where just about every little manufacturing company was, and they were certainly aware of Breene-Taylor, which made the famous Whizzer motorbike. They were also aware of Salsbury and their new deluxe streamlined motor scooter.

As soon as Fred heard about the Salsbury, he ordered a small fleet of them. He kept at least two for his personal use at

Fred Johnson wearing a boating hat and relaxing at home in Michigan riding his Salsbury 85 motor scooter. Passengers are son Rick and daughter Marilyn. Handlebar device is loud bell! (Photo Courtesy Marilyn Johnson-Smith and Robert Denton)

Rick and Marilyn Johnson inspect Fred's Salsbury in Florida. Fred's Cadillac is on right. (Photo Courtesy Marilyn Johnson-Smith and Robert Denton)

Fred and family ride Salsbury 85s in Florida winter. (Photo Courtesy Marilyn Johnson-Smith and Robert Denton)

Fred in Michigan with family and three motor scooters. Futuristic prototype on right was made at Creative. Headlight and seat were Salsbury. Handlebars, front fork, fender, and wheel were all from 1949–1950 CWC Roadmaster bicycle. Right grip was throttle. A 1948 Packard in background has 1949 license, Van Auken rear bumper guard.

his Delray Beach, Florida, resort. At least one other was kept at his home in Michigan.

At the very end of the war, Johnson quickly decided to go home to Denmark and survey the damage inflicted on the country by the Nazi army. Fred found heartbreaking devastation. There were thousands of homeless orphaned children and a devastated countryside and infrastructure. As a result, Fred promptly committed to building orphanages and vowed to help get the country back on its feet. He received awards for his kind generosity, but upon his return home to America, another thing remained on Fred's mind. There just might be a serious market for two-wheeled motorized vehicles. The only downside was that the window for this market might only exist for a short time. So the time to move had to be immediate.

Fred sat down and designed a series of motorbikes or lightweight motorcycles that he felt would meet his objective. At least one of the crossover engineers from Progressive who migrated into the early Creative Industries staff was put to work assembling prototypes that might fulfill Fred's vision.

Eventually the new prototypes went into three general types. The first was equipped to carry up to three adults in

Same engineer, colder weather, with a three-passenger Viking prototype. Center seat is Salsbury. Brick building behind was Creative Industries office. To left was East Outer Drive. Handlebar stem was from Shelby bicycle. (Photo Courtesy Marilyn Johnson-Smith and Robert Denton)

Early Viking prototype. Spring fork is European. Seat is American Mesinger motorbike. Fenders universal bicycle. Grips 1948 Whizzer "Twistgrips." Speedometer is Stewart-Warner bicycle. Handlebar, stem are bicycle. Fairings over motor and clutch were considered stylish.

Same engineer, three-passenger Viking prototype fully loaded. Could've substituted for car where none were available after World War II. (Photo Courtesy Marilyn Johnson-Smith and Robert Denton)

Fred Johnson with 1952 Viking prototype and visitors, possibly from Europe. Note seat backrest changed, rear completely enclosed with new taillight. Curved tails of lower fairing are brushed stainless steel. (Photo Courtesy Marilyn Johnson-Smith and Robert Denton)

Engineer must have been a beer lover: The baskets have four types of beer cases: Budweiser, Pabst Blue Ribbon, Blatz, and Miller High Life. Seat, headlight are Salsbury. Front sheet metal has mesh insert different from other versions. Note windshield and rearview mirror. (Photo Courtesy Marilyn Johnson-Smith and Robert Denton)

Fred Johnson with Rick, Marilyn, and last-known Viking prototype. Front end now is motorcycle type headlight, fork, fender, brake, wheel, and tire. Throttle, brake handle, taillight all appear to be the new design. (Photo Courtesy Marilyn Johnson-Smith and Robert Denton)

tandem. The second was designed to carry light cargo. in essence, a grocery-getter. The third ranged from stripped-down sports scooters to streamlined, enclosed bodies. One special fourth type was designed with a collapsible front end that allowed it to fit onboard Fred's small aircraft. These prototypes

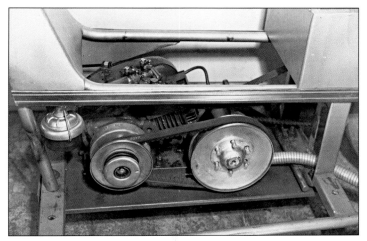

Detail view of CVT pulley on early Viking prototype clutch.

Engineer with passengers. Brick building was Creative Industries offices. Compare angular sheet metal on front to futuristic version shown earlier. (Photo Courtesy Marilyn Johnson-Smith and Robert Denton)

Early collapsible Viking prototype could be carried inside Fred's airplanes and was used at destinations. (Photo Courtesy Marilyn Johnson-Smith and Robert Denton)

were all under construction during the time that Creative was first opening. The name of the prototypes was a kind of homage to the bold adventurers from Fred's ancestral area of the world: Viking.

The three-seater version used a cobbled cushion on the rear and a Salsbury seat in the center position. The beer and grocery-getter version used an oversize American-made Mesinger saddle familiar to collectors today. This same saddle was used on various motorbikes and motorcycles of the era. It is unclear where all of the motors were derived.

The clutch was at least inspired (possibly made) by Salsbury. It was an ingenious continuously variable pulley and clutch assembly installed on all three types.

Engineer with grocery-getter Viking. Note seat and headlight are Salsbury. Front sheet metal different from other versions, has mesh insert. Note windshield and mesh saddle baskets. Car in background is parked on East Outer Drive. (Photo Courtesy Marilyn Johnson-Smith and Robert Denton)

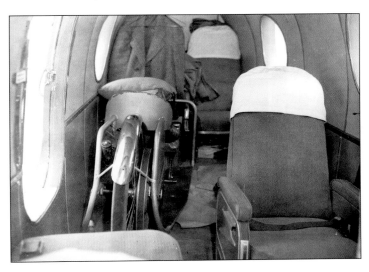

However, as it turned out, the window for motorized two-wheelers unfortunately snapped shut nearly as quickly as it opened in America. By the early 1950s, despite the Korean War, most of the people who wanted motorized bicycles, lightweight motorcycles, and motor scooters had already bought them. What people really wanted at that point was automobiles.

Even though there could have been a market in Europe for motor scooters and motorbikes, and even motorized bicycles, the costs to export there was tremendous. There were European import fees put up to protect those countries from domestic unemployment and flows of foreign (in this case, American) manufactured goods.

As such, the idea of the Viking motorcycle, motorbike, and motor scooter lines was eventually dropped. There was more than enough automotive work to go around in Detroit, and Creative Industries needed to be prepared for that future. And so it was. There were still other non-automotive projects that came in the door at Creative. But for the time being, Detroit's future was the future of Creative Industries.

The Magical Ironrite

One of Creative's early collaborations was with a Detroit area appliance maker. According to the Mount Clemons, Michigan, library, Ironrite began operations in the 1920s with Detroit's J. L. Hudson department store as the original retail-selling agent. Postwar manufacturing for Ironrite moved to the city of Mount Clemons.

By the 1950s, the Ironrite ironing machine was a very popular invention that could even be seen on the relatively new medium of television. It was a housewife's dream, and even my mother became starry-eyed every time the TV commercial came on. In those days, there was no "permanent press" in clothing, so virtually everything needed to be ironed. Anything that could reduce the labor in ironing was a welcome friend back then.

The Ironrite machine was composed of a soft, covered roller and a heated metal panel. It was built in a form almost like a consolette or a sewing machine and changed the entire concept and process of ironing clothes. Instead of spending hours having to stand at an ironing board and lunging back and forth with a hot, heavy iron, the user could now be seated comfortably in a chair. The only movement necessary was to simply lay an article of clothing on the intake panel, engage the roller and spin it slowly. The clothing was thus ironed as it was pulled in and rolled through the machine in a single sweep. The Ironrite was a wonder and the company sold thousands of them. Most went to hotels and laundry services. But a good number went to wealthy households. Had it not been for the obstacle of price, Ironrite would have sold three or four times as many.

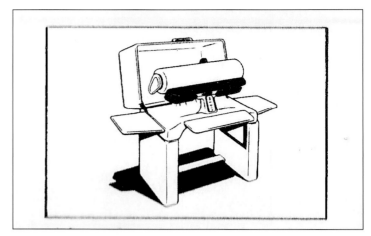

Ironrite console ironing machine for home, as pictured in 1956 Creative Industries brochure with no caption or identification.

So by the 1950s, the strategy was to make Ironrite a major household appliance as well. If the price could be reduced, manufacturing streamlined, and the machine sized just right for the home, the Ironrite people foresaw a bundle of profits to go with all of that laundry. All the while, nobody knew it, but Creative helped to design and reengineer these wondrous machines.

Today's recountings never mention the contribution of Creative Industries to Ironrite's history. However, the 1956 Creative Industries prospectus indeed simply illustrates a line drawing the Ironrite machine in the Product Engineering Division section. This work had been accomplished years earlier when Creative first opened its doors and Ironrite's assembly line in Mount Clemons was expanded. Creative remained as a source to Ironrite for years to follow, but as far as I know, Creative Industries was never mentioned in press coverage or histories of the machine or company.

Creative continued in its stealth role and served untold other companies in their quest for the best engineering and latest in technology. Of course, thousands of automotive components and accessories were developed, prototyped, even manufactured at Creative. Some, such as Van Auken bumper guards, are still remembered. Others are long forgotten. But most were things the public and even Creative's employees just never knew about.

As the 1956 Creative prospectus brochure stated, "For security purposes this division uses a special coding system. Jobs are identified by number only, and not even the employees of Creative Industries are informed of the name of the specific customer. Similar systems are used in other divisions when it becomes necessary." So after all these years, is it any wonder that the secret projects of Creative Industries are still mostly secret? After all, that's exactly the way they wanted it.

CHAPTER FIVE

THE EARLY YEARS, IKE'S COSMO AND THE MERCURY XM-800

C reative had agreements with many of their clients to maintain absolute secrecy. Few were the times that Creative was even mentioned in the work that they did. Like the unknown Motown Funk Brothers musicians who anonymously cranked out hit after hit, Creative did likewise for the car companies. Except for rare occasions, Creative's work went on without public acknowledgment. After all, Creative's job was to complete projects at the behest of their clients and not to gain fame via newspaper headlines. So in short, Creative was perhaps Detroit's best-kept automotive secret, and they were content to keep things that way. Aside from an occasional one-line blurb buried in a newspaper caption or trade publication, Creative's credit was the payment they received for a job well done. As for glory? That accolade remained sealed within the walls of the Creative buildings and (to a limited extent) inside the minds of their employees. And that was that.

Internally, Creative's people were given code names for contracts rather than actual names. This is not uncommon even at OEMs. Code names and numbers are a wise policy, and were even back in the 1950s. Of course, information leaks back then were nowhere near the wild levels of today. Furthermore, such coding policy easily builds in a facet that security people refer to as "plausible deniability."

At Creative, components of a car, for instance, were broken up and spread among several people or even over multiple divisions. In the end, only the people at the top usually knew what was going on throughout the company at any given time. Today, even after talking with key people involved in projects, it is often maddening to piece things together in a way that makes sense. Stories of who did what often zigzag back and forth or go in a confusing circle to nowhere and everywhere. Perhaps there is no greater example than the 1950 bubbletop Lincoln Cosmopolitan presidential limousine done for the White House.

Coachbuilder Henney Auto Body in Illinois supplied the first set of cars. Shortly after the time that Creative was opening its doors, legend has it that Ford tapped supreme classic coachbuilder Ray Dietrich in Battle Creek, Michigan, to do a

One of initial Henney-bodied presidential limos. Note padded hard roof, rear skirts, no "eyebrow" over rear fender. Also louvered metal running boards attached at rocker panels for Secret Service agents. (Photo Courtesy Thomas A. McPherson Collection)

convertible treatment on one of the 1950 Lincoln presidential limousines. But the Dietrich facility was winding down by this point. Could it really do all of the engineering and construction necessary to deliver such a car to the White House all on its own?

The real secret of the engineering and construction on this limo remains unknown to this day. Much of the work was done by engineers lent out from Creative Industries of Detroit. Later, a new bubble-top update with removable roof sections was ordered and completed for 1954 with the help of an automotive designer extraordinaire, and engineering from Creative Industries. Creative made the entire roof assembly. Although some say President Eisenhower thought the top made the limo interior too hot, the press and the public loved it.

According to Professional Car Society historian, Thomas A. McPherson, the bubble top Lincoln Cosmopolitan limo was designated "USSS." Collectors and historians know it today as "the Dietrich Lincoln." Of the fleet of Lincoln Cosmo limos, this was a very famous presidential limo indeed and had several distinctions.

Jumping back in time. Dietrich Cosmo with domed wheel covers. Note rear fender skirts, with chrome "eyebrows" installed. Also note light color top boot with dark piping; Secret Service agent step retracted. (Photo Courtesy Thomas A. McPherson Collection)

Dietrich Cosmo with folding soft-top fully raised. Prior to Creative conversion, top fabric was all one piece, light-colored fabric material. (Photo Courtesy Thomas A. McPherson Collection)

SPECIFICATIONS OF DIETRICH/ CREATIVE BUBBLE-TOP LINCOLN

The following data is courtesy of Thomas A. McPherson.

Engine, 336.7-ci V-8

Transmission, hydramatic

Passengers, 7

Top, power-operated folding and metal-framed plexiglass bubble assembly

Tires, 8.20 x 15 Good Year double eagle whitewall

Upholstery, genuine leather, pleated

Warning alert, siren located under hood, red lights on front bumper

Wheelbase, 145.0 inches

Overall length, 240.0 inches

Overall width, 89.5 inches

Overall height, 65.0 inches

Front tread, 59.0 inches

Rear tread, 60.2 inches

Curb weight, 6,450 pounds

Dietrich Cosmo enters U.S. Air Force C-130 aircraft. Note black full convertible top with tempered glass backlight window. (Photo Courtesy Thomas A. McPherson Collection)

The Lincoln Cosmo Limos

First, it served at least three American presidents: Harry S. Truman, Dwight D. Eisenhower, and John F. Kennedy. It was the car that John and Jackie rode in for President Kennedy's inauguration. The Dietrich Lincoln also carried British Queen Elizabeth II on her visit to the United States. Furthermore, at its introduction, this was the largest American-made seven-passenger convertible limousine.

Unlike the other Lincoln Cosmo presidential limos, this one had no gold plating in the interior, had no divider window, and no broadcloth fabric. The interior was upholstered only in genuine leather. Other distinguishing features were a continental kit spare tire on the extended rear bumper and pullout steps for Secret Service agents. Initially this car had skirts on the rear, but those were later removed. Additionally, chrome fender "eyebrows" used on the front fenders were repeated over the rear wheel openings.

The extremely complex convertible top mechanism incorporated a two-stage erection. First, a scissors-type mechanism lifted the top stack framework upward to height and then the top folded forward. The top framework bows were made of ultra-light magnesium and this was covered originally in a tan fabric, probably Orlon. The top and boot were later redone in black fabric.

According to Tom McPherson, the bubble-top Dietrich Lincoln logged approximately 100,000 miles on the ground and covered over 50,000 miles being transported aboard military aircraft.

Today, this vehicle resides in the Henry Ford museum. Signage at that museum will simply tell you that Ford built the vehicle. Other histories get even more elaborate but usually attribute all of the presidential Cosmo limos to Henney and stop right there.

Creative bubble top rear section assembly installed and rear seat raised, England's **Queen Elizabeth II** *sits next to President Dwight D. Eisenhower. (Photo Courtesy Thomas A. McPherson Collection)*

And remember those veteran coachbuilder companies mentioned in Chapter Four? Well, the firm of Ray Dietrich, Inc. was owned and operated by Raymond H. Dietrich, who had also run the famous coachbuilding firm of the same name. In his earlier years, Dietrich was also involved in the LeBaron coachbuilding company mentioned previously. LeBaron ended up under the wing of Chrysler Corporation, and Dietrich went on to other things. Among these were the startling electric Firebird guitars and Thunderbird basses for Gibson in the 1960s. Ray also had friends over at Ford and had done work for Ford Motor Company, Packard, and others much earlier.

Yet, when I walked into David Margolis' office at Creative Industries in 1962, there was an old yellowed news clipping of a Lincoln Cosmo presidential limousine in his big scrapbook. Of course I asked, but Dave wouldn't elaborate except to calmly say with a smile, "Oh yes, we did that one for President Eisenhower."

This was Dave's usual way of letting me know it was something he might acknowledge but couldn't discuss in great detail. Did this mean that Creative lent out assistance to Dietrich on per diem? Or did this mean that Creative only participated in the 1954 bubble-top conversion? It is certain that Creative Industries did this feature of the vehicle, but only this feature? You be the judge. Either way, Creative has not been openly credited for any of the work until now!

It was several years later when another member of Creative's staff once mentioned to me that Creative had "done some consulting" with Henney on the Cosmo limo project when the nine cars were being built. Another story popped up that Creative "may have helped Dietrich" a bit on this vehicle. Again, since Creative remained so very tight-lipped about what they did and did not do, this history is left for you to decide.

Still another former member of Creative's staff said in an interview, "Yes I do remember that car very well. I also recall that we hired a model to sit in the car with the bubble top when we were designing it. The reason was to have someone with exactly the same proportions and height of the Queen of England so that we could be sure there was enough headroom to clear her hat or crown under the bubble top!"

Former Creative co-owner Verne Koppin said, "I remember we had to raise the rear seat up several inches so it brought the Queen in a line so the people could see her more easily when they were driving."

A model of the dimensions and exact height of Queen Elizabeth II was found and extensive measurements and movement studies were done to ensure Her Majesty could sit in sublime comfort in the rear of President Eisenhower's limo. The clear bubble top was determined to allow ample clearance for the Queen to move and wave without any obstructions.

On yet another occasion back in the 1970s with famous designer William Schmidt, somehow the subject of the bubble-top Cosmo came up. Bill quickly volunteered, "Oh, yes, I did that one!" Of course, it is not commonly known that Bill Schmidt indeed also had a relationship with Creative Industries of Detroit in addition to Ford Motor Company.

A member of Creative's graphics division put it this way: "I have a recall very strongly of Bill Schmidt and work we did for him. When he went out on his own and created William Schmidt Associates after he left Chrysler, we, Creative Industries, did work for him, prototype work based on his designs. We did the builds and his firm did the designs. In fact, there were several different projects where Bill's guy and I worked closely together." Apparently this relationship between Creative and Bill Schmidt continued and lasted for the life of Schmidt's business.

So we have a Lincoln car, stretched and rebodied by Henney, for the president of the United States (with consulting

Quarter view of Eisenhower Cosmopolitan Lincoln car. Note top fabric here is black. (Photo Courtesy Thomas A. McPherson Collection)

Rear view of Eisenhower Cosmopolitan parade car. The boot fabric is black. (Photo Courtesy Thomas A. McPherson Collection)

Ford Motor Company technician demonstrates sectional latching of Creative-designed components Eisenhower Cosmo top. (Photo Courtesy Thomas A. McPherson Collection)

Another jump in time (same location, Ford Motor Company Styling, different time) Ike's Cosmo now has light colored soft top, light colored front soft sections too. Note different wheel covers, extended rear bumper, external spare. (Photo Courtesy Thomas A. McPherson Collection)

from Creative) then either redone or built by Dietrich but somehow with Creative's input and design from Bill Schmidt, who at the time was working for Ford! Are you getting the picture here? How could all of this be possible?

Creative Industries of Detroit was contacted as early as 1950–1951 regarding the possibility of constructing a see-through top for President Dwight D. Eisenhower. This top allowed the president to see and be seen in any kind of weather. "Ike," as he was affectionately known, had seen many a parade because he had served as commander of allied forces in Europe during World War II. He also knew from years of military planning as an army general that weather very well could cancel a parade or appearance, or make said event an exercise in wet misery. So the word came down that Eisenhower wanted an all-weather, see-through top on his Lincoln Cosmopolitan limo. The folding, soft fabric convertible top was nice and it was retained, but Ike wanted

Eisenhower Cosmopolitan Lincoln parade car in downtown Detroit, 1960. Note mid and front sections of roof are removed. Folded top fabric here is black. Building to left is the old Wayne County Building. And yes, Detroit Police Department rode Harley-Davidsons then!

Only known photo of Ike limo under construction at Creative. Staff member William Resztak sits in Eisenhower Cosmo passenger seat while completing construction of special bubble top assembly. Bill did much work on this vehicle, needed FBI clearance. (Photo Courtesy Jim Resztak Collection)

something better. And although this new top was not necessarily bulletproof, it still added a layer of protection in that regard.

Based on information I have assembled, construction began on the bubble-top conversion in 1953. Everyone involved with the project was required to obtain special security clearances and screening from Washington, D.C. No one was allowed to work on the project or to know details unless the government had cleared them.

According to Jim Resztak, whose father, William, worked on the Eisenhower limo at Creative, the FBI was very thorough in the background checks. They actually came and interviewed neighbors during the checks, all to ensure that anyone working on the president's car was not a security risk. Of course, Bill passed with flying colors.

Creative designed, engineered, and built the entire top mechanism and multi-piece clear bubble canopy for this historic automobile. I once saw the complete illustrations of the top and mechanisms, but I was told these were sent to Ford and to Washington, D.C. Sadly, all that is known to survive today as a visible record of Creative's participation is a photo of Jim's father, William "Bill" Resztak, sitting in the front seat of the Eisenhower limo in Creative's shop.

Of course, this was not Creative's only outing with a bubble top on a car. There were numerous dream cars for Ford and others that followed. More on these bubble tops elsewhere in this book, but for now, let's take a look at another project that was going on with Creative in 1953.

1954 Mercury XM-800

By the mid-1950s, auto shows were more than mere debuts for the new production models. "Dream cars" often became a rallying point of automotive fans at the shows. But the cars eventually became less dreamy and more like forecasts of things soon to come. In fact, auto shows became key style survey clinics where show cars were displayed and reaction gauged.

Such was the case of a 1954 show car, the Mercury Monterey XM-800. With the exception of Packard's Balboa-X, the XM-800 represented the ultimate attempt to gauge reaction and then move directly to production. It wasn't a gussied-up production vehicle. Yet it wasn't a wild and impractical dream on wheels. The XM-800 was about as production ready as any concept car up to that time had ever been. You will soon see just how close the latter actually came to reality.

Until very recent years and publicity over the XM-800, few historians or Ford people could previously seem to recall much about the background of the car or who designed it. But while interviewing old-timers back in the 1970s about the XM-800, two names quickly and regularly arose in discussions about the car. The first was Elwood Engle and the second was John Najjar. And although several different designers have been credited individually over the years and at one time or another, the XM-800 was apparently designed for the most part by Najjar. He also did the wild 1958–1960 Lincolns and Continentals and was involved in countless other Ford vehicles.

Back then, often the name of Elwood Engle was attached to the XM-800. But in possibly the last interview just before his death, Engle claimed otherwise. Mr. Engle told this writer, "There were very few times when only one stylist did an entire car, almost never. I headed a number of projects such as the XM-800, but several people worked on that one. A number of names come to mind: Gene Bordinet, Don DeLaRossa, and Jack Reith. But John Najjar probably was the most responsible for the design."

A 1954 Mercury XM-800 prior to interior installation. Interior done at Creative. Chrome-plated bumpers are fiberglass, not steel, which was Creative Industries' idea.

XM-800 side view prior to interior installation.

When I interviewed him in the 1970s, Najjar indeed seemed to have the most vivid memories of the XM-800 out of everyone I spoke with. And while he could not recall precise details of who did what and when and where, Najjar definitely remembered that Creative Industries of Detroit was involved in this vehicle, and more than once.

John Najjar picked up the story: "My earliest recollections of the XM-800 as a concept were full-size airbrush renderings done by Joseph Achor in our studios in 1953. At that point, we hadn't even decided on a name for the car, as was evident in the renderings. But the concept by then was pretty well set in place. We also had a derivative idea from the hardtop concept to a version with a stowable roof. This one would have been slightly shorter and even more sporty, like a two-passenger roadster.

"By the time we got the car into model form, the name 'Javelin' was stuck on the mock-up but this was dropped in favor of the XM-800 by the time the actual car was made. Why this happened, I don't recall. Several names were usually tossed out when we worked on a new car and decisions weren't always made on the name until development was well under way. I believe the 'XM' simply stood for Experimental Mercury, but I don't recall the reason for the 800 designation.

"Anyhow, we finished the clay model in full size and then pulled molds directly from the clay to lay up the fiberglass body for the actual car. Now, as near as I can recall, I think we did the original fiberglass work for the body right there

XM-800 rear view with interior. Rear deck antenna was futuristic in 1950s. Band over backlight became trim on 1955–1956 Mercury. Trunk held timer system to operate vehicle features for displays.

XM-800 version number-1 quarter view. Note large-diameter flat steering wheel.

Contemplated but never built: This was alternate two-passenger sports car proposal with stowable roof. No names on rear fender.

XM-800 clay. Note jack supports holding weight of clay model. Inlets on Dagmars were simulated. Concave grille was real.

Photo image from John Najjar showing XM-800 full-size clay model. Note name on rear fender is "Javelin." Name was coincidentally planned for Packard Predictor and Plymouth Plainsman.

Prior to "XM-800" name, note "Javelin" names and logo on rear fender.

Note "Javelin" name and logo. Ratcheting down support jacks holding clay body enhanced low stance.

Model, wearing beige gloves and copper color shoes, pretended to drive XM-800 version number-1. Note tinted plexiglass sun visors, copper color upholstery, and gauge faces.

Model pretends to drive XM-800. Note rolltop-style cover on console appeared later on 1967 Mustang. Bucket seats were considered futuristic, but by 1956, a big flat steering wheel, pointed radio knobs, and unpadded dash were at odds with the "Lifeguard Safety" program. Version number-2 deleted or modified these items.

at Ford, even though you mentioned some involvement of Creative Industries in the XM-800. I remember that, but I think if anything, Creative was certainly responsible for whatever update work that was done."

The mention that John Najjar made to my Creative Industries reference and the XM-800 was about a discussion we had from my own memories. I told John of seeing the XM-800 at Creative in the 1950s sitting in the narrow driveway between two buildings one day. Originally, I believed that Creative constructed the entire car. There remains some mystery here in this regard. Even John was not absolutely positive about the history. However, one thing is certain: Creative did something on the original Version 1 of the XM-800. And Creative also did the Version 2 safety-izing of XM-800. Although it is unclear what Creative's early work was, one possibility is very strong that Creative made and installed the handsome XM-800 interior on both versions. It may have also done the finish work.

An advance press release issued by Ford put it like this: "The XM-800, which was created by stylists of Ford Motor Company's engineering staff in cooperation with Lincoln-Mercury product planning and production engineers, is not a sports car, nor is it a 'dream' car of the distant future. Although it has the features of both, these features have been combined into a startlingly new but readily producible automobile."

Motor Trend took things even further in their April 1954 issue: "Mercury's XM-800, a hardtop show car designed to be built in quantity if the public likes it. The prototype is constructed of Fiberglas, but if the car goes into production, it will probably be metal." *Motor Trend* editors took issue with the front end design, likening it to "creation under the influence of Salvador Dali" but *Motor Trend* generally seemed pleased with the effort. *Motor Trend* editors concluded their remarks with an invitation to readers to write then-general sales manager Joseph E. Bayne at Lincoln-Mercury headquarters. *Motor Trend* followed up later in 1954 by featuring the XM-800 in an article about automotive styling. The overhead photo, though unlabeled, was unmistakably

Journalists criticized XM-800's Dagmars, calling them "battering rams," possibly one reason why "Javelin" name was dropped. Bumper was chrome-plated fiberglass, a Creative Industries idea.

the XM-800 in full-size clay model form. The photo depicted modelers and stylists (among them John Najjar) poring over the clay model from every angle.

During 1953 the revolutionary new Corvette bowed and suddenly plastic cars were no longer fanciful dreams when it came to production. Although the majority of auto manufacturers were content to let General Motors be the guinea pig for a fiberglass production, no one planned to be left sitting at the gate once plastic car technology was ironed out.

As a result, Chrysler unveiled a duo of plastics in the Plymouth Belmont and Dodge Granada of 1954.

Packard was also in the plastic arena with a fiberglass sports car of its own, the 1954 Panther. One of these cars created quite a stir of excitement when it set speed records at Daytona Beach, Florida.

Even embattled Kaiser-Frazer was producing the gorgeous Kaiser-Darrin fiberglass sports cars. If the company could turn out such a car in regular production, surely Ford could at least build a fiberglass show car.

So despite the hullabaloo over the XM-800's fiberglass body at the time, in the end, it was not such a big deal after all. Ford Motor Company's exercises in plastic cars and components have also been highlighted in Chapter Nine. Ford started research on plastic auto bodies all the way back in the 1930s. Although the first such Ford body product debuted in 1941 as fibrous reinforced plastic, it still paved the way for much of the fiberglass automotive technology to come. By 1953, Ford was certainly well capable of turning out plastic cars with ease, although they did indeed use Creative Industries to build FX-Atmos and others in addition to the XM-800.

Most people would be even less surprised at a fiberglass Ford car if they knew just how much Ford was involved in the material by the early 1950s. As John Najjar put it, "A lot of people may not know that Ford was a pioneer in fiberglass auto bodies. Almost all of our factory prototypes in those days were constructed in fiberglass. Many of the initial publicity photos and brochure illustrations were actually of fiberglass cars constructed long before actual assembly of steel production cars ever got under way! Differences were imperceptible in photos, but few ever even had engines. We weighted or jacked the cars to proper height levels for photo sessions. Looking back, it's really not all that unusual for the XM-800 to have been made of fiberglass. In light of what we were doing at the time, it was right in step." But for XM-800, the plastic body was just the beginning.

Underneath, the XM-800 featured a special chassis with a 119-inch wheelbase. This design allowed the car to sit lower with the body nestled into and over the frame rails. In fact, the overall height of the car (a total of only 55.6 inches) was substantially lower than even the lowest of production hardtops of the day.

Although it started with hot rods, Carson tops, and chopped 1949–1950 Mercs, XM-800 was one of the factory-built progenitors of the who's-got-the-lowest-hardtop-race of the 1950s. The Merc show car was soon eclipsed by others (Oldsmobile's experimental 1955 Delta 88 managed to shave its height to a mere 53 inches). However, the new XM-800 frame allowed the floors to drop, as did perimeter frames of later production cars in the United States. This drop in the floor provided adequate headroom even for a 6 footer. Ford claimed better road stability because of the lower center of gravity, but *that* would have been difficult to prove, no matter how logical it may have sounded. Why?

The reason is that by all accounts, the XM-800 was not an operable car, or at least not fully operable. No one we spoke with could seem to remember the car actually being driven. Some said the XM-800 was a "pushmobile," a display-only vehicle. Exactly why it was never set up to run remains a mystery. The show car had a nicely detailed, seemingly workable 312-ci V-8 engine along with a "Merc-O-Matic" automatic transmission. Suspension was put in place and gauges were even installed. The funny thing is that upon later inspection, the electricals under the dash never seem to have been hooked up. Just installed.

To get to the bottom of the story, it's necessary to skip over time to 1955. The XM-800 had been a highly successful show car during its first year out on the circuits. It was decided, therefore, to keep the car in circulation and to continue with appearances. During this period, Ford struck upon the idea of going all-out with a safety program. This program, as it turned out, dominated the 1956 marketing strategy. New models gushed with "Life Guard Safety" features such as padded instrument panels, padded sun visors, seat belts, and safety-dish steering wheels. It was here during preparation of the safety PR program that somebody took a good long second look at the XM-800.

It was bad enough that magazines were likening the front Dagmars to battering rams, but what about those lethal-looking pointed radio knobs? The two controls jutted menacingly out of the original hard, unpadded dash. The judgment came down that the radio controls had to go, or at least be modified. Ditto for the hard dash top. And say, that big ornamented flat steering wheel couldn't be tolerated any more if everything else at Ford was going to a deep-dish safety design! So in the space of little more than a year, production cars were already out-futuring the future car. By golly, the XM-800 would have to be safety-ized if it was going to be touring with padded and belted Ford production cars!

So XM-800 was hauled back over to Creative Industries sometime in 1955 (prior to the unveiling of the 1956 model lineup). During this time, and, pardon the expression, on crash scheduling, the Merc show car was revamped to reflect the new corporate safety theme. Changes included a new padded dash, seatbelts, and a new steering column with safety-dish steering wheel. Radio controls were lowered and regrouped in the center of the instrument panel. The interior and exterior paint was also redone.

The refreshed XM-800, now safety-ized and repainted, was rolled out for another tour of duty on the auto show circuits. It remained in auto show land through the debut of its successor dream car, the Turnpike Cruiser XM, and then abruptly dropped out of sight by the introduction of the 1957 production models. With no fanfare, the car that had been seen by thousands and cost a reputed $100,000 to build was now gathering dust in the back of a dark warehouse.

The XM-800 was too close to production. This fact, along with other reasons, is probably why it never went to production. In the rapidly changing car world of 1950s styling, the XM-800 was already outdated a year after it was unveiled.

The XM-800 had served much of its intended purpose. Some of the roofline and trim went into the handsome 1955–1956 Mercury Phaeton sedans. Its deep visor headlights probably inspired a number of cars that followed, Ford Motor Company and otherwise. The sculpted front fenders were used again on 1958 Lincolns and Continentals. Although the sculpted fenders like these were assassinated by critics, the design certainly influenced a volume of cars far too numerous to mention.

And the bumpers of the XM-800 were chrome-plated fiberglass. *This* was years and years ahead. Creative Industries had figured out how to chrome plate on plastic years earlier and now they were finally bringing this technology out in the light

of day to the public. Nobody realized that the bumpers were chrome-plated plastic until decades later. Even in the 1960s when manufacturers were trying such technology on bicycles, it looked rather marginal and was barely durable. Car companies weren't having much better luck as any restorer of early Mustangs can tell you. But Creative had the technology down cold by 1954!

And the XM-800 also had so-called Venetian blind dark plexiglass sun visors that were particularly unusual. As the visor tilted downward, fine internal louvering serrations refracted, filtered, or blocked light entirely. As it did so, the visor changed colors from green to gray to almost black. Similar visors were seen on at least one GM concept car and again on the production 1957–1958 Cadillac Eldorado Brougham. Furthermore, these same visors were rare options on 1958–1959 Continentals. A thinner, even more flexible version of this material exists to this day. Some 3M Manufacturing Company reps actually use a very thin version of it as business cards in recent years.

Ford, like most other automakers, routinely scrapped outdated show cars back then. Selling such cars to private individuals was usually beyond consideration. Between legal reasons and possible opposition from stockholders, selling the XM-800 was just out of the question. So what was Ford to do with this $100,000 (and that's 1950s money) obsolete car?

Reportedly there had been talk of cutting the car up, as unbearable as that may seem. So it was little wonder that most historians and car people presumed for decades that XM-800 had been destroyed. This notion was repeated in publications even into the 1980s. Fortunately, cooler heads at Ford prevailed after the XM-800's retirement and the car was actually donated to education.

By 1957, XM-800 became a resident of the University of Michigan School of Engineering in Ann Arbor, Michigan. Ford donated the car to the school with the idea it would be useful to engineering students as an automotive test-bed. So for a number of years, the XM-800 sat happily at the university's automotive engineering laboratory. It wasn't long, though, before the XM-800 was just too antiquated even to be useful for educational purposes, which by nature are geared more toward state-of-the-art.

Exactly what happened to XM-800 at this point remains somewhat shrouded in mystery. There were rumors that the car was turned over to a smaller learning institution. But sometime during the 1960s XM-800 was either given away yet again or sold at a surplus school sale. There are several stories trailing off from here, but one way or another the car supposedly ended up in the hands of an out-of-state owner who then reportedly stored it at a Michigan farm, then disappeared. It was just the beginning of a long and somewhat humiliating series of events.

The XM-800 had been saved from the crusher, but all was not roses ahead. In any event, the XM-800 now sat in a barn and then was moved outdoors, exposed to the weather for the first time in its life. The car continued to sit outdoors and increasing deterioration set in. And there it remained for nearly a 10-year period, waiting to be rescued.

I lived in Ann Arbor and attended the university at the time and knew of both the car and its eventual location, but I could never seem to figure out exactly who owned it. And remember, Creative Industries had lots of very strong connections with the U. of M. They hired football players for summer jobs. And Dave Margolis told me in the early 1970s, "You know, that experimental Mercury we worked on is still sitting alive up in Ann Arbor."

By the time I made a serious attempt to find the legal owner, the XM-800 had disappeared once again. Fortunately, another Michigan resident with a passion for cars had managed to obtain the car from the rural farmer.

The XM-800 was about to be restored to its former glory. But with surviving factory photos all showing the pre-safety-ized interior, the new string of owners presumed that the car had somehow been customized, perhaps by a private party. No one paid attention to the lone surviving photo of the XM-800 version number-2. Apparently no one else realized that there were two versions of the XM-800.

There were other surprises in store once the car was retrieved from the farm. The trunk was opened to reveal an elaborate electrical timer system. This system had been installed by Creative Industries and was part of a display activation for shows that included automatic opening and closing of the hood and trunk.

The first *new* owner told this writer that when he pulled the engine spark plugs, they appeared to be in pristine condition. It was as if the engine had never been fired. Then came the real shocker as it reportedly turned out there was no flywheel or torque converter installed! The final wow-wee came when the owner attempted to track wiring for the gauges only to discover there was none! Apparently the gauges were just dummies installed for looks. The only big harness in the car reportedly went to the timer. The XM-800 had been a lot of places, but apparently not under its own power.

Miraculously the XM-800 had stood the ravages of time and the elements. It eventually made it all the way back to being fully restored and even drivable in recent years. Looking at this dream car now, my mind drifts back decades ago to the prophetic words of the late Elwood Engle as he told me from his hospital room, "Leon, we'll never see those times again." How right he was.

Meanwhile, the list of automotive projects under Creative's belt continued to grow. Most were with metal bodies, as in the case of the famous Chrysler parade limousines. But the wondrous new material of what was then known as "Fiber Reinforced Plastic" (FRP), or what we more commonly know today as fiberglass, persisted. And this single development opened the floodgates on both dream car construction and production car development, as you shall see in Chapter Six.

Only known photo of XM-800 safety-ized version number-2. Taken at Creative Industries front driveway at 3080 East Outer Drive. The radio knobs were removed from the dash top and the car has a new-dished steering wheel.

DODGE GRANADA AND MORE ALLIANCES WITH MITCHELL-BENTLEY

*E*ven if you *thought* you knew the connection between these players, get ready for a few surprises in this chapter.

Dodge Granada

It was the early 1950s and Fred Zeder Jr., son of famous Chrysler engineer Fred M. Zeder Sr., was dreaming of making a be-everything sports car. This ultimate car would be like no other that existed at the time. It would combine old notions such as a long hood and the quaint old 1920s–1930s practice of swapping bodies on a chassis with a completely modern notion: a "plastic" body!

At the time, the words "magic" and "plastic body" had almost the same meaning in automotive circles. Actually the magazines back then usually called them "plastic bodies," but *fiberglass* is usually what they meant. And there wasn't a car magazine on the newsstands that wasn't talking about fiberglass bodies. It was futuristic and it was the buzz of the day.

In 1952, the great entrepreneur and car designer Howard "Dutch" Darrin (best known for the beautiful prewar Packard Darrin sportsters) tossed his hat in the ring by introducing a very sleek and novel two-passenger sports car. Power came from a Willys inline 6-cylinder engine, but this was just the beginning. Darrin's sports car had some wild features, such as a three-position convertible top and disappearing pocket doors that slid forward into the fenders. Although Dutch made only a few of these cars on his own, Kaiser finally took it on as an official model line in 1953 (dubbed a "1954" model). The industry held its collective breath. Just a few weeks later, General Motors unleashed their new fiberglass sports car, the 1953 Corvette (I discuss Creative's involvement later) and it was *game on*.

Don Mitchell, founder of Mitchell-Bentley, sits behind wheel of the Granada right after completion. Note the Dodge front emblem and Granada fender logos have not yet been installed. Mitchell's Panther and Balboa clone were both painted the same color, apparently his favorite.

Fiberglass body of Dodge Granada made at Creative Industries of Detroit. Final trim and paint were done at Mitchell-Bentley Company.

Author and Howard "Dutch" Darrin in 1970s. Dutch is sitting in one of his most famous creations, a Packard Darrin sports car. Dutch's arm is over one of his trademarks, a cut-down door with a "Darrin Dip" (beltline sweeps downward).

Things were heating up for fiberglass. But Americans were still largely skeptical of things made of plastic. In those days, most Americans only knew that plastic was fragile. It was either bendable and soft or hard and brittle. It could warp in heat, discolor with age, and could crack or even snap apart. And no common glues at the time could satisfactorily repair the stuff. This was the image that came to mind when Americans heard the word "plastic."

The depiction of Ralphie's dad struggling to glue his broken "major award" plastic lamp back together was hilarious in the movie *A Christmas Story*, but it was also true to the times. In those days there was no superglue. Once broken, most plastic just wasn't repairable. And when it came to car bodies, Americans still firmly believed that nothing topped metal for safety and durability. So? Fred Zeder Jr.'s idea was to make a car that offered the best of both worlds.

Having grown up with a father who was an engineering giant at Chrysler, Zeder's brilliant concept was in keeping with what he had learned, yet very trendy for its time. A lightweight, yet strong tubular chassis with racing potential combined with a powerful thundering Dodge Red-Ram Hemi drive train, all carrying a stylish aluminum sports car body. Now this was a theme that could get noticed in the auto world of those days.

When it came time to go racing, presto-chango! The metal sports car body could quickly be unbolted and the chassis slid under a super lightweight (claimed 150 pounds) fiberglass roadster body. In this amazing morphed configuration, Zeder envisioned that his creation could compete and command any track, virtually anywhere. And the best part of all was that Zeder's car could sell for *less* than the Ferraris, Jags, and anything else viable in racing at the time. Zeder was excited. But Dodge? They had other ideas, as we shall see.

Zeder Sports Car

An actual Zeder sports car was completed in Italy by coachbuilder Bertone. The Zeder arrived in New York in 1953 and was ultimately whisked off to Chrysler headquarters in Highland Park, Michigan.

Dutch Darrin's other famous design, the Kaiser Darrin sports car, built of fiberglass. "Pocket" doors slide into front fenders rather than swing out.

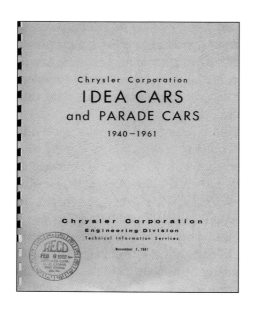

Cover of Chrysler's corporate compendium book on their concept cars. Book mysteriously avoids any mention of Creative Industries, Mitchell-Bentley, and Granada itself!

The car was now dubbed "Zeder Storm-250" and there was great anticipation that the Storm would become Dodge's Corvette competition. It made sense, especially in light of the Vette's rather anemic 6-cylinder engine. The Zeder's power-to-weight ratio was surely far superior, especially in the fiberglass configuration.

According to a 1994 article by Michael Lamm in *Special-Interest Autos* magazine, the car was then turned over to Fred's uncle, Jim Zeder, who was an important figure in Chrysler engineering at the time. There was great anticipation, but once in the hands of Uncle Zeder and Dodge, something very odd took place that has mystified car people to this day.

Instead of the joyful acceptance and eager adoption expected, the Zeder Storm was mysteriously hustled off into deep storage in a garage. There it remained a closely guarded secret for several years. According to the *Special-Interest Autos* article, Chrysler personnel were reportedly told neither to touch the car nor to discuss it. And that was that.

Why wasn't the Storm adopted as a Dodge? Why was it kept hidden away for years of obscurity in Highland Park? These have always been nagging questions that no one could answer. Although the real reason may never be confirmed, there does seem to be a simple explanation to this mystery.

Around this same time, a sporty new fiberglass convertible was secretly being planned as a Dodge concept car. Fred Zeder didn't know this and modern speculators have never contemplated the history in its entirety.

To have the privately built Zeder car steal thunder away from the secret corporate concept would have been like Dodge shooting itself in the foot. Further complicating the possibility of a Zeder/Dodge Storm was the fact that Chrysler was also working on a set of handsome little two-passenger sports cars that appeared later, to be called "Falcon."

The Zeder Storm was kept hidden away and simply allowed to die on the vine. Between being possible competition for the upcoming Dodge concept, the upcoming Chrysler Falcons, and being an N.I.H. (Not Invented Here), the Zeder Storm was likely doomed. Meanwhile, the new Dodge plastic mystery concept was proceeding full speed ahead.

Now, if you were a car company in Detroit in the early 1950s and you wanted to build and engineer a special one-off car out of this new wondrous plastic material, who would you turn to? Who had the engineering and problem-solving prowess, along with expertise in fiberglass? One name quickly came to mind: Creative Industries of Detroit. Creative had serious expertise in this new material and their engineers had been toying with it since the dawn of the 1950s.

There was also a deep Chrysler connection. Despite the passage of time since Fred Johnson (Creative's founder) left Chrysler in the 1930s, Johnson continued to be widely known as a "Chrysler engineer."

Rex Terry had formerly been assistant chief engineer of Chrysler commercial car engineering. He had spent a lot of time in the Dodge division. And one of Terry's right-hand men at Creative, Verne Koppin, had also previously worked for Rex at Dodge. So the Chrysler connection remained strong.

Mitchell-Bentley was also included in this project. It was a fairly large Michigan firm and had great expertise in interior trim, short production runs, and convertibles. Mitchell had plants and facilities in several locations around Michigan at the time. Via their Ionia Body Division, Mitchell-Bentley had been building certain station wagons for General Motors, Ford, and Chrysler since the 1940s. And Mitchell's Don Mitchell hung out with Fred Johnson, Rex Terry, and William Newburg, who just happened to be head of Chrysler's Dodge Division.

Ultimately, it was really no surprise when a decision came down pairing two companies under contract to Dodge for a dream car. Mitchell-Bentley partnered with Creative to produce the new plastic Dodge concept. It was completed by 1954.

It remains unclear who suggested the name of the new Dodge concept car. One thing that remains clear is that by the mid-1950s, Chrysler Corporation decided their concepts would now have names representing themes. The new policy was a move away from robotic, uninspiring names, including "K-310" or "C-200," and onward to more exciting titles such as "Falcon," "Plainsman," "Adventurer," or "Flightsweep." Whenever possible, the new policy dictated that design elements be incorporated into the concept that carried out the theme in a visual sense. In the case of the new Dodge dream car, its name would have to be European, sporty, and with a wistful tinge of romance. And 2+2 seating. This concept would also be powered by the same kind of Red Ram Dodge Hemi engine that the Storm carried, an engine that any potential buyer could order in their new Dodge. Ultimately this new dream car was known as Granada.

The Mysterious Missing Granada

As a Chrysler Corporation concept car, Granada occupies a very strange rung on the ladder of concept car history. For years there was an official list of what Chrysler termed "Idea Cars." This list was rarely seen by outsiders.

In 1961, the Engineering Division Technical Information Services section of Chrysler Corporation composed a booklet summing up their concepts program. It included the aforementioned listing. The title of the booklet was *Chrysler Corporation Idea Cars and Parade Cars 1940–1961*. It is dated November 1, 1961, and was originally distributed internally, as well as to some public relations people.

The first page begins with an explanation of Chrysler's philosophy of concept cars and the fact that the corporation referred to them as "Idea Cars." Later, in Section I, there is a full page listing of concepts from Dodge, Plymouth, De Soto, Chrysler, and Imperial. The booklet goes on to show and describe virtually every concept listed, even the 3/8-scale model De Soto Cella. So you would think that Granada was included in this listing, but no. Granada is missing.

– 4 –

BODY AND DIMENSIONS

Car Name	Body Style	Year Intro-duction	Over-all Dimensions			Wheel-base	Tire Size	Page No.
			Length	Width	Height			
Thunderbolt	Retr. H.T.	1940	N.A.	N.A.	N.A.	127.5	7.00 x 15	6
Newport	Phaeton	1940	N.A.	N.A.	N.A.	145.5	7.50 x 15	7
Plymouth XX-500	4-Dr. Sedan	1950	N.A.	N.A.	N.A.	118.5	6.70 x 15	8
Chrysler K-310	2-Dr.Hardtcp	1951	220.5	76.0	59.0	125.5	8.00 x 17	9
Chrysler C-200	Convertible	1952	220.5	79.3	58.0	125.5	8.00 x 17	10
Chrysler Special	Sport Coupe	1952	214.0	72.5	55.0	119.0	7.00 x 16	11
Chrysler Spec.(Mod.)	Sport Coupe	1953	204.0	75.3	57.5	125.5	8.20 x 15	12
Chrysler GS-1	Sport Coupe	1953	204.0	75.3	57.5	125.5	8.20 x 15	13
De Soto Adventurer I	Sport Coupe	1953	189.8	67.0	53.5	111.0	6.70 x 16	14
Chrysler D'Elegance	Sport Coupe	1953	204.5	74.0	54.5	115.0	7.60 x 17	15
Plymouth Belmont	Roadster	1954	191.5	73.3	49.3	114.0	6.70 x 15	*16
Plymouth Explorer	Sport Coupe	1954	185.2	76.9	54.5	114.0	7.10 x 15	17
Dodge Firearrow	Roadster (1)	1953	188.8	75.5	46.3	115.0	7.10 x 15	18
Dodge Firearrow	Roadster (2)	1954	194.0	76.3	50.9	119.0	7.10 x 15	19
Dodge Firearrow	Sport Coupe	1954	190.6	76.5	55.0	119.0	7.10 x 15	20
Dodge Firearrow	Convertible	1954	189.6	75.8	54.9	119.0	7.10 x 15	21
De Soto Adventurer II	Sport Coupe	1954	214.3	77.9	55.5	125.5	7.60 x 15	22
Falcon	Roadster	1955	182.0	68.3	51.2	105.0	7.60 x 15	23
Flight-Sweep I	Convertible	1955	207.0	70.4	53.5	120.0	7.10 x 15	24
Flight-Sweep II	2-Dr.Hardtop	1955	207.0	70.4	53.5	120.0	7.10 x 15	25
Plainsman	Station Wagon	1956	208.0	79.4	60.2	115.0	7.10 x 15	26
Norseman	2-Dr.Hardtop	1956	227.5	82.0	56.0	129.0	8.20 x 15	27
Dart	Retr. H.T.	1957	223.0	80.0	54.0	129.0	8.00 x 15	28
Plymouth Cabana	Station Wagon	1958	215.8	80.0	55.9	124.0	8.00 x 14	29
Imperial D'Elegance	4-Dr.Hardtcp	1958	228.0	79.3	52.3	129.0	9.50 x 14	30
De Soto Cella I	Hardtop	1959	- 3/8 Scale Model - Dimensions N. A.					31
Plymouth XNR	Roadster	1960	195.2	71.0	46.0	106.5	8.00 x 14	32
Dodge FliteWing	2-Dr.Hardtcp	1961	215.6	77.9	52.8	118.0	8.50 x 14	33
TurboFlite	2-Dr.Hardtcp	1961	218.0	75.4	52.1	118.0	8.00 x 14	34

Chrysler's official listing of Mopar "idea cars" mysteriously had no mention of Zeder or Granada.

An announcement in the *Detroit News* written by veteran automotive newsman Ralph R. Watts and dated January 1954 clearly stated the contrary. The published newspaper account published under the headline, "2 FIRMS PARTICIPATE" was worded as follows: "Participating with Dodge in the styling and construction of the car was Ionia Manufacturing Co., Ionia, Mich., and Creative Industries of Detroit." Why this information and Granada itself were later eliminated from the record is unknown. But this same story was picked up and published by other newspapers nationwide. So, confidentiality issues aside, the information about who made Granada was clearly known and out in the public, at least for a while.

Who Did What?

Over the years, confusion has reigned over the real parenthood of Granada. However, credit for the main engineering and fiberglass work for Granada rightfully belongs in large part to Creative Industries of Detroit. Certainly there was some input from Dodge Division, but from all those who were there, the lion's share was done at Creative. Most of the engineers behind the car, whether they were geographically in Detroit or Ionia, were still largely employed by Creative Industries, even if on loan to Mitchell-Bentley.

Nobody stepped forward to take credit for the bodylines, but they were initiated by Dodge Division and largely completed between Creative and Mitchell-Bentley. The result leaned a bit in the design-by-committee direction.

David Margolis of Creative Industries told me once that Dodge apparently had only sketchy ideas of what they wanted to do for this concept car in the beginning. Some of the engineering hard points were obviously dictated by the chassis and engine used, but the rest was a huge gray area. In the 1970s when I talked with him, Bill Mitchell repeated a lot of what Dave said, except to claim greater input from Mitchell-Bentley.

Not yet painted, Granada as it looked in 1953 when completed and partially assembled by Creative Industries, ready for shipment to Mitchell-Bentley. Note rear seat, side glass, and top stack are not yet installed.

Origins of the Name

Granada, the famous city in Spain had a long history. It was fought over and occupied by ancient cave dwellers, Romans, Christians, Jews, and Arabs. It ultimately fell to Christians under Spanish Queen Isabel and King Ferdinand.

Perhaps then it is no wonder that Americans in the 1950s who were thinking of a Euro-design theme for a car might find inspiration in a Spanish name like Granada. Why not? The name sounded like such a grand and romantic title to Americans at the time. And inspiration was everywhere, even in Detroit.

In fact, in those pre-expressway days, if you drove west across Detroit from Chrysler headquarters out past the Lincoln-Mercury plant to the De Soto plant, you almost certainly had to also pass the beautiful, majestic old Granada movie theater. It was located on West Warren Avenue.

Regardless of who made the choice (and where) it is clear that the concept name had been chosen at least by January 1953, a full year prior to debut. How do we know this? Because Don Mitchell's daily calendar had hand-written entries as follows:

"January 2, Friday
8:30 AM . . . Mr. Newburg . . . Dodge Main
11:30 AM . . . William C. Newburg President of Dodge Division Chrysler Motor
. . . Discuss Granada"

Of course, the Spanish aura at Chrysler Corporation didn't stop here. Chrysler already had De Soto and what was the icon of that brand? A Spaniard wearing a conquistador helmet with a sweeping brim that came to a pointed peak in front! So one way or another, Granada came to be the name of the new Dodge concept. And in keeping with Chrysler's new theme policy, a visual cue, a connection, was included somewhere within this design.

According to Creative insider Gary Hutchings, at first there was an idea to cover the headlights of the Granada with clear plastic bubbles. But why not use the shape of the sweeping curvilinear line of the Spanish helmet around the headlight instead? So finally that peaked, curved De Soto conquistador helmet brim found a way into the

Headlight opening of Dodge Granada evokes questions today and some may even criticize the design, but knowing the De Soto inspiration for the design may provide the viewer with a new and different perspective.

design. Yes, it was De Soto, not Dodge, but it was all in the family.

A Spanish helmet inspired the peaked opening of the Granada headlights, whether it is understood or translated well into automotive styling. So if one looks at Granada today and the front end leaves one wondering, wonder no more.

Pages from Don Mitchell's business diary reveal Granada name already was intended a year prior to debut. Date was January 1953 and it was a business meeting. Notes state, "William C. Newberg, president of Dodge Division, Discuss Granada."

Promotional Direction and
Packard Cross-Pollenization

Meanwhile Dodge decided *its* promotional line on the Granada was to emphasize the one-piece body construction in media releases. After all, a plastic car with a one-piece body back then sounded like science fiction. Dodge wisely figured this was enough of a *wow* factor to make the public sit up and take notice. The one-piece story worked, and to this day, it is the tag line most associated with the Granada.

As construction was about to commence, the Granada still had no taillights and the design needed a conclusion. The word came down that Chrysler's new upcoming corporate design theme was going to be fins! Exner tailfins. So fins had to be worked into the Granada design. But what about taillights?

Dave Margolis of Creative told me that this was a detail that migrated from down low on the rear to high up into the fins. Apparently early taillight proposals were low on the rear and looked somewhat like Pontiac's Club de Mer concept. But this configuration was neither loved nor unanimous in fans. There was just no clear agreement on proposed designs of the rear that was satisfactory until someone took a good look at the Panther taillights. The Panther units, affectionately known as "sore thumb lights" (which themselves were adapted from the upcoming 1954 Packard Clipper), were an inspiration. The shape of the Granada's fin could indeed predict and project the new Exner "Forward Look." A nice sculpted, angled-in taillight could help draw attention to the fin while completing the rear. And so it was.

The Granada pieces were designed and engineered at Creative's plastics shop on East Outer Drive. According to Gary Hutchings who worked on the car, the actual full body assem-

Granada taillights were inspired by Packard Panther (see Chapter Seven) but are very different. Also note thickness of rear quarter interior trim panels and narrow rear seat width. Clear evidence of folding top. Also note that steering wheel, other parts, and boot were originally white. Dodge added exposed exhaust pipe tips after construction.

bly was also done at a special facility that Creative once had over on the northern end of Mt. Elliott Avenue.

Once the body was completed, actual vehicle assembly went rather quickly. The body was mated with the chassis, wired, windshield installed, and even bare front seat frame (no rear) installed. Stock optional Dodge/Plymouth wire wheels (made by Motor Wheel Company, not Kelsey-Hayes as so often stated) were installed along with whitewall tires. It was only at this point that Granada was shipped out to Mitchell-Bentley's Ionia factory to be painted and trimmed.

Once at Ionia, the body was carefully prepped and primed for paint. It was then done up in Don Mitchell's favorite color: turquoise. Officially, Dodge called Granada's color "Seafoam Green" or some such name, but the actual color was more like turquoise.

Frankly, the references to "green" were questioned so much internally that the advertising agency doing the press releases wisely went so far as to attempt to clarify what "green" really meant. Press releases were carefully worded so as to describe the color as "turquoise-green."

Side glass for the doors and a power-operated top-stack assembly were all engineered at Creative but installed at Ionia. But as far as we know, the white folding top was

DODGE ONE-PIECE PLASTIC CONVERTIBLE

Said to be the first one-piece, all-plastic-body car ever developed by the automobile industry on a convential chassis, the Dodge Granada has a width of 76⅛ in., a height of 55½ in., and a length of 211 in. Ionia Manufacturing Co. and Creative Industries cooperated with Dodge in the joint styling and construction venture. There are no immediate plans for production of the car, Dodge points out.

AUTOMOTIVE INDUSTRIES, *February 1, 1954*   35

Granada as it appeared in February 1954 issue of **Automotive Industries** *with emphasis on "one-piece plastic convertible."*

Tail fins were mostly an afterthought in the Granada design. They were added late as a tribute to Virgil Exner and Chrysler's "Forward Look" theme.

never seen at shows or photographed in raised position. There was a reason. Many dream cars cut corners somewhere along the way. In Granada's case, it all came down to the folding top. The soft-top assembly for Granada was never very attractive, but there were some serious reasons why.

From an aesthetic standpoint it was pure love it or hate it. Due to the fact that there were no quarter side windows, the top had a blind quarter in the raised position. Depending on your preference (or point of view) the raised top either had a chic limo/1940s Continental look to it or a heavy, blind look that changed the entire nature of the car. Largely for this reason, the Granada was not officially photographed with the top raised.

Because an existing top stack framework was adapted and series of existing parts used, there were some obvious compromises in the top and everything related to it. For instance, the windshield header was a modular piece based on existing parts. It was nearly identical to the header used on the Panther. Even the Granada's sun visors were virtually identical to the ones on Packard Panthers, all of which used the same chrome-plated hinges installed on production Packard Caribbeans (also built by Mitchell-Bentley).

And the Granada's interior rear quarter trim panels were unusually thick. This was obviously to allow a top frame (that was actually quite narrow) to retract into the body, while still retaining a more bulbous exterior quarter. Of course, the reality is that a narrow top stack frame dictates a narrow rear seat. It was all a matter of physics and geometry. So for a car as wide

as the Granada, a surprisingly tight, narrow rear seat was fitted. But this confirms that the Granada once had an operating soft top. Otherwise the rear seat could have been made much wider and more visually appealing. And the interior rear trim panels could have been much thinner.

All these factors were a compromise for a concept car that would normally be seen with its top down anyway. So there was no urgent need for rear quarter windows. The upshot of the compromise also saved some serious cash since it meant no need for quarter window mechanisms, glass, sealing, special trim, and more. It also meant that a top could merely be adapted from existing parts rather than completely engineered and fabricated.

There was one final touch of cross-pollenization from Packard Panther: the radio antenna. Originally, the Packard Panthers were first conceived to have no visible radio antenna. Today this design fact is confused when people look at the last two Panthers with external twin rear antenna masts. However, the original Panther format indeed carried the radio antenna hidden under the deck lid.

This very same system was adopted for the Granada. The end result was a clean, uncluttered body. Of course the benefits of the fiberglass body combined with the rearmost mounting of the antenna meant that static transferred from the engine was virtually nil. In those days, AM radios on some cars picked up so much engine static that the radio could be used as an audio tachometer! And the Granada had a big hemi engine under the hood, which was a sure source of static via the ignition system.

So the Granada's advanced trunk-mounted radio antenna was considered not only very high tech for its time, but also practical.

As Mitchell-Bentley put the finishing touches on Granada, it was rolled out in front of that company's Ionia building entrance for the first of what was many photos. At this point there were no "Granada" logos on the front fenders and no Dodge emblem on the fascia of the car. There were also no exposed exhaust pipe tips at the rear. These items all appeared later but before the car was sent out to the press and auto shows.

Even Don Mitchell took a turn being pictured at the wheel wearing a suit and a large felt hat. With Mitchell and the hat towering over the windshield header, the first upshot of *this* photo was to lower the seat when the Granada went right back to Creative for a quick once-over in Detroit.

Jim Resztak, son of the late Bill Resztak, commented that his dad had worked on a car body that he thought might have been a Packard. That car turned out to be the Dodge Granada. All he could remember was that when the car left Creative, it came back with the driver's head projecting well above the wraparound windshield. Since the windshield was a focal point on the car and wrap-around windshields at that time were all the rage, it was feared that people might react badly and think this had something to do with the new kind of windshield design. Bill told his son that there was some debating about what to do to correct the problem. Resztak, in his usual get-it-done style, took one look and simply said to lower the seat frame and tracks. Then he walked away, back to his work area. As he saw it, it was an obvious solution. And indeed, that's what they did.

Somewhere during this period, Granada logos and Dodge badging were added. The glove box face also received a "DODGE" block-letter logo.

Official press release photos were also taken with Detroit model Janet Lewis Hoffmann smiling behind the wheel in several poses. Janet also wore a hat and a chic striped outfit complete with a string of pearls and gloves! Look very closely and you can see what appears to be a man wearing a light-colored V-neck top directing Janet in the reflection on the driver's door.

Downtown Detroit's magnificent Guardian Building was the site of feverish activity from Dodge's advertising agency. It cranked out press kits and releases through the holiday season for 1954 and all early January to prepare the press for Granada. Now it was the agency's turn to spread the word as Dodge and the industry sat in anticipation of the Granada's debut on January 15, 1954, at the Los Angeles Auto Show.

For the rest of the year, the Granada was off on a whirlwind tour. It was seen in shows and at dealerships nationwide. In fact, dealers were reportedly clamoring just to have the Granada displayed at their showroom. One dealer claimed his walk-in traffic and car sales shot through the roof on the weekend when Granada was exhibited on his salesroom floor. A tireless small crew was kept busy ferrying the Granada from venue to venue, cleaning and prepping in between.

By the time a year had passed, the Granada had logged thousands of miles traveling coast to coast. And the Granada had thrilled thousands of viewers all over the United States. But after all that traveling, poor Granada was starting to look just a little tired. However, the life of a show car in those days was judged on how much it was in public demand and what kinds of crowds it could draw. Fortunately, the Granada was still an attention grabber. So, there was only one thing left to do.

During the 1955 season, the Granada was called home, or actually back to Creative Industries. Other cars, such as the Packard Panther, were already getting refreshenings there, and now it was Granada's turn.

Little was changed visually on the Granada, but there *were* modifications/upgrades that took place during the update.

It is known that the Granada was sent out again on tour for several months but then by 1956, a whole new flock of concept

PARTIAL GRANADA TOUR SCHEDULE

City	Date
Los Angeles, California	January 15–24,1954 (LA Auto Show)
Akron, Ohio	March 19, 1954 (Anniston Motor Co.)
Anniston, Alabama	July 21–22, 1954 (Anniston Motor Company)
Panama City, Florida	August 14, 1954 (Carver Motor Company)
Sarasota, Florida	August 30, 1954
Sarasota, Florida	August 31, September 1–2, 1954 (Shay Motors, Inc.)
Sarasota, Florida	September 9, 1954 (Ben McGahey, Inc.)
Miami, Florida	September 10–12, 1954 (Tutan Motors, Inc.)
Palm Beach, Florida	September 18, 1954 (Joe Blank Motor Company)
Daytona Beach, Florida	September 22–23,1954 (Volusia County Motors, Inc.)
Spartanburg, South Carolina	October 12, 1954 (City Motor Car Company)

cars was unleashed from Chrysler. Eventually the Granada was lost in the shuffle.

Sadly, this rule was especially swift and severe for 1950s dream cars. Many of these cars had painfully short periods of exposure only to disappear permanently thereafter. Such a fate usually amounted to the vehicle's destruction at the wrong end of a saw or blowtorch or in the jaws of a crushing machine at some wrecking yard. But the Granada was one of the lucky ones. Somehow it managed to hang on, if only just barely. But the ensuing years were not kind to the Granada.

Version number-2 Granada rear at auction. Rear bumper is fiberglass. Chrome-plated metal plates on deck lid were not original and have since been removed. Turned-down tailpipe extensions are also not original.

Refreshening Changes

The following is a list of the changes made by Creative to the Granada:

- Exterior door mirror was removed
- Interior rearview mirror was added Exner-style for the first time (mounted on I.P.)
- Heater and ventilation controls were changed
- Medallion panel above radio deleted
- Defogger and ventilation louvers (production style) were added atop the I.P.
- Bright metal cladding was added to the lower section of I.P.

Updated version number-2 of Granada included newer HVAC vents mounted atop the instrument panel. Rearview mirror was also relocated, Exner style (with bracket identical to that used in Rex Terry's Panther).

Version number-2 mods included removal of medallion above radio head and "Dodge" name from glove box door. Pressed metal cladding was added to lower instrument panel.

Version number-2 Granada, details of new HVAC vents and rearview mirror mounting.

Granada Version number-2 heads off to restoration after auction. Bon Voyage!

As the clock ticked on, the Dodge dream car was rumored in various locales and with numerous owners. Wherever it was while it drifted along, the Granada suffered very serious deterioration. Fiberglass doesn't rust, but steel chassis surely do, and this one had developed some very nasty corrosion damage. Various parts such as the convertible top assembly and door window glass disappeared along the way. Other areas such as the deck lid and wheels had been modified. By the time the car arrived in the hands of a collector in more recent years, to say that the Granada was in bad shape was an extreme understatement. As the sad hulk was pictured in magazines, Granada looked as if it were a candidate to take the dirt nap.

But once again, the amazing Granada defied death and finally made its way home. This time Granada arrived back at Mitchell Corporation and the hands of William Mitchell, son of Don Mitchell. As a tribute to his father, Bill was determined to put the Granada on display in his private Mitchell museum. Somewhere during this period, Granada underwent a cosmetic restoration.

The door glass and convertible top assembly were still missing, but at least the Granada now *looked* presentable. The best part of all, the time of indignity was finally over and Granada was once again being admired.

Repainted, trimmed, and at least looking good, the Granada remained parked in the Mitchell Museum in Owosso, Michigan, until shortly after Bill Mitchell's death, when everything was auctioned off in 2014. It had been a journey of more than 60 years but fortunately, the Granada continued safe in the hands of a caring new owner once again.

As luck would have it, the present owner has now taken the Granada full circle with an intense frame-off restoration. With meticulous attention to detail, each part of the Granada has painstakingly been returned to the grand condition it was in when it debuted in 1954. Correct Motor Wheel wire spoke wheels were located and are now back in place as of this writing. Modifications made over the years have been removed and returned to original. Door glass and even a convertible top have been fabricated. And the chassis is now good as new. So the resurrection of the Granada is complete.

In the final analysis, was it not the raison d'être of these cars to make us all dream? To imagine? To convert *what if* into reality? To add a dash of romance? By all these criteria, the Granada succeeded magnificently. Whether or not you like the styling in today's realm, it accomplished exactly what it was intended to do. And now, the Granada has survived like an old soldier.

CHAPTER SEVEN

MOPAR PACKARDS OR PACKARD MOPARS

 In this chapter, you will see that the spheres of Detroit car companies not only intersected, sometimes they also overlapped.

The Plastic Packard, Plastic Dodge and Plastic Mopar X

During the planning for the Dodge Granada, another development took place that also involved fiberglass sports cars and ultimately, Creative Industries. This one involved Packard Motor Car Company, but in a way, it also involved what ultimately became yet another component of Chrysler Corporation: Briggs Manufacturing Company.

Packard's new president, James J. Nance, had just come onboard in 1952. Nance had successfully built the Hotpoint appliance brand into a powerhouse of sales for General Electric. His aim was now to do something similar for Packard Motor Car Company.

Jim Nance was on a crusade to return Packard to the level of a top luxury carmaker while creating a fourth alternative to the Big Three automakers. His ambitious plan included a merger with Studebaker and ultimately with American Motors: in effect creating the Big Four. Of course, for many complicated reasons, the latter part of this equation never took place. But there were lots of things happening with design proposals at this point.

When Nance first arrived, Packard's body supplier, Briggs Manufacturing Company, had a staff of top designers sitting around dishing out ideas. One of these ideas was a fiberglass sports car.

The design of the car that finally came to be is now credited to designer Bill Robinson, who insists today that it was done only for Plymouth. However, somewhere along the way, Briggs' design chief Albert Prance apparently pitched a slightly different version of the same design to Packard.

Whatever James J. Nance felt about the Prance/Briggs proposal, *somebody* at Packard thought enough of the design to feed it to a car magazine. Perhaps it was intended as disinformation. Maybe it was a sly way to test the waters. More likely it was an idea being championed by the head of Packard design, Edward Macauley. But either way, it happened. A slightly modified illustration of the Briggs sports car complete with the same deep bombsight-type headlight bezels, long hood, rear-looking bumper (mounted on the front), concave front fenders, and

Packard Panther under final assembly at the Mitchell-Bentley Ionia Division. Some members of this team were Creative Industries employees working on a per-diem basis. Only four deck lids were shown in the series of photos, again pointing to the number built. (Photo Courtesy Dr. Gerald Perschbacher Collection)

kicked-up rear quarters appeared in *CARS* with a Packard grille in 1953. The caption read, "Sketch from design section reveals lines along which Packard is thinking."

But for a number of reasons, Nance didn't warm up to it. Outspoken Nance was never one known for tepid reactions. He had very strong opinions about car design, especially when it applied to Packard. Nance's term for the existing Packard taillight design was one that shall go down in the annals of automotive history. He minced no words as he derided the design, referring to it as part of a bull's anatomy. One designer quipped that Nance thought the Briggs plastic Packard proposal looked like a new Ford going backward.

So at that time, anyone trying to impress Nance was wise to have a seriously interesting design to show. Otherwise it could go down in flames. As it turned out, the Briggs proposal never made it past the magazine appearance. Nance believed that Packard could come up with something better, and he was determined that the design would be done in-house.

Also one must understand that several factors had all come into play about the same time. Packard had slipped from

Plastic Makes Perfect

Designs by George Walker, Arthur Fitzpatrick and John Reinhart

THREE Detroit automobile designers here present their conception of cars of tomorrow. Lighter, and therefore more economical to drive, they will be quieter and more comfortable—for plastic insulates against noise as well as weather, while "living room" is increased. Most of these are small-wheeled cars with small tires which afford the proper turning radius in view of the fact that a portion of the side panels comes beyond the wheel and eliminates wheel housing. These body panels are complete compression moldings and can be molded in sections so they may be easily replaced in case of accident. Vision is improved by the use of transparent "plasticglass" tops, and by the lighter pillar support which is required in the windows and windshields.

Opaque colored plastic panels; rear engine motor; chromium steel around lower panels incorporates grille and bumpers. Rear plastic panel has ventilation to cool motor. Rest of the top is clear plastic material incorporating windshield. Concealed head lift lights. 5-passenger.—by George Walker.

Sport coupé designed for front or rear engine has free flowing lines. Lamps flush with front fenders. Air intake above fared in bumper. Body panels of molded plastic. Top over front seat can be screened by concealed blinds. Rear part of top could be made to fold.—by Arthur Fitzpatrick.

6-passenger large plastic body sedan. One-quarter opaque top and the balance in clear plastic material. A chromium bumper runs completely around the car, also including an integral grille. This is a front motor car with draft ventilation coming through the rear compartment for cooling.—by George Walker.

6-pass., rear-engine sedan. Plexiglass top, has concealed curtains. Built-in bumpers with air-conditioning intakes. Trunk under front bonnet. Wheels encased by shrouds; front shrouds turn. Color through body panels obviates repaint.—by John Reinhart.

3-passenger car, motor in rear. Lower, opaque plastics; three-quarter clear plastics on top include windshield. Chromium louvers at rear cool the motor. Chromium bumper and grille in front. Chromium band completely around car staves off stones.—by George Walker.

5-pass. rear motor car. Tan opaque plastics form one-quarter of the top; balance is in clear plastic and an opaque body incorporates color within the plastic. Grille treatment also an integral part of the bumper. White rubber inlay in the center of the bumper encircles the car.—by George Walker.

3-pass., 3-wheeled; opaque plastic body, clear top; chromium door frames. Bumpers embrace front, include cooling grille. Rear chromium piece shields rear wheel, forms bumper. Chromium at rear for cooling.—by George Walker.

6-pass. sedan, front-engine chassis; cooling grilles abolish radiator shell; body contours replace fenders. Corrugated panels form base. Curved plastic windows and windshield; light pillar construction increases vision. Leather and cloth interior.—by John Reinhart.

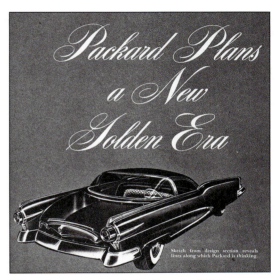

pioneering predictions of a future in plastic cars in 1941 (as in *Esquire* magazine) all the way down to playing catch-up in 1953.

To add insult to injury, upstart Kaiser-Frazer was about to unleash its own production fiberglass sports car. And to make the insult even greater, Kaiser-Frazer was using former Packard sports car design guru Howard "Dutch" Darrin (of Packard Darrin fame) to do it all!

The 1953 Corvette introduction quickly followed, cementing the fact that plastic cars were now in the big leagues. Furthermore, General Motors was also busy unleashing a slew of plastic concept cars. There were four fiberglass Cadillac LeMans sports car concepts and numerous other concepts including a handful of Corvette-based models. Ford was also busy preparing fiberglass-bodied concepts, the FX-Atmos and the Mystere, both of which were actually built by Creative. Mercury's fiberglass XM-800 was also built at Creative, as was the Dodge Granada and others that were in the works. In short, it was a fiberglass frenzy in Detroit.

Richard "Dick" Teague

Jim Nance immediately assigned hot new designer Richard Teague on a rather crash project of creating a fiberglass sports car. But first there were several issues that needed to be resolved and another car that had to be done.

Teague had preceded Nance at Packard Motor Car Company, but his direct boss was famed Edward Macauley, who at that point was in charge of Packard design. Jim Nance apparently regarded Ed Macauley as having retired on the job. As Nance saw it, all that Macauley had done since the 1940s was to endlessly tinker with the styling of his personal "Phantom" or "Brown Bomber" experimental car. Like a Hollywood star that didn't know when to stop having plastic surgery, Macauley's personal rolling testbed sports car was the epitome of the phrase "too much is never enough." Apparently, every time Macauley got a new idea, the Brown Bomber was hustled into the design and engineering

Packard Styling Chief Ed Macauley at the wheel of his plexiglass roof Packard "Phantom" at Packard's Proving Grounds in the 1940s. This one-off experimental was later simply known as "Brown Bomber" (with all due respect to boxer, Joe Louis). (Photo Courtesy Stuart R. Blond and The Packard Club)

facility and out came the torches and the bars of lead.

The Bomber changed every year, and sometimes underwent numerous changes during the same model year. So photos of the car depict numerous morphings. Suffice it to say that the Bomber was a constant work in progress and Macauley was never satisfied with the vehicle. Just as soon as it was updated, Ed might drive the Bomber around Detroit for a while, take some photos on Belle Isle, then decide he didn't like the fenders or the wheel openings. So? It was back to the drawing boards.

By the early 1950s, Ed Macauley came up with a replacement for the Brown Bomber. This new replacement was first known as the "Saga-Macauley" and then later "Panther" (more on *this* Panther later).

This Macauley "sportsman's car" was based on John Reinhart's body design that debuted in 1951. Once completed, it wasn't long before Macauley was back to tinkering endlessly with the new car. But the new Packard president wasn't impressed with Macauley's ideas and tinkering.

The outspoken Nance reportedly referred to the 1948–1950 Packard as a "pregnant elephant," and we've already

Packard Styling Chief Ed Macauley sitting in his custom-built, ever-morphing Packard Phantom. Better known to some as "Brown Bomber," as it looked in the late 1940s. It first appeared in early 1940s and was altered numerous times. Forward top section was tinted plexiglass designed by John Reinhart. (Photo Courtesy Stuart R. Blond and The Packard Club)

Late 1940s view of Ed Macauley's hugely morphed Brown Bomber. Headlight treatment was so far ahead it was still being used on several imported cars up until recent years. (Photo Courtesy Stuart R. Blond and The Packard Club)

mentioned his feelings about the 1951–1954 Packard taillights. As he surveyed the situation at his arrival, the only exciting car he could see with a Packard nameplate hadn't even been originated at Packard. It was the 1952 Pan American concept car (see Chapter Ten). But this concept had been penned by outside designer Richard Arbib and executed for Packard by coachbuilder Henney Motor Company.

The Pan American had won wide acclaim for its beauty. Some even say that the rear of this car inspired Ford's new Thunderbird. But back in the hands of Ed Macauley, the Pan American had morphed into a "whatzit" of ponderous styling with no particular direction. This was hardly an endorsement for Packard's in-house design prowess. Outside designs from outside companies and status quo just wouldn't do anymore.

Macauley's morphing never stopped. His Brown Bomber was always in a state of transition. If it wasn't being cut and welded or molded with lead, it was being slathered with (brown) clay to create a new shape. Here the deck lid and rear bustle are being toyed with in clay. Apparently the decision to do this was so spur-of-the-moment that the real taillight was simply left in place and covered in clay. (Photo Courtesy Stuart R. Blond and The Packard Club)

Saga-Macauley Speedster as it looks today. "Panther" letters on grille originally said "Packard" but were changed by Ed Macauley. Chrome ridges on fender tops were a late addition and mimicked Briggs, proposed flange covers.

Nance wanted to shake up the design department at Packard. It was a breach of protocol, but Richard Teague now largely received his marching orders directly from the new Packard president. This move ultimately involved Creative Industries.

The Packard Balboa

First, Nance challenged Teague to come up with a cost-efficient but very pleasing Packard redesign for limited production. This new design would be released and sold as a prestige sports convertible. This new model would also be inspired by Richard Arbib's Pan American design. Like the Pan American, it would also be based on Reinhardt's body design and related hardware but with a bold new and sporty look.

To hold costs down, this new car would eliminate most of the hardcore bodywork like channeling that was done on the Pan American. This sporty convertible would be known as the Caribbean, and it would be built by the Ionia Body Division of Mitchell-Bentley.

Once the limited-production Caribbean was under way, Teague's additional project was an exciting new concept car that was known as the Packard Balboa. This concept debuted in 1953 as the first clear evidence that Jim Nance had arrived.

According to people I knew at Creative, the futuristic new roof of the Balboa was pressed out and welded at their facilities. The inside story goes that the wooden armature, the clay form, tooling, die work, and the actual sheet metal forming were all done at Creative. The company had numerous presses, including one huge press (inherited from Progressive Welder Company) that had been used for everything from aircraft, to trucks, to automotive hoods and roofs. So Creative certainly had the capability. And nobody knew welding better than the descendent company of Progressive Welder, right?

People on Creative's staff indicated that Briggs built the basic body and sent it over to Packard on East Grand Boulevard. From there the body was transferred over to Creative, where the new roof was pressed out and welded onto the structure of the Briggs body. When the additional metal work was completed at Creative, the bare body, painted only in primer, was taken back to Packard building 38 off Concord Avenue. Here the new body assembly was inspected and reviewed both for engineering and styling. The Briggs/Creative body was then mounted on a chassis with an engine.

With this being Dick Teague's major styling debut for Packard, and with Ed Macauley wanting every detail double-checked, and with a new Packard president to please, Balboa was (as one person put it) reviewed, reviewed, and then reviewed again. Once

![Packard engineer Bill Graves looks on while Ed Macauley points to a unique reverse-slant Balboa backlight window.]

Packard engineer Bill Graves looks on while Ed Macauley points to a unique reverse-slant Balboa backlight window. Noticeably absent in these photos is the man who actually designed the Balboa. Staged photo was taken in front of the Detroit Institute of Arts.

Early rendering by Richard Teague of Packard Caribbean proposal slightly different from eventual vehicle. One idea was for tempered glass backlight with chrome trim. Illustration was done so early that "Caribbean" name had not yet been decided, thus reference to simply "Sports Model." This was one of many images in Creative's files that were eventually destroyed. Author has reason to suspect Teague did much of Caribbean styling work away from Packard and at Creative's East Outer Drive location.

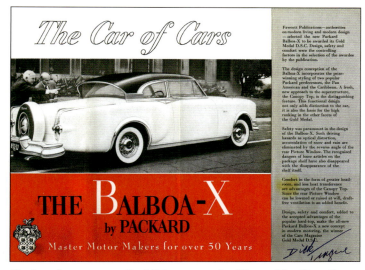

Early references called this concept with roof by Creative "Balboa-X," later shortened to "Balboa." Packard engineer Bill Graves points out the reverse-slant backlight to Ed Macauley. Noticeably absent is actual Balboa designer who autographed this brochure, Richard Teague.

approved by Nance and his staff, the basic vehicle was shipped, along with some pre-conversion Packard Caribbean convertibles, to Mitchell-Bentley's Ionia Division in Ionia, Michigan. There the beautiful, luxurious Ionia interior was made and final paint and trim were done.

Balboa was originally intended to have a retractable rear window glass that could be lowered behind the rear seat backrest. It certainly could have easily worked with the glass retracting down at the same angle behind the backrest. And yes, there was room to do it, even if the window could only move down partway. Anyone who has owned a 1958–1960 Continental can tell you how this is possible.

According to David Margolis and Gary Hutchings, Creative had already worked out the details to do the retracting window using an American Bosch reversible electric motor. A similar little motor was used later in making the 1957–1959 Ford retractable hardtop convertibles and in the 1958–1960 Continentals with similar reverse-slant backlight glass. These Continentals indeed had retracting reverse-slant backlight glass.

Unfortunately there was no money to fabricate the mechanism and perform the work necessary to get the Balboa's rear glass operating. No budget was ever created to fund the testing and installation, and worse, they just plain ran out of time.

The Balboa had been a rush project from the beginning and it was thought that the rear window could be made

Balboa just after paint and trim were completed at Mitchell-Bentley's Ionia Manufacturing Division.

Balboa's interior trim as seen when first completed. (Photo Courtesy Gary Thomas Collection)

Early Balboa just after completion. Note "Mitchell-Bentley Corporation" lettering on brick entryway.

A 1953 Caribbean prototype undergoes conversion from a standard Packard convertible body at Mitchell-Bentley with engineering assist from Creative Industries. Power convertible tops were another Creative specialty. (Photo Courtesy Gary Thomas Collection)

Front view of a 1953 Caribbean prototype during conversion from a standard Packard convertible. Wood template on floor was a guide for rear wheel radius cuts. Black strips on fender and door were created when the original stainless trim was removed and the holes filled with brass and smeared with lead. (Photo Courtesy Gary Thomas Collection)

operable during a refresh at Creative for the 1954 auto show season. So a power backlight was postponed. Meanwhile, the backlight window operation could merely be stated. Why not? Ford Motor Company was using this same kind of PR in spins on their concepts at that time.

But Jim Nance didn't like what he viewed as fakery and was not happy with this development. It was the first of a series of disappointments and setbacks for Nance. Nance vowed that the next such backlight glass would indeed retract.

Unfortunately, by the time a refresh could take place at Creative, Packard was in even worse financial position due to the alarming discoveries made in the merger with Studebaker.

Don Mitchell (left) discusses production with son William Mitchell at Packard Caribbean assembly line at Mitchell-Bentley.

And as concepts went, the Balboa was already long in the tooth. So the idea was dropped, and it all stopped there.

As the Caribbean assembly line finally got humming at Ionia Body Division of Mitchell-Bentley, the Balboa concept (originally known as "Balboa-X") was also released with great fanfare. Newspapers all over the country ran stories with pictures of the Balboa. But back at Packard headquarters on East Grand Boulevard, there was trouble brewing.

According to Gary Hutchings of Creative Industries, there was an unspoken but very bitter rivalry borne out of the Balboa creation. Richard Teague had done the re-style of Packard's existing convertible, probably inspired by Chrysler's K-310 concept. But Ed Macauley had wanted to go in a different direction with the styling based on an evolution of his own cars, including the Brown Bomber or maybe the Saga-Macauley.

In the end, and despite Teague's work and ideas on the Caribbean, patent number D 175845 was issued in the name of Edward R. Macauley. Now, this was not altogether unusual since Mac was the Director of Design at Packard. But it also revealed where the power resided, regardless of who designed what, at least for the Caribbean and the time being.

It was remarkable that Ed Macauley appeared prominently in Balboa press photos. But oddly, there was no sign of Richard Teague in images that were sent out to newspapers and magazines.

As chief of design, Edward Macauley still held sway at Packard despite the new presidential regime. Macauley didn't much like the idea of young Teague usurping what the senior Packard man felt was *his* territory. Macauley was insulted by Nance's breach of protocol. But then Teague had his orders straight from the top, so what could he do?

Although Macauley was said to be a very quiet, reserved, and nice man, Gary Hutchings and others at Creative indicated there was friction. Disputes between Macauley and Teague (Nance) over styling directions eventually reached a boiling point. Almost immediately after one of these first encounters, Teague eased first himself and later, a couple of trusted colleagues, over to East Outer Drive and the headquarters of Creative Industries. The excuse given at the time was that it was all due to remodeling being done at Grand Boulevard. But at least part of this was just a cover story. Some former Packard design people were told that the company would lease temporary space over at Creative while the areas over at the plant were being re-done.

Either way, Packard ended up having a physical presence at Creative and so did Richard Teague. The official Packard area reportedly was upstairs in the rear, close to Moenart Street and was designated as a "loft." However, the Teague area was downstairs in a locked, corrugated metal partition.

From this point on until almost the end of his career, Teague kept a secured area surrounded by corrugated metal walls set aside in the back of Creative's workshops. Employees at Creative came to refer to this enclosed area as "The Teague studio." It was here where the Panther work was finalized, away from the prying eyes and meddling that was going on back at Grand Boulevard and the Packard plant.

At Creative, Teague covertly polished all of his Packard (and other) design work away from interlopers. No published history has ever stated this, but talking with Creative's old employees confirmed the story repeatedly. And remember my history of Creative Industries for *Car Classics* in December 1978? One quote from that history had Dave Margolis talking about how "Dick Teague and his boys were in recently working on some super-secret goodie." So Teague's ongoing relationship with Creative was a fact.

In the end, when Packard Balboa patent number D 176962 was finally issued (and this after some unusual delay), it came in the names of both Edward R. Macauley and Richard A. Teague.

There are also claims that Dick Teague somehow worked for Mitchell-Bentley. However, Dick had his hands absolutely full at the time just working for Packard. And the patent on Balboa invalidated any other claims about anyone else owning or selling the design rights. Creative did engineering, roof manufacture, and assembly. Ionia Division of Mitchell-Bentley indeed did the final trim on Balboa, but that's all. Packard and Macauley had the U.S. Patent on the design.

Packard Panthers

With Balboa completed, it was now full speed ahead on to the Packard fiberglass sports car. Dick referred to this new car idea as "a lunchbox project," squeezed in during spare moments between various other pressing issues (of which there were many at the time). And who would Nance turn to in order to make this fiberglass Packard concept? Creative Industries of Detroit.

Initially the name for Packard's new plastic sport car was to be Gray Wolf II (after the famous early Packard racing car). But this name was nixed at the last minute due to some rather volatile (if not silly) internal company politics.

According to Richard Teague, someone on Packard's board (or perhaps the person who liked the Briggs design) took issue with the Gray Wolf name, citing that it invoked images of old men chasing young women. This odd protest came so late into the program that chrome-plated metal logo names had already been made and installed on the first car. These nameplates were quickly removed and the new Packard was finally dubbed Panther.

Detroit News automotive columnist Ralph R. Watts wrote an introductory story about the Packard Panthers in February 1954. In his article, Watts said, "Panther has been under construction for the past 36 months by company engineers."

Photo replaces a thousand words. Dick Teague is not only included in the Packard concept pics, but now is shown seated at the wheel, while Ed Macauley merely looks on with engineer Bill Graves. Photo taken on Concord Avenue outside of the Packard plant. Note the "Gray Wolf II" lettering already made and installed here prior to the forced name change to "Panther."

If the gestation time listed here is accurate (it was likely just a slight bit of puffery), this pushes initiation of the Panthers back to 1951. In reality, while Packard engineers (plural) were likely involved in the early plans for the Panthers, there was really a total of one known Packard engineer assigned to the Panthers for their final assembly. His name was Lester Shoemaker. According to Creative's Lynn Griffin, Les had come over to Creative from Packard and became an employee of Creative Industries, which then lent him to Mitchell-Bentley, where he worked at Ionia. That's where Les supposedly ended up (yes, it's a lot to keep up with, but also reveals the tangled web of links no one outside ever knew).

So as with the Dodge Granada, Mitchell-Bentley assisted Creative by doing the final trimming and completion of the Panthers. Mitchell-Bentley was already doing the Packard Caribbeans. And don't forget that there were engineers and designers from Creative already camped out for years at Mitchell-Bentley, so subcontracting Mitchell-Bentley was little different than contracting Creative. It was all family. Of course, there were also other benefits.

Macauley might not have been warm and fuzzy over the Richard Teague/Jim Nance situation, but Macauley sure liked

With "Gray Wolf II" logos removed but holes still visible, the Packard Panther concept is shown next to another wall of the Packard plant in Detroit. Note the special louvered wheel covers and Packard's first wraparound windshield.

Passenger-side view with "Gray Wolf II" logos removed but holes still visible.

Don Mitchell. Both men fancied themselves as sportsmen and both liked sporty cars, and once they had one, both had the same proclivity for endless experimentation and morphing of the design. Neither man was ever satisfied with their personal vehicles and ended up constantly modifying the cars.

So right from the start, it was a good bet that with Mitchell-Bentley's manufacturing capacity, Mitchell-Bentley likely had a hand in the making of the Panthers.

Creative's Gary Hutchings related to me back in the 1970s, "We did all of the original Panther bodies from molds we made off a full-size clay done at Creative. I know that we turned out the bodies in a special shop we rented over on Mt. Elliott and that was where we did all of our fiberglass work at the time."

According to Steve Koppin, this Mt. Elliott operation was run by a fellow named Bud Mick. Adjacent to this shop off McNichols (6 Mile Road) and in the same building, at least for a while, was the graphics and designs department. This unit eventually became a separate company known as Creative Universal.

Driver-side view with folding top raised and "Gray Wolf II" logos removed but holes still visible.

Final assembly of Don Mitchell's Panther, painted a turquoise blue. Behind it was Rex Terry's Panther awaiting final assembly. (Photo Courtesy Dr. Gerald Pershbacher Collection)

Some of these people were from Creative Industries, but they were working at Mitchell-Bentley. Many of them worked on the Packard Panthers. The fellow on far right wearing a bowtie is Lynn Griffin, who had an incredible automotive career beginning with Creative and ending with Shelby Mustangs. (Photo Courtesy Linder Griffin Collection)

Creative also had a staff of clay modelers that was par excellence. Some had cut their teeth at the Big Three car companies and these people were all razor sharp. They were among the top clay pushers in Detroit and had studied under GM's Harley Earl.

So coincidentally, at the same time the Panthers were taking shape hidden behind a set of rippled silver metal partition walls on East Outer Drive, another crew was pushing clay on a Dodge Granada armature. This armature was actually lurking in another part of the same Creative facility, but on the other side of the building behind yet another rippled metal partition.

And since Creative already had both a Packard connection and a joint project with Mitchell-Bentley going on with the Granada, it was inevitable that the two would also do the Panthers. But aside from those at the very top of the company, nobody in general knew that these two projects were taking place in the same building at the same time. Work began on the Panthers at Creative in 1953 as a full-size clay model.

Then there was another question: Who would get design credit for the Panthers? In the interim since the Balboa, things had changed. First, a Panther patent was issued around the same time as the Balboa and, likewise, it was listed in the names of both Macauley and Teague. But *this* time, Dick Teague was indeed shown in factory press photos, not merely *in the photo* of his Panther creation. Furthermore, Teague was now pictured seated *at the wheel* with Macauley looking on, more like a bystander than the boss. As the saying goes, photos often say a lot more than words.

In a personal letter dated February 10, 1972, Richard Teague wrote to Gene Grengs, the current owner of Panther number-2: "Yes, I did design the Panther, although I'm not particularly proud of it. I guess all designers would like to see

their creations changed to some extent after they see a few put together. I'm no exception for sure and would give a month's pay to have had the chance to do a full-size clay model of that car rather than the 3/8 clay that was the case. I knew when the small model was completed that very substantial changes should have been made, however, time was running out and our executives liked the car and the way it was and, therefore, that most important phase (full-size clay) was eliminated.

"Creative Industries were then given the task of doing all the full-size surface work and the male full-size model at their shop without much needed necessary modifications.

"You will find it of interest to know that up to the very announcement of the car, it was to be called Gray Wolf II after, of course, the famous 1903 racing car that was designed by Charles Schmidt, the first chief engineer of Packard. This name was changed at the last minute because of the aversion of one of our management people to the name. His feeling was this was demeaning and referred to a lecherous old gray-haired girl chaser; idiotic, but that's what happened, so help me!"

As for that Briggs plastic sports car design mentioned earlier here? No matter what company or name it was intended to carry, it was something Creative would not have done.

Although Creative respected Briggs' effort in making a fiberglass car, they thought the construction method and aesthetics left a lot to be desired. The level of fiberglass expertise at Creative was already years ahead in sophistication and skill. These people were setting the high water mark in automotive fiberglass at that time. Creative's designers and engineers didn't like what they saw as a quick-and-dirty, unsophisticated exposed flange mating of fiberglass panels on the Briggs fiberglass proposal. So it was clear that Creative was going in a different direction for both Panther and Granada.

Creative's David Margolis once told me, "That Briggs body looked too much like a kit car; the flanges ran really obvious, along the fender tops, covered in chrome strips. We just didn't like that. And we really didn't want to go 'bathtub' style either, even though it would have been easier. Whatever we did had to look the way a steel fender might look."

Creative, fresh from their experiences with the Ford FX-Atmos concept and Corvette, quickly determined the best approach was to meld both the Granada and Panther bodies into one large unit rather than multiple pieces or exposed flange construction fenders.

So the Panthers were constructed as smooth, light, one-piece assemblies that could be lifted by one man and ride on

Panther one-piece body built by Creative Industries was light enough to be lifted by one man. Photo was never used because similar photo was also taken of Dodge Granada body being lifted. Packard backed off on this notion and chose to promote Daytona speed record aspect of Panthers. (Photo Courtesy Dr. Gerald Pershbacher Collection)

a basically stock 122-inch-wheelbase Clipper chassis. But wait, the same construction was also being applied to the Dodge Granada. And there was the same claim that it could ride on a stock chassis.

From Creative's position, there were some delicate decisions and coordinations that needed to be made. With the same company engineering and making the fiberglass bodies for both, how could one possibly avoid cross-pollenization? What was the hook for each car that the PR types could hang their hats upon? The folks at Dodge were looking for possible publicity angles on their fiberglass Granada concept. Likewise, so was Packard with their Panther.

Business was business, but in the end, diplomacy and civility had to reign, along with cleverness. Creative wanted and needed friends who would continue to bring them contracts. It was not in their interest to create friction. After all, this was the 1950s, not the 2000s. Let's just say that in those days when courtesy and business civility was more highly valued, a gentleman's agreement was reached.

Luckily, Packard had lots of publicity angles for a fiberglass car. Most important among these was the heritage of the racing car whose name it was first intended to carry. Then came Packard's many years of talking about plastic cars, and more. So there was wiggle room in choosing a way to promote the Panthers without obvious leakage from the Granada. And vice versa.

In the end, Packard wisely backed off on the one-piece-body angle, even though at first they had a photographer snap a shot of a man lifting a bare Panther body. Instead, Packard went for the speed angle and proceeded to set a record (131.1 miles per hour) with a Panther running the sands at Daytona Beach in Florida. After that, the factory Panthers grew a longer name,

Panther-Daytona, and emphasis remained on speed first and the plastic body second.

How Many Panthers?

Over the years there has been much speculation, myth, and rumor as to how many Panthers were made. There has even been discussion of supposed memos regarding a fifth Panther, followed with claims it was also destroyed. The biggest problem with the Panther destruction story is that a fifth car had to be built before it could be destroyed. There may have been a chassis, floor pan, and engine assigned, but the people who fabricated the bodies over at Creative never knew about it, or at least not that anyone could recall. And with the people who did the building not knowing anything about a fifth car, this makes for a tough set of possibilities regarding destroying one.

There was also the tantalizing illustration of an odd Panther apparently drawn up for Earle C. Anthony. "E.C." (as he liked to be called) was Packard's longtime West Coast distributor and huge car dealer. He was also a member of the PMCC board of directors. Anthony had his own ideas about how a Panther ought to be made. His version would have included both throwback cues from the past and design from the future. E.C.'s Panther had built-in dual side mount spare tires with a classic Packard radiator-style grille surrounded by a 1958 Packard Hawk–style mouth. The rear quarters and taillights would have been based on what were intended to be 1959 Packard taillights and mini-tailfins.

But no one I've spoken with over the years from either ECA, Packard, or Creative Industries has ever been able to confirm if this car was actually built. As far as I know, his Panther

Panther chalk and charcoal rendering of proposed 1957 Panther was shown twice in reversed photography. It was reportedly influenced by Packard board member and West Coast distributor Earle C. Anthony. Remember the Briggs concept sculpted indentations? Dual side-mounts and extended nose could have been supported by either Anthony or Macauley. But no one knows if this Panther was ever built.

Mitchell Panther after 1955 re-styling by Creative Industries. Photo reveals a lot. Roll-up side windows (side curtains are shown here) and vents were engineered and installed by Creative at same time they were doing likewise on Corvettes. Two-toning rage included here with color changed from Danube Blue to Roman Copper and Corsican Black. Unlike today, roof was originally black for this update. Tire casings here are brown rubber. Why the change to so much brown? It was Packard styling chief Ed Macauley's favorite color!

Three gold V symbols were leftover Creative Industries logos when Jim Nance didn't sign up for Creative's Panther update. Remaining set of "V" symbols ended up here on Rex Terry's Panther. Meaning there were four sets for four cars. Photo shows my friend Dave Margolis of Creative at wheel somewhere in Detroit's Palmer Park near where I grew up.

illustration was only shown twice where outsiders could have seen it and it was done at Creative.

After decades of following this story and talking with people who actually worked on the Panthers, there was no actual fifth Panther that anyone can recall, not even if it was ever discussed. And there were no engine numbers or body numbers assigned to a fifth Panther, at least not by the time the project reached Creative Industries. There was no chassis assigned, at least not one that made it outside of the Packard plant.

Construction photos show four deck lids. There were no parts to make a fifth car. Thus, there was no fifth Panther destroyed, or at least not one that could have reached the stage of construction at Creative.

As further and perhaps final evidence of the fact that there were only four Packard Panthers made, take a good look at Don Mitchell's 1954¼ version of the Panther. On the tail of the rear quarters you will find a stack of three offset "V" symbols. The offset "V" was Creative's trademarked logo. One of these same gold "V" symbols was on Rex Terry's 1954½ Panther. So do the math. Four again. These four sets of "V" symbols were made up in hopes that Packard would want to update the factory's remaining two Panther-Daytonas that were still sporting 1954 Clipper taillights. The plan was that four updated cars receive one set each of the Creative scripts and gold "V" symbols, as if to say *Body by Creative*.

But when Creative shopped the Panther update idea to Jim Nance, he turned them down flat, despite the fact that he liked the new taillights and handsome re-style. There just wasn't any money available at the time for such frivolity. Packard's accountants were already getting some sad, shocking surprises in Studebaker's numbers after the 1954 merger. Then there were the huge outlays that had been made for Packard's engine and transmission plant in Utica, Michigan. This was bad enough, but then came another shocking surprise at the eleventh hour that Briggs would no longer be supplying Packard bodies. The company had been acquired by Chrysler. It all must have seemed like a very bad dream for Nance.

So a new Packard assembly plant was shoehorned in during a lightning-fast miracle conversion of the Briggs east-side plant. This new Packard plant now occupied the former Briggs body facility on Conner and East Warren Avenues. Meanwhile, the original Packard plant stopped making cars on East Grand Boulevard at the end of the 1954 model year production.

Yes, this move and installation cost a pile, but there just weren't many viable options at the time. And speaking of time, there was none. Add all this to the legendary quality and assembly issues that followed over at Conner Avenue and you've got the picture. All Creative could do at this point was to hold on and hope that the checks kept cashing. Besides, the next Packard concept car kept Creative busy for a while and Packard continued to rely on the skills and facilities at Creative more than ever before.

But a Panther re-do at this point just wasn't a high priority. Bottom line, only two were upgraded, both by Creative, and both were the privately owned Panthers. Nance already had his game plan. He was banking on the upcoming 1955 Packard Request and the even wilder 1956 Predictor that was in the planning stages. Investment in updating the Panthers just couldn't be justified.

Ed Macauley's Packard Panther

Next came Edward Macauley's Panther, which adds to the confusion. This car, originally done in connection with popular *Saga* men's magazine, was first only known as the Saga-Macauley Speedster. For years, it *never* said Panther anywhere on the vehicle. In fact, the original design of this concept with its very long trunk was touted as a sportsman's dream vehicle. The trunk, while it may appear odd today, was made extra long to accommodate rifles and fishing rods, and it even had a bed for plush sleeping out in the wilderness. So the idea of this car suddenly sprouting a Panther name on the grille where it once said Packard was purely Ed Macauley's way of following the trend. The Macauley cars, whenever they were and however they started out in life, always had a habit of morphing every time production designs changed. And yes, Creative assisted with some of the morphs. Gary Hutchings never differentiated in descriptive details beyond stating, "We always helped Macauley out with work on his sports cars." Of course "sports cars" encompassed at least three known vehicles. We already mentioned the Phantom/Brown Bomber and now the Saga-Macauley Speedster. But there was more.

For instance, Macauley's 1952 Pan American Number One eventually ended up with 1955 senior cathedral taillights, along with a 1955 instrument panel and steering wheel, all courtesy of Creative Industries.

So when the fiberglass Panthers became the latest talk of the town, Ed Macauley's Speedster did the usual and morphed from a sportsman's luxury SUV to a Panther sports car. But it was not a true Panther and certainly not the origin of the model name for Packard.

Placing the name "Panther" and installing a supercharger on the Saga-Macauley Speedster was likely Macauley's last grasp

Another Ed Macauley one-off, ever morphing Packard, the Saga-Macauley Speedster (later renamed Panther) at Packard Proving Grounds in Michigan. Light on roof was spotlight, operable from inside the vehicle. (Photo Courtesy Stuart R. Blond and The Packard Club)

at holding onto his fading power as head of Packard Design. Packard designer Fred L. Hudson wrote a revealing article that appeared in *The Packard Cormorant* magazine in 2009. According to Hudson, Edward Macauley spent his declining time at Packard huddled in his office, reading the *Wall Street Journal* and clipping coupons. During those last few months before the arrival of new design chief William Schmidt, Ed Macauley sat ignored and powerless in his office in what the Japanese would call a "window seat."

As Hudson put it, by the end of 1954, Ed Macauley "never ventured into the Styling Studio. Until, one day, he was no longer there! A gracious, soft-spoken gentleman, Ed Macauley was an 'old school gentleman' personified. His 'daily driver' was the 'Panther,' a 1951 Patrician with a Mayfair roof welded up to it, which transformed the car into a coupe with an enormous rear deck. He drove his Panther back to Grosse Pointe for good. No good-byes, no nothing. Perhaps about the time of Bill Schmidt's arrival on the scene."

The torch had quietly been passed, but Creative Industries continued to interact with Ed Macauley, providing him at least one 1955 Caribbean hardtop: a car that was not officially produced by Packard except as a convertible. You can see just the rear tip of this car in the official Creative Industries of Detroit photo of the general offices building. It was painted in non-stock colors and sometimes could be seen sitting in Creative's driveway at 3080 East Outer Drive.

Simply put, James Nance had bypassed Edward Macauley beginning with the Packard Balboa concept. Nance continued to back Teague and Teague's design direction over Macauley and the styling direction where Macauley was headed. Macauley's services were no longer valued and that was how it ended.

Changing Panthers

The first two Packard Panthers were built just as originally intended. Panther number-1 was originally painted metallic silver-gray. As thus it was carrying out the Gray Wolf II theme. The interior was always orangish-red and silver, not the plain solid gray that has recently been executed on one car. The bench seat was done in bright orange-red bolsters with silver leather inserts. These inserts were done in thick, deeply pleated genuine leather. It was said to be incredibly comfortable to sit on. This deep pleating of leather was a Mitchell-Bentley specialty, and they were quite proud of this method that they claimed to have invented. So proud was Mitchell-Bentley over this seating that they took official photos of it.

Although early black and white promotional shots and a few color transparencies were taken of Panther number-1, the silver-gray exterior color of Panther number-1 only remained for a very short time. Once the Gray Wolf II name went away,

Mitchell-Bentley was so proud of their deep-pleated leather Panther seat that they took a photo. Seats were reportedly extremely comfortable. Two original factory Panther-Daytonas had bright orangish-red bolsters with silver pleated inserts.

Panther number-1 with Gray Wolf II colors still intact pictured here with "Panther-Daytona" logos installed. (Photo Courtesy Stuart R. Blond and The Packard Club)

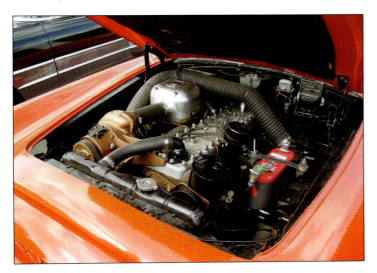

the body color was quickly changed because there was no longer a reason for it to be silver-gray. It was then decided to paint Panthers number-1 and number-2 in a bright orange-red, extending the interior colors to the exterior.

Meanwhile Panther number-2 was immediately sent down to Daytona Beach, Florida, for a special speed trial on the

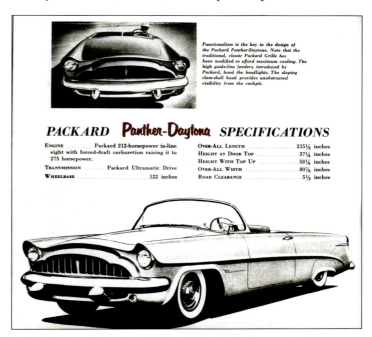

Panther foldout brochure shows driver Dick Rathman seated behind special racing windscreen temporarily installed for record run.

Panther foldout brochure cover, autographed to author by Panther-Daytona number-2 owner, Gene Grengs.

Panther-Daytona straight-8 engine with supercharger in Panther number-2. This car actually ran at Daytona Beach and set the speed record of over 131 mph. Author had the pleasure of driving this Panther in recent years.

Panther fun at Fred Johnson's resort in Delray Beach, Florida. Children are Pamela Terry, Marilyn Johnson, and Rick Johnson. (Photo Courtesy Pamela Terry-Bonk Collection)

Jim and Delores Shank frolic in Rex Terry's Panther at Fred Johnson's Holiday House in Delray Beach, Florida, during the mid-1950s. Jim was a Chrysler executive. (Photo Courtesy Pamela Terry-Bonk Collection)

famous sands. In the old days Daytona was like a mini Bonneville Salt Flats, attracting famous racers from far and wide.

Such was the case of Packard Panther number-2, which visited on February 16, 1954. The occasion was the old Daytona Speed Week races. The Panther, with noted driver Dick Rathman at the wheel, rocketed over the sands at a speed of 110.9 mph. In an effort to cut wind resistance and reduce weight to the absolute bare minimum, Panther number-2 was not fitted with the wraparound windshield with metal header frame. Instead, a tiny windscreen was specially installed directly in front of driver Rathman.

According to author Nathaniel Dawes in his book *The Packard: 1942-1962*, Rathman wasn't satisfied with this official speed and later arranged to have his own unofficial run made. With the Panther horsepower of the Packard straight-8 already pumped up from 212 hp to 275 horses via its supercharger, Rathman was convinced the Panther could do much better. He firmly believed the engine power boost coupled with the lightweight fiberglass body could dust the first results he had been handed. As it turned out, Rathman was right. This time, the Panther went though the traps at 131.1 mph, much to Dick Rathman's and Packard's delight.

Thus, shortly after Rathman's run at Daytona, the Packard Panther was rechristened "Panther-Daytona" to capitalize on the speed run. Since no automobile in its class had ever traveled that fast, it was a record, official or not.

With this new speed record in hand, the first two Panthers were immediately slated for nationwide promotional tours. Panther number-2 was brought back to Creative in Detroit, where it was then fitted with a wraparound windshield and quickly sent out on tour to shows and dealerships. Sharp eyes note that this car originally had no provisions for windshield wipers and, in fact, was not actually street legal. This was changed later.

Panthers Go to Don Mitchell and Rex Terry

Four cars were certainly ordered (or at least built), but the amount of money required to field a fleet of show cars on tour was enormous. Not good in Packard's dire financial condition of massive cash outflows. So after the first two cars were completed, it was decided not to do any further Panthers for the circuit. Instead (and it remains unclear exactly how this was handled) the two remaining Panther cars were turned over to the heads of the companies that had worked on them. Don Mitchell of Mitchell-Bentley got Panther number-3 and Rex Terry got Panther number-4.

Although Mitchell-Bentley did the final trim assemblies and paint, it is important to remember there was a significant contingent of per diem Creative staff members at Mitchell-Bentley. Also, these last two Panthers were *never* rechristened Panther-Daytona and neither received a supercharger.

Only the first two Panthers had superchargers and orange-red paint. And henceforth only those first two Panthers were officially known as Panther-Daytonas. The last two Panthers were simply Panthers. The things that came with the Daytona part of the name were not included in the last two Panthers. So references to these last two cars today as Panther-Daytonas are simply mistaken.

Mitchell's early Panther had a white and turquoise interior. The exterior was actually painted Danube Blue (a 1956 Packard

Panther number-1 or number-2 showing off new "Panther-Daytona" logos after record-setting run at Daytona Beach, Florida.

Don Mitchell's Panther as it first appeared in Danube Blue.

Driver-side rear-quarter view of Don Mitchell's Panther as it first looked. Note wire wheels, which were later deleted in favor of wheel covers (Mitchell got tired of cleaning the spokes). Note white seat bolsters.

Don Mitchell in his Panther in front of Mitchell-Bentley's Ionia headquarters. Don quickly had "Packard" logos removed and replaced them with "Mitchell." Sharp eyes will see circular holes under lip above grille. This Panther was driven on streets in hot weather and had tendency to overheat, so extra holes were added.

Mitchell Panther morph number-3 showing off new root beer brown paint, two-piece side curtains with vents by Creative Industries and removable hard roof. This car was soon wrecked after this photo and 1955 Packard tail-lights and exhaust bumper were installed. Paint was then changed to two-tone.

production shade). It was one of Mitchell's favorite colors and basically the same as the color on the Dodge Granada. This color also turned up on other things that the Mitchells owned at the time. It was a very popular shade in the early 1950s and could even be found on other concepts, such as GM's Oldsmobile Starfire.

Don Mitchell, ever the promoter and always seeking ways to draw attention to his company, decided to rename *his* Panther. The history of this car became very confused in the minds of historians from this point, but here is what actually happened.

Early in the life of Panther number-3, off came the Packard logos, only to be replaced with new ones in a similar font. Only now these logos stated "Mitchell." We're not sure what Packard thought about this brash move, but it was apparently done with no major complaints. As I said, Don Mitchell had friends in high places, and Packard had bigger fish to fry with all of its financial woes, new plant, merger with Studebaker, etc.

Then, like his friend Ed Macauley over at Packard, Don Mitchell got even busier morphing his Panther. According to Creative design engineer Lynn Griffin, an Ionia employee named Don Funky was assigned to design a removable hardtop for the Mitchell Panther. But according to Gary Hutchings, the top was actually laid up at Creative's facility in Detroit. There is strong credence to Hutchings' claim because the addition of a hardtop was accompanied with the complicated addition of two-piece vented side curtains in the doors. Like Corvette at this time, the Panthers were only fitted with side curtains that had to be plugged into the doors. There were no roll-up win-

dows. Although this change truly made Panther number-3 a fully all-weather automobile, it required some serious engineering to accomplish.

Although this is totally unknown, Creative had already done something similar with removable hardtops for Chevrolet's Corvette. They did at least some work on the incredible Corvette Corvairs and the first removable hardtop Corvette concepts for 1954 along with the door window mechanisms.

Once the new Panther hard top was designed and fitted, roll-up door windows with side vents were installed for a while with triangular vents. For unkown reasons, these were removed. Then the entire car was repainted a solid metallic brown, which was coincidentally Ed Macauley's favorite color. At this time, Mitchell's Panther was still equipped with the 1954 Clipper "sore thumb" taillights.

Rear view of Mitchell Panther right after taillights, rear bumper, two-tone paint, and slight body modifications performed by Creative Industries. Note 1955 license plate.

Mitchell's Panther shows 1954¼ front clip modifications and two-tone paint. New hood scoop in contours of Packard radiator cusps; Yankee Pacesetter fender mirrors. Round holes under hood lip were changed to triangular-shaped air inlets.

Rex Terry's Panther showing off new 1954¼ front clip modifications and two-tone paint. Hood scoop in contours of old Packard radiator cusps was new. So were Yankee Pacesetter fender mirrors, but no air inlets under hood lip.

Rex Terry's Panther shows off 1954½ modifications and two-tone paint. Note wire wheels were retained; steering wheel and interior here were white.

With the new hardtop and paint job in place, Don Mitchell and son William decided to show off the new look of Don's Panther and drove it over to attend a football game at University of Michigan. That was when disaster struck.

The scene was Ann Arbor, Michigan, in the fall of 1954 and football was on the minds of Don and Bill Mitchell. Lynn Griffin tells the story: "They [the Mitchells] didn't drive the car very much; it had only 11,000 miles on it when it was sold to Homer Fitterling later [after Don passed]. Anyway, Don and Bill were at a game and a lady rear-ended them. The damage to the car wasn't that entirely bad overall, but that fiberglass just disintegrated where it got hit in the rear, into the quarter.

"So Don sent the Panther down to Creative in Detroit for Rex Terry to do a repair job on it. Rex installed those 1955 Packard taillights and liked the look so well that he decided to change his own Panther too!" So this is how the 1955 Packard cathedral taillight assemblies and twin-exhaust rear bumper ended up on

two Packard Panthers. What started out as a repair job quickly snowballed into a restyling makeover. The look of the last two Panthers was now substantially changed, and now the bodies just begged for a two-tone paint job, which was all the rage in Detroit at the time. I refer to these modified Panthers as "1954½ models."

Gary Hutchings flatly stated, "I remember sawing off the old taillights and molding in new ones, but this was done only on two of the Panthers." This restyling was done at Creative's Mt. Elliott Avenue facility, where the bodies had originally been made.

Yet another odd coincidence occurred at this same time. Over at De Soto two designs were being readied for building into a new pair of concept "idea cars." These were to be known as Flightsweep I and Flightsweep II. But looking at these cars and then back at Creative's Panther updates, the air can only be filled with question marks.

Despite the fact that the entire industry seemed blind to the similarities of the updated Panthers and De Soto

Photo taken at home of Creative employee William Resztak who worked on Panthers. The 1954½ modifications are plexiglass wind wings, seats with white bolsters, black pleated inserts. (Photo Courtesy Jim Reszstak Collection)

Creative employee William Resztak, who worked on the Panther, sits in passenger seat of Rex Terry's Panther. Note Creative "V" symbol logos and end of rear fender. Color here was silver over black. (Photo Courtesy Jim Resztak Collection)

PANTHER NUMBER-3 AND PANTHER NUMBER-4 MODS

Following is a list of the modifications made to these vehicles by Creative:

- New extra cooling ports under the body lip above the grille
- New hood scoop molded in the shape of a Packard radiator top with cusps
- New body side crease with upsweep at the rear (paid homage to Creative's logo)
- Senior Packard 1955 cathedral taillights and exhaust port rear bumper added
- Reverse-gear back-up lights in rear license plate nacelle eliminated (switched to existing reverse gear light in cathedral taillight assemblies)
- Exposed twin rear radio antennae (not same as Caribbean) added on top of rear fenders (deck lid antenna deleted)
- Yankee Pacesetter chrome mirrors installed on front fenders (factory mirrors deleted)
- Packard (Motor Wheel) wire spoke wheels deleted on Panther number-3 (replaced by disc wheels and 1955 Packard senior wheel covers)
- New two-tone paint job. Panther number-3 was painted Packard Corsican black on the hardtop roof and below the body side sweep crease. The remainder of the exterior was done in Packard Roman Copper. Even the whitewall tires were specially constructed of brown rubber instead of black. Interior was re-done in bronze and black colors. "Mitchell" logo was moved from front fenders to roof C-pillar. (Bucket seats presently in this vehicle were added later. Around 1959 the Corsican Black was changed to a cream yellow, and it remained like that until hitting the auction circuit in more recent years. Although the present colors have been returned to include Corsican Black, the roof has been changed to bronze.)
- New two-tone paint job. Panther number-4 was painted silver with Corsican Black below the body side sweep crease. This color scheme lasted only a very short time and during construction of Packard Request, silver was changed to Rinshed-Mason murano iridescent white pearl (same color as used on the Packard Request and Packard Predictor).

Flightsweeps, those similarities were (or should have been) striking. But for whatever reason, nobody seemed to notice openly.

Creative was already busy constructing the next big Packard concept, the Request. And while Don Mitchell continued to tinker with his Panther Packard's fiberglass experiment, Creative Industries had done its job.

Today all four Panthers survive in remarkably good condition. And while the recent silver-gray auction car (Panther number-1) has slipped off the radar for the time being, the whereabouts of the other three Panthers are known. Panthers number-3 and number-4 are in New Jersey, owned by Ralph Marano and his famous Toy Box Museum. The Daytona record car, Panther number-2 resides at Gene Grengs' Cavalcade of Cars Museum in Wisconsin. Panther number-2 is undergoing a restoration as of this writing, despite already being a good-looking, good-running automobile. I know because I've driven it.

Oh, and remember the fiberglass sports car that Briggs had promoted earlier to Packard? The illustration shown in *CARS* magazine? It didn't die. It just came to the light of day with a different grille and the Plymouth name attached to it: the 1954 Plymouth Belmont concept car.

CHAPTER EIGHT

MANLY MEN AND BEHIND THE SCENES WITH THE CORVETTE LEGACY

*C*orvettes, Corvettes, Corvettes. Creative really does know Corvettes.

GM's Deep Secrets

There is hardly a history ever written on Corvette that does not eventually touch upon the concept/dream and semi-dream Corvettes of the mid-1950s. These include the Waldorf Nomad, the Corvette Corvair, and the first removable hardtop Corvette concepts.

But how many of these cars were actually made? Where were they made and who made them? Most would say that only General Motors was involved in GM dream cars. Some are steadfast and insistent that no one else, no other entity, could ever possibly have been involved. And with GM's huge, prestigious Tech Center on Mound Road, north of Detroit, this notion would seem infallible. But is it?

Author David W. Temple's book *Motorama–GM's Legendary Show and Concept Cars* reveals several interesting stories. Temple attempts to unravel the maddening twists, turns, myths, and mayhem, all to reveal facts or fiction behind the early Corvette prototypes and concept cars. Of particular note are the so-called Waldorf Nomad, the removable hardtop concepts, and the fastback Corvette Corvair.

With Temple's masterful research into these cars and the many write-ups they have already received elsewhere, there is little value in walking these same well-worn footpaths once again. However, with this history acknowledged, there are still some important and unknown bits of information that exist. And as you well know by now, some of this just has to involve Creative Industries of Detroit.

I vividly remember pictures I saw at Creative Industries of Detroit decades ago, and among those were many of the Corvette Nomad and the Corvette Corvair: the 1954 Motorama fastback adaptation of the 1953 Corvette body.

Whoever did it, *somebody* built at least two or more of these Corvairs. I remember seeing the actual cars. And according to David W. Temple's *Motorama* book, there are factory records that have been uncovered in recent years indicating as many as *five* of these Corvairs were built.

One of several Corvette Corvairs, this one debuted in GM's Motorama held at Waldorf-Astoria Hotel in New York City, 1954. Although most immediately dismiss outside involvement in these cars, it is clear that Creative Industries contributed something in the project. (Photo Courtesy GM Media Archives)

Another Corvette fastback Corvair, this time in pale blue. Headliner featured chrome bows as did all GM hardtops. Aside from sleek fastback roof, other differences from production Corvette were hood bulges, louvered front fenders, and roll-up door windows with modified ends of windshield. Creative indeed engineered and installed roll-up door glass. (Photo Courtesy David F. Temple and GM Media Archives)

Detailed view Corvair interior. Seat upholstery and interior differed from production Corvettes. Also production models never had roll-up side windows. (Photo Courtesy David F. Temple and GM Media Archives)

Overview of 1954 Motorama Corvette-based concepts. First three to right all have roll-up side windows. Yellowish Corvette with roll-ups and removable hardtop was prediction of things to come because these features were not yet available on production models. Tiny images of at least two of these vehicles were featured in rare 1956 Creative brochure. (Photo Courtesy GM Media Archives)

According to what I was told in the 1960s, Creative engineered and assembled some versions of the early Corvette with removable tops and roll-up side windows. General Motors was certainly capable of doing such work, but who is to say what got farmed out and why? Our purpose here is merely to report.

Few remember today, but the early Corvettes of 1953 to 1955 had no side windows, only plug-in side curtains. This was a common format with what were thought to be *real sports cars* back then.

When it came to sports cars, the auto industry was still clawing its way out of the dark ages. It was imagined that if

Note differences from Corvette concepts such as no door buttons, handles, etc. On the set of movie The High and the Mighty. Famous actor John Wayne (light uniform center) told author's friend he got this Corvette new, gave it to actor Ward Bond (Wagon Train TV show) left, and Ward sold it to an LA dealer.

you drove a sports car, you'd insist upon the thrill of the open air, always and everywhere. Side windows built into the doors? Who needed 'em? As such, primitive features such as side curtains (as ancient and troublesome as these were) continued with barely a thought as to doing away with them. Most never dreamed of having roll-up side windows in a real *sports car!*

If you had a sports car, especially a European import, folding tops that didn't fold easily and barely kept out rain, heaters that didn't heat, and antiquated side curtains (if you had any at all) were all just part of the package. Sports cars were for *real men!* Or so the industry thought. But the industry had to wait for Ford's elegant 1955 Thunderbird to come along and break all of the old rules with what were then considered downright luxury features.

So the Corvette was released with side curtains in a postmounted plug-in metal frame. Of course, as side curtains went, these were pretty advanced, with an operable vent window. Still, when not mounted in the doors, these cumbersome assemblies took up most of the trunk. As truly beautiful and modern as the Corvette was, the side curtains were clumsy relics of a bygone era.

Meanwhile, even the Packard Panthers fell under the same macho thinking. They also came with side-curtains, not rollup windows. But when Don Mitchell and Rex Terry got their Panthers, the side-curtain issue was particularly troublesome. As far as anyone recalls, Rex never used the side curtains on his Panther unless caught in bad weather. Even then, the Panther usually remained parked at Creative and Rex would take some other car. And who was more manly than Rex, the former lifeguard, boxer, and pilot?

For a time, Creative was considering getting into removable hard roofs for sports cars. San Diego, California, company got them out first, made early removable hard roofs for early Corvette, designed to work with side curtains. Shape of top and backlight window was very similar to that used on Don Mitchell's Packard Panther. Insiders said Creative did not want to upset stealth relationship with Chevrolet Division, so they decided not to get into this business for aftermarket.

Front view of California-made removable hard roof.

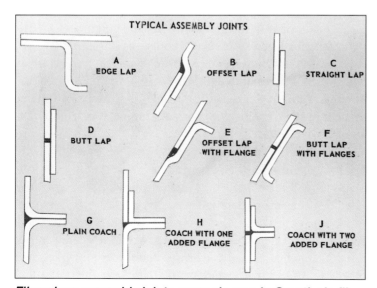

Fiberglass assembly joints example was in Creative's files.

Don Mitchell didn't see the macho aspect of a sports car either. He had the vision to see beyond the old ways and foresaw the Thunderbird direction as having great validity for the future. Mitchell was a golfer and sportsman, and rode horses that he bred. Yet when it came to driving a car, he was far more interested in comfort. So being forced to deal with a soft top and side curtains just wasn't his cup of tea. Mitchell made up his mind: he wanted a removable hardtop and roll-up side windows, and by golly, he was going to get them. In a nutshell, the side-curtains were just too much trouble. Who wanted the hassle?

By 1954 there were aftermarket firms already popping out removable fiberglass tops for the Corvette. Rex Terry had connections and "moles" everywhere, especially in California, which was the hotbed of new trends for custom features back then. Scott Manufacturing of San Diego, California, was already making an interesting hardtop for Corvette and was starting to sell a few. Rex and his people at Creative sensed that a trend was emerging.

Creative quickly had two ideas for removable Corvette hardtops. One of these was a clear bubble top; the other was a painted fiberglass top. I saw both tops in illustrations at Creative and one bubble top prototype. Since an aftermarket company eventually began selling such a bubble top, I have no idea whether the two were somehow connected or if it was completely separate development. With Creative having such mastery in both fiberglass and clear bubble tops, it would not be surprising to discover links somewhere back in the mists.

An unconfirmed rumor also indicated that Creative was somehow working on the Corvette roll-up windows for General Motors. This feature eventually appeared in production for the 1956 model year. But in the meantime, some of this work was clearly performed on Don Mitchell's Panther, which indeed acquired roll-ups for a while. At the same time this was happening, Lynn Griffin, Creative's man at Mitchell-Bentley, has said that Mitchell-Bentley's Donald Funky had designed the removable hardtop for the Mitchell Panther. And Gary Hutchings said the Panther top was laid up at Creative.

The work on the Mitchell Panther roll-up windows took place at the same time as the building of Corvettes with removable hardtops and the Corvair fastbacks. Can this be proven? The time frame? Yes. The Corvette part? No. Were these the Corvettes shown at the GM Motorama and pictured in press photos? I don't know, and it is unlikely that anyone alive today would have absolute certain knowledge of these issues, fact or fiction. Was there simultaneous work being done at both General Motors and Creative on the Corvette roll-up windows? Possibly. Was some of this work jobbed out? According to what I was told, very likely. But again, I cannot prove any of this outright. We do know the Panther mods were done at Creative. And we do know the time frame.

Early Corvette assembly technician smooths clamped and bonded joints.

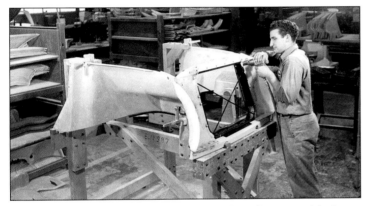

Radiator core support done in fiberglass is assembled with splash wells for early Corvette.

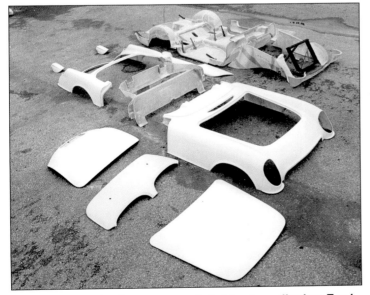

Early Corvette body components laid out on display. Ford was good with fiberglass, so was General Motors. But Creative had the technology down cold.

The system and the secrecy thereof were all purposely constructed precisely just to prevent anyone who should not know from knowing. In politics, finance, and big business, it is called the principle of "plausible deniability." And frankly, there were contracts and relationships and money involved. People in the industry knew where Creative's headquarters were. They knew Creative's expertise. And there were certainly personal friendships. And some even knew that Creative was doing work for General Motors and the rest of the Big Three. A few even knew that Creative had some kind of, well, something, somehow to do with Corvette. But nobody who was talking could ever say or even admit exactly where, how, and how much.

The only certainty is that there were engineering and job shops scattered all around the Detroit area from the 1940s until now. But out of this, Creative Industries was the real Detroit "skunk works." So think of it all perhaps as a kind of automotive Area 51. But there are some bits of evidence that have not been lost.

Dave Margolis once took me back to a room at Creative's headquarters on East Outer Drive. He showed me hundreds of pictures, illustrations, line drawings, and mechanical drawings. There were lots of color illustrations; some were the kinds of visual things related to the Corvette. Dave's words to me were something like, "I know you were in communications in Viet-Nam and there were things you just didn't talk about. So for now, same thing here. Nothing here leaves the building. You are free to look, and you will then know about our involvement with Corvette to that extent. But we have to keep most of this confidential, at least for now. The future? Who knows?"

I picked up a big binder filled with photos and flipped to a section filled with Corvette photos. These included assembly pictures, artwork on assembly techniques, and more. There were also 8 x 10 glossy photos of a Chevy Cameo truck

From Creative's files, women examining early Corvette components, location unknown.

Again, from Creative's files. All Dave Margolis would say is "we worked on that program" but no more. Author has reason to believe this Vette was used to set up removable hard roof Motorama concepts. Note this Vette has no wire mesh screen covers over the headlight openings (nor provisions for screens), just the heavy chrome bezel. Leading top edge of passenger door has been cut, and then patch screwed on over the hole. Also note severe wave in right front fender.

Rear view of same early Corvette outside of Creative rear shop building. Note exhaust routes through fender ends. This feature would not arrive until 1956. Also note screwed-on fiberglass patch on passenger door on forward beltline area.

A 1956 Corvette prototype image from Creative's files shows exhaust now routed through rear fender ends, but different rear bumper and new taillights. Roll-up side windows debuted for 1956 production along with power top, another Creative specialty.

New fastback roof returned on Corvette in late 1970s. Creative did the setup and Gary Smyth (later of Mazda R&D) worked for Creative on this project that changed the look of Corvettes.

showing details of its fiberglass bed construction. When I pointed at the photos with an amazed, quizzical look on my face, Dave said, "That was the first Corvette and we did some work on it." When I asked what exactly Creative did, Dave just responded, "I can't tell you." When I asked what happened to the one car in the first photos, Dave responded, "I can't tell you that either, but I do know it isn't around anymore."

Of course, this was in the 1970s. Dave did give me several construction photos that appeared to be from General Motors. However, there were two extra 8 x 10 glossies in another section of the binder, and these were the ones that really had my attention riveted. These two images showed the 1953 Corvette and had Creative's photo numbers on them, meaning Creative's official photographer had taken these photos. But the Corvette in the images was different from anything I had ever seen. So naturally, I was filled with questions. But Dave simply said, "This is all you can have. Nothing else you've seen ever leaves the building."

The photos show an early Corvette, but not exactly as it was produced during 1953 to 1955. Although this car indeed had more prominent chrome surround rims as on production headlights, it did *not* have wire mesh screens over the headlights. And the right front fender had a pronounced set of what I call "greetings" on the sides. In other words, huge waves in the fender.

The right-hand passenger door had been cut and cobbled. A crude screwed-on patch was installed along the beltline edge that butted up below the trailing end of the windshield. And there was a tantalizing difference at the rear.

Normally an early Corvette rear exhaust routed out through a valance panel below the trunk lid for 1953 to 1955. Instead, the exhausts on this Corvette neatly exited out via a hole in the bumperettes on the tail end of the rear fender pontoon. Otherwise, this position was normally occupied by a chrome bullet. The production car did not have this exhaust feature until years

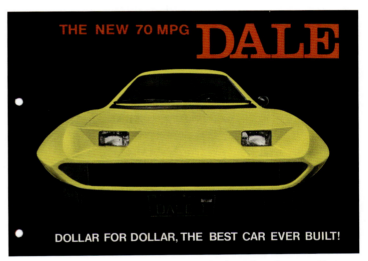

The infamous Dale car emerged during the desperation of the 1970s. It claimed 70 mpg and was an attempt to say and be all that car dealers desperate for vehicles to sell during the oil embargo crisis and customers wanted to hear.

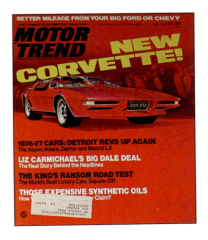

Aluminum Corvette built by Creative made the cover of Motor Trend in red color. Appeared in the same issue with "Liz Carmichael" and the Dale car (see Chapter Fourteen).

later in 1956. Of course, by then, the taillights had been substantially changed and did not look at all like the 1953–1955 taillight I saw in the photo.

From what little Dave and others at Creative told me, I believe this car was used to set up the exhaust ports for 1956 production models. I also believe it was used to set up doors and roll-up windows on the Corvair and Motorama concepts

Aluminum Corvette mock-up sits in GM's Tech Center design courtyard. Note Datsun 240 Z sports car to left and Opel GT to right.

Side view of aluminum Corvette mock-up in GM's Tech Center design courtyard. Note Datsun 240 Z sports car to left and Opel GT to right.

Aluminum Aero Corvette clay in raised position at GM's Tech Center design studio. Note Vega GT.

with removable hardtops, or at least a version of them. I further have good reason to believe that while this engineering was being done, the roll-up door windows for Don Mitchell's Packard Panther were also being done. These roll-ups were later removed from the Panther for reasons unknown.

Corvette and Creative

In the mid-1970s I was again visiting Creative and talking with David Margolis. Dave took me to one of the shops in the rear of the facility and opened a corrugated metal door. His intention was to show me some projects for accessories that were not so confidential. In the meantime, someone opened an adjacent door and that's when I saw it. Of course, by now Dave and Creative knew they could trust me. He turned and saw the look on my face. "Yeah, that's the next Corvette. You can't take any pictures and you can't describe to anybody what it looks like, but I'll let you see it. But what you see stays here. We do the updates on Corvette every year, but nobody knows it." Dave told me this after knowing him for 20 years or so. I remember very vividly this car was in the back of the facility inside a rippled metal enclosure.

A few years later, I had yet another encounter regarding Creative and Corvette. This was, ironically, via my position at Mazda Corporation R&D Advanced Engineering division in California. At the time I reported to a new fellow who had just come onboard from Detroit. As it turned out, he had also worked for a while at Creative Industries. One of the major projects he had worked on for Creative was, you guessed it, the new fastback Corvette of the 1970s.

His name is Gary Smythe, and he knew Creative well. He had come up though the maze of jobbers and OEMs in the Detroit area and could talk for hours about all of the goings-on with cars such as the Corvette.

"My first big assignment at Creative was working on the Corvette. I was a contract engineer; this was in the mid-1970s. I worked with Al Bederka at Creative and later over at Aero Detroit. We were a small engineering group within Creative. We were doing exterior panels, upgrades, and evolutionary design on the Corvette. Basically we were doing the 1978 Silver Anniversary, 25th Anniversary Corvette. This was when the roof design changed from the flying buttresses style to the big fastback wraparound backlight in the 1970s. They also introduced the glass T-tops as an option. I was involved with these T-tops. Before then the top panels were all fiberglass. These were aluminum frames with glass bonded to it. The 1978 Corvette was also chosen for the Indy 500 Pace Car.

"They had all of these secure partitioned areas in the building where different programs were going on. The Ford SVO program was going in one area, which I worked on. And then the

Creative's Prospectus Brochure

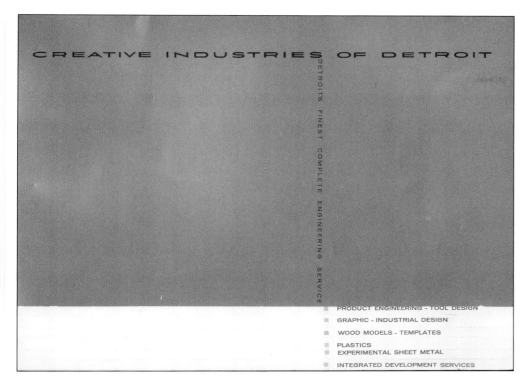

Cover of 1956 Creative Industries gold prospectus brochure shows amazing things and explains a lot if you look closely. Inside were notes and images ranging from concept cars to project security. Every facet of Creative's operation and irrefutable evidence that Creative built concepts and prototypes for the Big Three and independents is contained.

An incredibly detailed prospectus brochure about Creative was published in late 1956. It had brilliant gold covers and inside pages done up of the trendy color of the day: turquoise. In-depth information about each Creative department and division was listed along with photos of facilities, equipment, staff, and management. This publication was strictly put together for distribution to industry people. Today it is one of the rarest paper items on Creative.

Here is what this Creative Industries brochure says on the page listing Plastics, Experimental Sheet Metal, and Integrated Developmental Engineering: "Shown are some experimental and prototype automobiles built to customer design, complete with interior and exterior trim." The arrow next to the text points to five images that obviously have been hugely reduced in size. None of these images list a name, but each is clearly identifiable. They are as follows: Ford FX-Atmos; Ford Mystere; Dodge Granada; Corvette Corvair; and a composite image showing two Packard Panthers, one of which is Don Mitchell's early version with the first hardtop and Rex Terry's Panther. The special effort to show the Mitchell Panther in its early configuration with the removable hardtop right next to the Corvair is something to think about.

This important brochure would have been put together by the graphics department. One individual formerly from graphics was very adamant that anything used in such a publication had to be very carefully checked, authorized, and approved. And Creative steadfastly avoided mentioning deep details or claiming credit to the public for most of its work. The graphics person also insisted that nothing would have been posted here that was false. The penalties were just too severe and there was certainly no need to bite the hand that fed the company. The same brochure *also* featured a line-art reduced photo of a 1956 Corvette on another page with similar wording. And none of this was by either coincidence or by accident. Perhaps you may remember those old TV commercials that said, "Only her hairdresser knows for sure"? Consider the same logic as your answer here.

Corvette. When I left Creative I went to Aero Detroit and ended up working on the GM S-10 truck program. I was also on the truck and bus program."

One final but important person I can't leave out is Larry O'Dowd. Larry was manager of Creative's Sheet Metal Prototyping division, and when the subject of Corvette came up here's what Larry had to say: "People always think of Corvette being done in fiberglass, but we made one of them out of aluminum!"

That aluminum Corvette Larry referred to indeed was produced and was known as one of the AeroVette concepts. It was ultimately featured in *Motor Trend* for July 1975 in a piece written by later coworker and Mazda Miata pioneer, Bob Hall. Dubbed with several different names and slightly different backlight designs, one version appeared on the cover in red right next to a headline about Liz Carmichael and the infamous Dale car. But the actual Corvette was silver-gray.

Various sources have claimed that this car was somehow built by Reynolds Aluminum, but the story more appropriately might be that it was made out of Reynolds Aluminum.

Creative's files had images of this Corvette in clay and several Creative people recalled building the car there. And, as Al Bederka has already said, the Corvette was to continue for many more years in a relationship with Creative Industries.

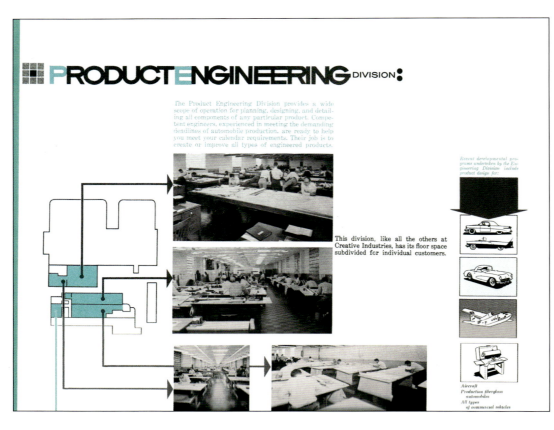

Product Engineering section of 1956 Creative Industries gold prospectus brochure shows very early version of Packard Panther with removable hard roof installed. Below it is 1956 Corvette. Tiny wording above line images says, "Recent developmental programs undertaken by Engineering Division include product design for . . ." According to former Creative staffer, this prospectus had to be very carefully worded, and there is no mention of Chevrolet or GM but you can plainly see the Corvette.

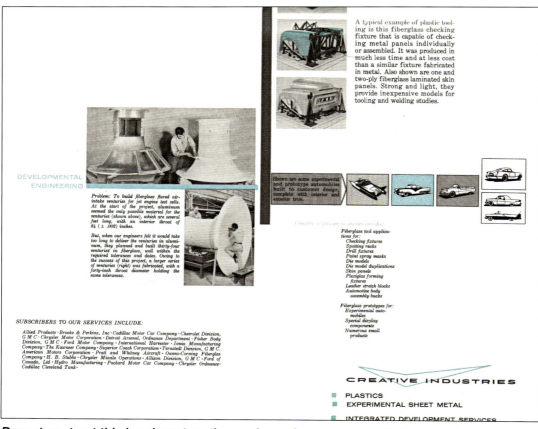

Developmental Engineering section of 1956 Creative Industries gold prospectus brochure. No connection with Corvette or Corvair? Take a look. Tiny wording reads, "Shown are some experimental and prototype automobiles built to customer design, complete with interior and exterior trim." Shown are Ford FX-Atmos, Ford Mystere, Dodge Granada, Corvette Corvair, and two versions of Packard Panthers. Elsewhere on the same page (to left), Chevrolet Division is listed under "Subscribers to Our Services" section. No connection to Corvair and Corvette? You be the judge. Creative's Graphics Department put this brochure together and says it was very carefully worded and reviewed prior to release and went only to industry professionals.

CHAPTER NINE

FORD FX-ATMOS AND CREATIVE'S MASTERY OF FIBERGLASS

lastic car bodies and gas turbine engines were once the wave of the future, but at Creative, the future was always now.

FX-Atmos

A. J. Middlestead was not an American household name in the early 1950s. There were few car designers who could ever lay claim to such a status. But a lucky handful became legends in the automotive world and some, even in the minds of the general public. Unfortunately, Middlestead remains largely unknown today, but he deserves better.

Of course, it has always been highly unusual that a car designer can conceive a concept or production vehicle and actually see that design achieve reality. But A. J.'s FX-Atmos was one of those rare instances when the planets aligned and the powers that be gave their blessings. There were others involved in some design refinements, but Middlestead was the primary principal designer. What began as a sketch on his drawing board in Ford's studio became a legendary American concept car.

I first saw the FX-Atmos up close and personal on the turntable at the Ford Rotunda. And it was an amazing sight. People standing around the display were blown away and the comments went on nonstop. At certain intervals, a man appeared with a microphone and gave a brief spiel on the car. It didn't matter that Ford's press release stated there was no engine in the car. All that I heard from people standing around the display were imaginations running wild. Indeed, this was the very essence, the purpose of a dream car: to excite the mind and inspire. It was the kind of thing that could only have happened in the 1950s before the cynicism of the 1960s set in.

The FX-Atmos was a brilliant masterpiece. The name was taken from the word "atmosphere" and the FX part stood for "Factory Experimental." Atmos sat very low on a 105-inch wheelbase. It was 220½ inches long and it was very wide (almost 80 inches) with an interior designed for only three occupants. The driver was seated forward in the center position while the two passengers sat slightly rearward. All were seated in thin-shell bucket seats.

The "future" has arrived. Instead of a grille, front of FX-Atmos was a full-width headlight bar. Antennae were for self-guidance system Ford called "Roadar" Note canted fins on rear. Fender-top scoops have not yet been blacked out. (Photo Courtesy Ford Motor Company)

Quarter view of FX-Atmos reveals driver position in center front. Close inspection here reveals center section of bubble canopy is missing. Doors were only simulated. Occupants at shows or photos were lowered into interior from above. Driver here is often mistaken for famous pinup model Bettie Page but reportedly was actually a Ford Motor Company secretary. (Photo Courtesy Ford Motor Company)

Directly in front of the driver was a very advanced 1950s-style semi-navigation system that Ford dubbed "Roadar" (a play on the term "radar"). This system featured a monitor screen that was claimed to graphically show the road ahead and was sup-

The Ford Rotunda

A visit to the Rotunda gave me about the same elated feeling as going to one of the fabulous old Detroit movie theaters.

As you approached from the outside, the Rotunda had the appearance of the base of a gigantic Grecian column. At night it was illuminated with floodlights and soft, indirect, glowing lighting around the top. Inside, above was more beautiful indirect lighting and at your feet were highly polished floors. Displays changed with the seasons.

At Christmas there was a holiday fest that was legendary among Detroiters. This yearly festival was a giant twinkling bacchanalia and usually featured some kind of special cars. This Rotunda at Christmas display went on for weeks, fascinating both adults and kids. It was the kind of innocent pleasure rarely found today.

When Ford's dream cars were not on duty at auto shows, it was a very safe bet that you could find at least one or two at the amazing Ford Rotunda. Detroiters simply referred to it as "the Rotunda" and everyone knew what that meant.

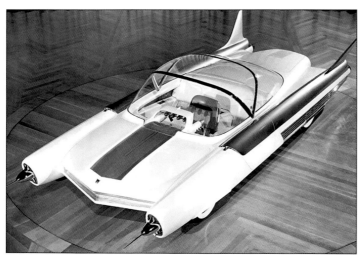

View from above on Ford turntable clearly shows unusual center-front driver's position. Logos have yet to be added to front fenders. (Photo Courtesy Ford Motor Company)

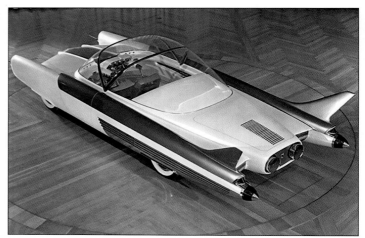

Wild from any angle, rear view from above on rear of vehicle clearly implied a rear-mounted gas turbine power-plant. Logos have yet to be added to front fenders. (Photo Courtesy Ford Motor Company)

posed enhance safety by predicting possible obstacles. The two antennae in FX-Atmos' front fenders were claimed to be part of this system that assisted the driver in high-speed motoring.

Atmos was filled with other interesting ideas such as "wrist-twist" steering. Here there was no steering wheel, but rather a pair of handgrips as you might find in recent years on a computer game.

But it was the genius of Creative Industries that actually made the FX-Atmos a reality. I knew both David Margolis and Garriston "Gary" Hutchings, who worked on the car at Creative. I met Dave in 1962 during my first formal introduction to Creative. Years later I interviewed Dave and Gary for a magazine history I wrote for the great Dean Batchelor and a magazine called *Car Classics*. This was the first and perhaps only history of Creative Industries ever written until now. This is just how far off the radar that Creative continued to remain, despite its many amazing automotive ventures.

Although Ford personnel drifted in from time to time, Dave Margolis supervised the mold-making and overall construction

of the FX-Atmos. Gary was one of the actual crew who worked on the Atmos molds and construction of the vehicle itself.

Even when I interviewed both men in the 1970s, Dave was still vigilant about the secrecy of Creative's projects and interactions with customers. He talked about Atmos but was guarded in how much should be published. In the end, we decided not to say much about FX-Atmos in terms of behind-the-scenes details. But you get more now.

Dave Margolis said, "Ford had done the basic clay over in Dearborn and had it hauled over by truck to our facility on Outer Drive. From that point we made a few refinements to the clay and prepped it for making full-size molds. That's where Gary's crew took over and splashed the molds. It all went along quite smoothly. Once the molds were done, those were taken out to Mt. Elliott and the body was laid up."

By that time, Creative's plastics people were razor sharp in their knowledge of making fiberglass car bodies. Creative's people had even figured out ways to chrome plate on fiberglass, and this was on the order of science fiction at the time. In fact,

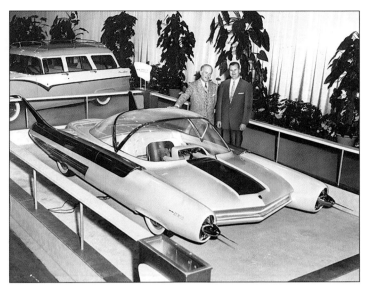

Later version of FX-Atmos on its display stand. Note bubble top with fluorescent light inside appears to be hazing. A 1955 Ford station wagon with rare factory roof rack and skirts in background.

some of the pieces on Atmos that appeared to be metal indeed were chrome-plated fiberglass!

Like the Packard Panthers and the Dodge Granada, Creative made the FX-Atmos as a one-piece body. This was especially important since Atmos contained no conventional inner structure. Everything was done just for show and as such, no engineering of the structure that bolstered it as a normal car had really been allowed. But this was a fateful decision that likely contributed to the eventual deterioration of the car.

Dave continued, "As we saw it, a one-piece body was the best way to achieve strength and a more finished look to the vehicle. From this point on, Gary's crew did an actual assembly of the car. It wasn't easy because of the fact that it had a lot of details for a pushmobile, even a basic electrical system. Atmos was fully lighted. Also we had to make a lot of lenses for the taillights. Oh, those were complicated. And headlights and that big bubble top."

Although there has been debate over how the FX-Atmos got its final colors, I was always told that the red, white, and blue were Creative's suggestions, particularly the white. The colors on the finished car were done in iridescent mother-of-pearl white and metallic blue with a metallic red insert out on the hood. This pearl-white finish became Creative's unofficial trademark. Though few noticed or realized, Creative repeatedly used this color on many top concept cars they built.

Gary told me that he did much of the interior installation. Of course, this was done without the bubble top in place, but it was still hot and tight inside doing the assembly. "We wanted to do opening doors and a motorized lift for the bubble top,

and we were ready to use some pieces from a convertible top to do it. We had it all worked out too. But Ford didn't want to spend another penny on the car at that time, so they told Dave no. Even if there had been a budget, there was no time. So the only thing we had left was to make the middle section [of the top] removable by hand and then lift somebody into the cabin. We weren't happy with that, but it was all we could do."

Pushmobile or not, Ford still wanted to photograph and display the car with people inside. Since the driver's seat was in the middle up front, it wasn't too difficult to drop a lady in, which was what everyone envisioned for the shows. Or so Creative thought. Creative figured a thin, light female model would be used when the Atmos went on display. So that was no problem. However, Ford surprised Creative later by using a man for the shows!

The decision to make the top totally inoperable almost backfired when some less imaginative, more cynical editors and writers got a peek behind the scenes during show setup preparations. A few were not so impressed with what they obviously saw as fakery.

Of course, while Ford never talked about the doors and top not working, they didn't hide the fact that FX-Atmos had no engine. This part of the Atmos story was definitely not a secret. Indeed, several newspapers published the fact that this concept had no engine. But some even seemed to make light of this fact. One lead-in quipped in uppercase, "LOOKS GOOD. But No Engine!" Another no-nonsense news account went even further past engine talk to the extent of almost poking fun at the overall pushmobile aspect.

This publication took a stance more common in today's tell-all cynical world where the media often *does* "pay attention to the man behind the curtains," and some try to tattle every titillating little secret. "When the car was displayed here, part of the transparent top had to be unscrewed while a 'driver' was lifted in. And he took off his shoes to avoid damage to the delicate finish. But Ford insists the car is not fantastic." That was a pretty hardcore critique and even mockery for the 1950s, but in some ways, it too reflected what was yet to come in the future.

You can only wonder what would have happened had Creative been allowed to make the doors open and the top work. A functional car would have been stronger and more endearing too, and who knows how that might have figured in the long-term survival of the FX-Atmos? Perhaps it might otherwise still be around today. Certainly, Creative could have done it all in terms of making the Atmos operable, but it was not to be.

Who Put the "T" In T-Bird?

Although it is rumored that A. J. Middlestead envisioned a conventional rear engine mounted in Atmos, the buzz of the

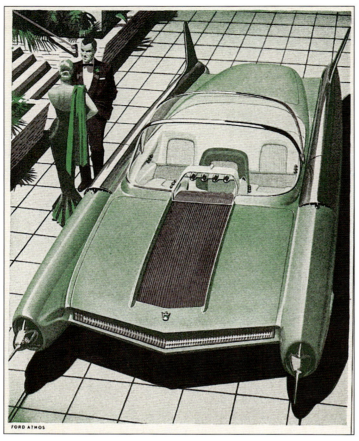

Quaker State Oil advertisement depicted FX-Atmos out on the town in the future in green and black with rear seats in white.

day was two words: gas turbine. There wasn't a car magazine in those days that had not talked about turbines and the fact that they were seen as the next wave of automotive technology. So while Ford openly proclaimed that Atmos had no engine, the real secret was that they were simply playing their cards close to the vest. And frankly, there has been much debate about Ford's 1950s dream cars having turbines.

There is at least some credence to this notion. More than one Ford designer openly alluded to turbine power in the FX-Atmos. Alex Tremulis once told me from his home in Ventura, California, that somebody, somewhere along the way, had actually talked about dropping a turbine into the Atmos and the Ford Mystere that followed. As in making them actually run.

Perhaps Dave Margolis provided the rest of the story to Alex Tremulis' mention of turbines. Dave continued, "Keep in mind that we were under contract to Ford, so we could only make suggestions, but we had a lot of ideas. Ford was insistent that no engine was intended for the car and we were to devote no time to engineering in that regard. The car was already running over budget and they just didn't want to spend any more on getting it running, especially since the primary purpose was to have it on turntables for car shows. But a couple of our guys who were working on some aircraft projects with clients just couldn't resist. Somebody here drew up some roughs on installing a real gas turbine in the rear. They figured it would run beautifully, and just as good as anything General Motors or Chrysler had, but it never got beyond that."

What few people ever knew was that Creative was also contracted to Boeing. So the imagination here can fly in numerous directions. The FX-Atmos rolled out into the light of day without an engine. But while noting these obvious facts, something *not* so obvious was also taking place about the same time. Although it is neither openly shown nor talked about in Thunderbird histories, a 1955 Thunderbird was indeed fitted with a Boeing gas turbine engine and made drivable. A good photo of this car was shown in the Bill Carroll book *Automotive GAS TURBINES*.

Lenny Williams, a former engineer at Boeing, passed more photos taken in front of Ford buildings to me years ago. Len built his own gas

Installation of Boeing gas turbine engine in 1955 Thunderbird. (Photo Courtesy Lenny Williams)

FX-Atmos Scale Model

Creative was not just a master in making full-size pushmobiles, they were masters with scale models too. One other thing that Creative did with the Atmos was to construct a small-scale model of the car. This beautiful little model was kept in a boardroom at Creative's headquarters at Outer Drive.

This highly detailed scale model was finished in full color. I took photos of it on one of my visits to Creative back in the 1970s. David Margolis was even kind enough to take a photo of me sitting at the head of Creative's boardroom table with the FX-Atmos model. In later years, this model sat on Dave Margolis' desk. I last saw it in the 1980s.

In his later years, Dave once called me at my office in California. Creative had only recently left Outer Drive and moved into a new headquarters building in Auburn Hills, Michigan. He telephoned to let me know they had changed addresses and then said, "You know, you're so crazy over this model, one of these days when I retire I'm gonna pack it up and send it to you!" Unfortunately, I was spending a lot of time out of the country in Japan then and working an extreme schedule in the United States. This was during the development of Mazda Miata.

FX-Atmos scale model on the boardroom table at Creative Industries general offices on Outer Drive in Detroit.

Suffice it to say that we lost touch for a lengthy period. Sadly, during this time, Dave became ill and passed. Also sadly, the FX-Atmos model was somehow lost in the shuffle of things. To this day, the whereabouts of Creative's FX-Atmos model is anybody's guess. Wherever it is, I can only hope this beautiful little dream car has managed to survive and is in caring hands.

Detail of FX-Atmos scale model on the boardroom table at Creative Industries general offices shows early wheel covers differed from actual car pieces designed later. Model preceded actual completion of full-size car.

FX-Atmos scale model rear view on the boardroom table at Creative Industries general offices on Outer Drive in Detroit. Note large globe and drapes in background. Two levels of drapes allowed either only sunlight or complete darkness for high security meetings and unveilings.

Author seated with FX-Atmos scale model on the boardroom table at Creative Industries general offices on Outer Drive in Detroit. Photographed by Creative's David Margolis in 1970s. Model was promised to author but disappeared years later. Whereabouts today is unknown.

turbine hot rod out of a 1932 Ford back in the 1960s, and that turbine hot rod survives today at the LeMay Family Automotive Museum in Spanaway, Washington.

Although it was not publicized, Ford indeed had a team of engineers working on Boeing-based gas turbine engines. According to the Carroll book, the first engine was dubbed "701" and was installed in a 1954 Ford sedan. The next went into the Thunderbird. Now, this Thunderbird installation was rather crude (most were in those days, no matter who did them) with a pair of large, exposed raw turbine exhausts poking out of the front fenders. But it was built and it operated.

So was talk of a gas turbine in the FX-Atmos and the Mystere merely talk? All that I *can* say for sure is that *somebody, somewhere* was playing with turbines in Ford's advanced automobiles at this time.

End of the Dream and the Atmos Legacy

FX-Atmos was immortalized in newspapers and on the covers of numerous magazines such as *Motor Trend*. As time went by, "FX-Atmos" logos were installed on the front fenders. It is also known that the paint was touched up at least once and other freshening done at Creative.

But eventually the life of a pushmobile is even more limited and tentative than that of an operable concept car. For whatever reason, there eventually seemed to be no more storage space to tuck Atmos away. Exposure to the elements simply accelerated the deterioration and thus the decision to destroy the FX-Atmos became increasingly easy to make. The cruel rule of dream cars had finally caught up with the FX-Atmos, and it lived no more.

But in the end, the FX-Atmos really did predict some of the future. Yes, bubble tops and "wrist-twist" steering never quite caught on, at least not in cars. But how about those huge twin taillights and canted upright fins on the Atmos rear?

Today, if you look at these design features and something clicks in your head, but you just can't quite put your finger on it, try this. Take a gander at the rear of an F-14 Tomcat fighter jet taking off and think for a moment. Does that bubble-top canopy with the metal partition framework remind you of anything? Do those big twin jet exhausts and twin canted vertical stabilizers look familiar? Of course they do.

Boeing gas turbine engine in 1955 Thunderbird. (Photo Courtesy Lenny Williams)

CHAPTER TEN

YESTERDAY, TODAY AND TOMORROW: THE PACKARD REQUEST AND THE PACKARD PREDICTOR

ackard's brave last stand and final wonders from East Grand Boulevard actually came from Detroit's East Outer Drive.

Packard Request

Richard Teague's new design for the 1955 Packards was well under way and his third assignment was being developed and was likewise well along and appeared for the 1955 model year. There were a lot of issues to consider, despite having the overall 1955 body pretty much dialed in: Teague's reputation as a designer, Nance's challenge to design, and whether the Request would also be an appropriate answer to Packard customers. Dick was still faced with the daunting task of how to resurrect the classic upright Packard radiator grille and make it look good on a modern 1950s design.

As Teague once told me, "It was one thing to stick an upright 1930s-style grille on a 1950s Packard. But it was quite another to come up with something that would at least be easy on the eyes, if not beautiful."

And there was still the issue of those old taillights that J. J. Nance despised. The Request was ultimately based on a preproduction pilot 1955 Four Hundred coupe body. But it was so early that production tooling for Teague's famous Packard cathedral taillight had yet to be completed. In fact, the taillight had been a nagging sticking point all along.

Well after the basic 1955 body was almost set, Teague had designer's dilemma. He was still noodling with the new taillight design, and Nance was still grumbling about the old one. According to an interview with Stuart Blond, editor of *The Packard Cormorant* magazine, Jim Nance finally gave a directive to Teague on Good Friday of 1954. Dick got right to work on the solution and had a moment of inspiration.

As the story goes, the design for the beautiful taillight came to Teague when he was attending church on Easter Sunday, 1954. The architecture of the church cathedral's structure ignited a spark in Dick's sense of design. He went right home afterward and penned what came to be known as the Pack-

Driver's side view of Request reveals 1955 Caribbean-type side trim, special cloisonné center medallions on spoke wheel caps, metallic gold/copper finish in center trips and roof.

ard cathedral taillight. It became the hallmark of the 1955 and 1956 senior Packards. Had Packard survived, this taillight would have continued as a design theme into the 1960s.

A new 1955 preproduction pilot body (serial 5587-1003) on a rolling chassis was taken over to Creative on Outer Drive. But there were no taillights. Of course, *you know* that nonexistent taillights were certainly no problem for Creative Industries. Although this was many decades before stereo lithography and 3-D modeling, they simply made a set. This is how things used to get done. After all, Dick had the drawings and the specs were set on paper; and Creative had their own metal foundry right there on-site. This was a valuable leftover from the days of Fred Johnson's Industrial City and Progressive Welder Company. So casting a set of prototype 1955 Packard cathedral taillights was a snap.

The Request's hand-built taillights are indeed quite different from the production units. They *look* the same at first glance, but close inspection reveals the differences. Without an injection mold to make fresneling inside the lens, Creative's plastics craftsmen found a way to scribe the fresneling on the inside of the lens. To this day, most people who have viewed the Request have never noticed the taillight differences.

By 1955, Packard was focused on a return to upright Packard grille. Plans for the future were not influenced by Edsel as some have said; plans were influenced by Packard customer requests and Request dream car built by Creative Industries. (Photo Courtesy Stuart R. Blond and The Packard Club)

Detail of Request taillight (left) compared to normal production taillight. Casting is slightly different toward bottom. Red lens on Request is scribed inside with a grid. Production lens (right) is fresneled and features circular lens aligned with bulb. (Photo Courtesy Stuart R. Blond and The Packard Club)

According to David Margolis, the design for Teague's magnificent taillight, was hustled over to both the foundry and the plastics shop in the Creative building. There, a small crew got right to work whipping up cast housings and the large red plastic lenses for the lights.

"We pulled some plugs for those lights over in our foundry and castings area. We were not happy with the first pulls and they had a lot of handwork that was needed to make everything go together. But we got it all done and they turned out beautifully!"

Like much of the rest of the special Request design features, the massive front bumpers were hand assemblies and were cast, welded, and shaped all at Creative. The vertical fins of the grille were individually cast and shaped. A bend at the bottom

Beautiful Packard Request on turntable in Packard Styling studios off Concord Avenue between Grand Boulevard. and Harper. Body was based on early pilot production 1955 Four Hundred hardtop. However, most of the front and many timepieces had to be hand-fabricated by Creative, including the two entire taillight assemblies.

Request taillight (left) differs from 1955 actual production taillight. Casting is different toward bottom. Red lens on Request is scribed inside. Production lens (right) has molded-in fresneling and features circular lens aligned with bulb. (Photo Courtesy Stuart R. Blond and The Packard Club)

Here is exactly what I first published in *Car Classics* back in 1978, quoting Gary Hutchings: "We had a heck of a time finding a place with tanks big enough to plate those huge front bumpers. We finally got 'em done over in Hamtramck." Gary told me that the chrome pieces for the Request grill, front trim, and bumpers took a tremendous amount of work to complete. There were problems with bubbling chrome and other issues. It would have only been worse had they tried plating fiberglass.

By the way, the headlight surround doors that appear to be stamped metal production Clipper units are not. And yes, even these components actually added more weight than needed. But it couldn't be helped. Although the design was based on the Clipper parts, again those were not yet in production and therefore no tooling was available. So? Creative simply cast up a set especially for the Request. Of course, all of this was being done under a "we-need-it-yesterday" kind of deadline.

The Request hood was then the next big question. Gary Hutchings: "We got a plaster mold made from the clay and took it out to our Mt. Elliott facility where we molded the hood. We didn't have a lot of time to do it exactly the way we wanted and the budget was limited. So we went with what we had. It certainly was not production spec; it was just to get the right look for shows." Again, while Request was made as a functional automobile (one of Creative's pet preferences), nobody ever imagined that this dream car would actually be driven out on the street as a normal car!

was inserted so as to give a pleasing tuck-under and finished appearance.

Yes, it was all very heavy. People unfairly make a big fuss about this today in write-ups about the Request. None of these complicated pieces would have been made this way and so heavy in weight for mass production. But this was a one-off vehicle, and there were expenses and time to consider. The Request was intended to be viewed, not unleashed out onto the public highways.

Detail of Request taillight reveals no molded-in fresneling, no circular lens. Bulb is clearly visible behind lens. (Photo Courtesy Bud Juneau and The Packard Club)

Head-on view of Requests show intricate details of beautiful upright grille traditional Packard customers begged for. Pay close attention to the light pods in the bumper ends and take note of the fluted ribs on each.

Newspapers and magazines were still trying to get a handle on what to call this wondrous new material. Some were still calling it plastic. Others moved to more sophisticated references such as FRP (an acronym for Fiber Reinforced Plastic). In the end, it was primarily what we know today as simply fiberglass.

Whatever you choose to call it, the entire hood for Request was made of this material. It was ungainly when raised, but beautiful when lowered into normal position.

For a while there had been various proposals as to how the hood should open. One of these even included a center-folding hinge, but this was quickly discarded since the fender tops were so high that there was no real advantage to a side-opening hood.

Originally the massive fiberglass hood was attached to the spring hinges via sheet metal bolts. These bolts were then screwed into chunks of two-by-four wood glassed in to the hood tail underside. This arrangement was ultimately changed and strengthened, but for the purpose of appearance, it worked. And Creative, contrary to their usual stealth posture, continued to be mentioned in the press for their automotive plastics expertise. And likewise, so was Richard Teague.

So here was yet another area of friction between Teague and Macauley. Newspapers never mentioned Mac at all in coverage of the Request. But they did mention Teague and his youth. One put it this way in April 1955: "Richard Teague, Chief Stylist in the new, young styling section at the Packard division, specified glass reinforced polyester resin for the hood and modifying the front fenders of a special non-production model, the 'Request.' The Request features modifying front fenders and hood made of reinforced Plaskon polyester resin, a product of Barrett Division, Allied Chemical & Dye Corporation. These parts were molded by Creative Industries of Detroit. 'In the Request,' Teague, who is 30 years old, said, 'Packard has achieved again some elusive style objectives.' Teague heads a group of stylists at Packard who are doing advance research on working with plastics, both for parts and dies."

This unusual article was topped with a photo of Richard Teague standing next to the Request in Packard's styling studios. You can come to your own conclusions, but the minimization of Ed Macauley was obvious. Conversely, the importance of Teague at Packard and the connection between Creative and Teague was maximized.

Several hues were originally suggested, including (you guessed it) a brown metallic. Thankfully, Creative's suggestions prevailed. The Request was finally painted an iridescent murano pearl white from Rinshed-Mason, custom-mixed at Creative. The Request's roof and body color band stripe were done in a medium goldish-copper color (this was changed to a darker color during a refreshening at Creative). This same original color and scheme had also been used by Creative on the Mercury XM-800, but nobody seemed to notice. Iridescent mother-of-pearl back in those days was stunning on the turntable and floodlights at the auto shows. It was something new to the public and (as I have told you) Creative was a pioneer in this color. I can assure you that on a turntable during show time, the Request flashed brilliant glints of blue, pink, red, silver, and orange as it turned in the lights. It was far more striking in real life than any black and white photo could possibly convey.

Chrome wire wheels made by Motor Wheel Corporation were installed with specially modified center caps. Dark red cloisonné on chrome center medallions from older Packard wheel covers were installed over the top of the caps, transforming their look. The resulting rich appearance gave Request a unique traditional Packard look with just the right blending of 1950s modern in the mix.

The Request interior was basically carried over from a 1955 Caribbean convertible except that the rear seat was wider (due to no intrusion from convertible top mechanism) and based off the 1955 Four Hundred hardtop underpinnings. Packard designer Mary Ellen Green's Posture-Perfect seats were done in genuine leather supplied by Lackawanna Leather Company. The lower cushions were done in thick white pleats with bulging colored bolsters.

When the car was refreshened for 1956, a standard tan and brown 1956 Four Hundred interior was installed. That interior remained until recent years.

By now, if you are a Packard fan, you probably want to know some additional information that ties directly into Creative's work on the Request and its interior. As V-8 Packard aficionados know, there was no official hardtop Caribbean for 1955. Right? Well, kind of.

Yakima, Washington, 1970s. Author Leon Dixon with newly restored Packard Request in storage. Friends Larry Dopps and Richard Comstock found the car in Oregon and spent a couple years restoring it. Some parts came from author. Dick Comstock, who was part owner at the time, took this photo with my camera.

Actually Creative made a batch of them; the precise number is unknown. One of these was built specifically for Ed Macauley. Again, according to Gary Hutchings: "We built up a special Caribbean for Ed Macauley. It had special paint and a different interior. I think it was a hardtop." These were not official models with a special serial number or any other indicator. They were simply specially trimmed Four Hundred hardtops that looked like Caribbeans.

So what happened to the Request? Rumor has it that someone from Packard simply drove off with the dream car during the confusion that ensued as Packard was shutting down. Richard Teague once told me that for a time, the car had been used as a driver in Florida by the wife of a Packard executive.

I was convinced that Packard never destroyed the Request because I saw it in Chicago in the 1960s. But I had to wait many years later to be vindicated when a friend, Larry Dopps of Washington state, found the car sitting in weeds in Oregon. It had apparently been in at least one good collision and was partially disassembled.

Larry, together with his brother Orville and another friend, Richard Comstock of Yakima, Washington, managed to do a very decent cosmetic restoration on Request.

Eventually the Request was sold and ultimately became part of the famous Ralph Marano collection in New Jersey, where it remains to this day.

In the meantime, Jim Nance's master plan for dream cars was proceeding just as he had envisioned. The Packard Request had been built in 1954 to debut at the 1955 auto shows. Just as Jim Nance had suspected, the Request drew many favorable reactions. Although the press did not fall over itself in praising the car, traditional Packard customers viewing the Request as it toured the country seemed to love it. Some gushed in their praise. They could often be overheard saying things like, "Now *that's* how a Packard ought to look!"

So by 1955, based on all those letters and public reaction to the Request, it was clear that Packard's styling direction was going to include some kind of vertical grille theme for the future. That was all Jim Nance needed to know.

Packard Predictor

Finally came the crowning jewel in J. J. Nance's Packard concept car strategy: the Packard Predictor. No, Creative

Packard product planner Roger Bremer discusses Packard Predictor with President James J. Nance at Packard's styling studios.

Famous designer Bill Schmidt points out Predictor's vertical grille to Packard President James J. Nance. Design was actually a spring-loaded bumper. When impacted, the vertical section would simply retract into the hood and then spring back into position.

Fabulous Packard Predictor in Packard styling studios with stylist Bill Schmidt and Packard President James J. Nance. Predictor was probably one of the most popular dream cars and was repeatedly imitated over the years. Nance hoped it would be a PR bonanza, but it was too late to save Packard as a carmaker.

The Packard Request and JFK's Lincoln Continental

Afinal point on the Packard Request that nobody knows today has to do with Creative Industries and the JFK assassination Lincoln Continental. Creative's Bill Resztak, who did much of the work on the Eisenhower bubble-top Lincoln Cosmo parade car, had some interesting news clippings saved in his collection of Creative Industries souvenirs. One of these items was a clipping about the debut of the John F. Kennedy Lincoln. This special Lincoln Continental parade limo was a convertible that featured another plastic bubble top similar to the one fitted on the earlier Eisenhower car we discussed in Chapter Five. Although the clear bubble top was not in place on the fateful day of November 22, 1963, when Kennedy was assassinated in the car, it nevertheless had one. So one can say this is merely a logical coincidence and progression of the format theme of a presidential parade car.

But there was always something odd about this car in the front and here is yet another mystery you can add to the grassy knoll and the rest of the stories.

If you remember the Kennedy car in the films of that terrible day in Dallas, one thing striking in the frontal view were the two flashing red warning lights mounted on the front bumper.

Yes, supposedly Hess & Eisenhardt of Ohio built this presidential car for Ford Motor Company and the White House. And yet we know that bubble tops were a Creative specialty and they had already done one for the previous presidential Lincoln. We also know that Bill Resztak had a government security clearance and was approved to work on the Eisenhower car. So why did Resztak have a news clipping about the debut of the Kennedy car in his Creative Industries memorabilia? Just residual interest left over from his previous work you say? Perhaps.

But now back to those warning lights on the front bumper of the Kennedy car. They were no more standard to this car than was the custom bubble top. So where did they come from? Take a good, very close look at the housings. Then take a close look at the parking light housings on the Packard Request. I believe the Kennedy car warning light housings were modified from dies or die models used to make the light housings on the front bumper of the Request.

And if you're chuckling or clucking right about now, note the very sharp ridges on both sides of the light pods. Then take a good look at the sharply creased ribs on the Request housing, then look back at the ribs on the sides of the warning light housings on the Kennedy car. Look familiar? Yes, the warning light housings are

Close-up detail reveals just how intricate Request front design is. Headlight doors look like pressed metal 1955 Clipper units but were actually cast, handmade parts fabricated by Creative. Each vertical bar was individually cast and bent. Packard medallion on hood was recessed and entire hood assembly was made of fiberglass. See those light pods? Again, remember how they are made with the ribs on sides. Now take a look at the next photo.

Look familiar? Recognize the overall pod and pinched rib on the side? The casting has obviously been modified on top and brought forward to give a visored effect, but there is a familiar size and shape here. Know what it is? (Photo Courtesy Thomas A. McPherson)

smooth on top and droop into a more visored opening. This aspect differs. But this would have been easily accomplished simply by modifying an existing die or mold, which is another thing that Creative was well known to do. So am I saying the Packard Request and the assassination limo are connected? Perhaps it is all speculation, but there are a lot of coincidences here. And it was not the first time that Creative was involved in a presidential vehicle but did not get the credit.

Yes. President John F. Kennedy's infamous Lincoln Continental assassination parade limo. Take a good look at the warning light housings on the lower front bumper. See the ribs in the side and overall shape? There is reason to believe these were supplied to the credited company via Creative Industries. Made from modified castings used to make the Packard Request years earlier. (Photo Courtesy Thomas A. McPherson)

Packard Predictor struts its stuff in Packard styling studios next to Continental Mark II. The Continental was the most expensive car sold in the United States (including Rolls Royce) in 1956. Predictor was longer, lower, wider (the ultimate in 1950s automotive marketing) and made the Mark II look old by comparison. Predictor was also one of the first cars seen in public with thin-line whitewall tires.

Industries didn't build Predictor. Ghia of Italy did. But it was Creative that got the Predictor show-worthy. They did this by rebuilding parts of the car, rewiring the electricals, upgrading the faulty power windows, fabricating damaged components, and repairing the retractable roof sections. Creative also serviced, maintained, and otherwise hovered over Predictor during its brief show career.

My friend Tom Beaubien (yes, of the old Detroit family with the street named after them) was one of two Packard employees who built the original Predictor scale model.

By spring of 1955, Tom Beaubien began work along with Jim Flory on a large-scale model of Packard's new dream car for 1956. And while Dick Teague has often been credited as sole designer on this car, much of Predictor was Bill Schmidt.

One Last Fling for Pan American Number-1

And there was still one more Macauley-Creative collaboration. Sometime along the way, Ed Macauley acquired ownership of the Packard Pan American number-1. As was Macauley's fashion, he immediately decided it needed "updating" and dug into the car repeatedly.

Having seen what Creative had done with the Panthers, particularly on Don Mitchell's car, Mac got itching once more. This time he decided to do a total revision on his Pan American too. The car was taken over to Creative and a total revamp was ordered.

Like the gun mansion in California with the endless remodels, stairs that led to nowhere, and doors that opened on walls, so ended the original look of the Pan American number-1. This quirky, ungainly restyle included the 1955 cathedral taillights with exhaust-port rear bumper, a 1955 instrument panel, and numerous other changes. The rear fenders were modified with exactly the same step ridge that Creative used on the two Panthers it had modified.

After all of the modifications, the Pan Am number-1 was eventually sold and ended up in the collection of J. Bell Moran. Upon Moran's death, the Pan American number-1 was willed to the City of Detroit, which owns the car to this day but has it out on loan to museums. This hugely customized Packard dream car currently resides along with the Pan American number-2 (which is also much modified) at the National Packard Museum in Warren, Ohio.

A 1952 Packard Pan American dream car on display at Pan Pacific Auditorium in Los Angeles, California. This was Pan Am number-1 as it originally looked before undergoing years of modifications.

Pan Americans number-1 (top) and number-2 (bottom) as they look today under the ownership of City of Detroit. Both have been much modified over the years. I believe roll-up (and later, power) side windows were changed over to this car from Don Mitchell's Panther. (Photo Courtesy Stuart R. Blond and The Packard Club)

The PREDICTOR'S Promise to You

IN ENGINEERING

When you open the *Predictor's* doors, sliding roof panels over the doors automatically and silently roll back for easy exit and entrance. The roof panels can also be opened for ventilation while the doors remain closed.

Swiveling front seats add to the ease of entering or leaving this all-new car.

The wrap around, wrap over windshield provides the ultimate in visibility.

A hooded Packard Balboa-type rear window is fully retractable providing maximum ventilation.

Four headlights—two especially designed for country driving, two especially for city driving—are recessed behind power-operated hood openings.

Jet pods in the rear house the back-up lights and the four exhaust ports.

Powered by an advanced Packard V-8 engine rated at over 300 horsepower.

Electronic Push-buttons control the powerful Ultramatic transmission.

Rear deck lid raises and lowers hydraulically for your convenience.

Pedestal for all major operating controls is located between the two front seats.

A control unit for operation of roof panels, radio antennas and courtesy lights is located in the rooftop convenient to both driver and passenger.

Of course, the Predictor brings you Packard's famous Torsion-Level Ride, like so many other advanced features already available on Packard-built cars.

IN STYLING

The sculptured-in-steel Packard Caribbean design is typified by crispness, sharply defined forms and smooth-flowing lines.

A contemporary version of the world-famed classic Packard grille with a floating vertical blade that is both a shock absorber and bumper guard.

Individual contoured seat cushions and back rests that are reversible, with natural pliable leather on one side and beautiful fabric on the other.

Satin finished aluminum mouldings that begin at the base of the grille and flow smoothly around the body.

Beautiful opalescent pearl body enamel that assumes the color of the light playing on it.

Crisp molded hood lines that flow unbroken from the top of the grille terminating at the instrument panel.

New trend-setting proportions. The Predictor is 222 inches long by four and a half feet *low*.

A circular window to the rear of the passenger compartment combines a courtesy light with a jeweled escutcheon.

TO A GOOD FRIEND, 9/25/07

Predictor foldout brochure autographed to the author by Tom Beaubien, who made original scaled model sent to Ghia.

Side view and shaping up original Predictor scale model by Tom Beaubien and Jim Flory under construction at Packard. Rear wheel basic disc is inserted but not yet in final form. Side sculpture here was not final and was later filled with ribbing. Note genius in subtle design of slanted lines that carry through and repeat (rear roof line repeats in taillight angle leading C-pillar line follows through to body sculpture, repeats windshield A-pillar line). Eye tends to see extremely long straight line enhanced by flowing angles that tend to imply motion and low sleekness.

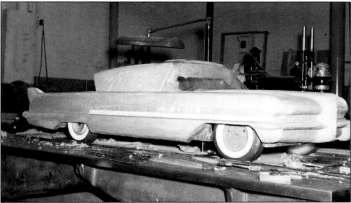

Original Predictor scale model by Tom Beaubien and Jim Flory under construction at Packard.

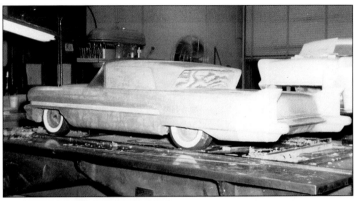

Rear view of original Predictor scale model by Tom Beaubien and Jim Flory under early construction at Packard. Model in background was Raymond Loewy project for Studebaker. Note precision plate model sits on is scaled down from the plate actual full-size scale models use for precision measurements. Clay model tools are basically the same as used on full-size clay models.

Right rear view original Predictor scale model by Tom Beaubien and Jim Flory nearing completion at Packard. Can you read what it says on the rear license plate?

Finished! Original Predictor scale model by Tom Beaubien and Jim Flory at Packard prior to being sent off to Ghia in Italy to make the full-size Predictor.

Can you read it now? The license on Predictor says "Javelin," which was the original Name Richard Teague wanted to use on this dream car. Of course, designers at Ford were thinking of using the name on what became Mercury XM-800 (see Chapter Five) and Chrysler was also considering the name for their concept station wagon that became known as the Plainsman!

Plymouth Plainsman went on the show circuit in 1956, appearing in some of the same shows as Predictor. Both might have ended up being named "Javelin."

But an even bigger surprise is that, according to Tom Beaubien, the primary principal designer of Predictor was Dick Macadam, who later became VP of Design at Chrysler.

The illustrations of the Macadam design were expertly translated to dimensional drawings by former World War II bomber pilot Frank Wild. Beaubien and Charles Flory used these precise drawings to build an actual three-dimensional scale model.

By the time that the engineering drawings were done, there was really nothing major that changed from that point forward. As Beaubien tells the story, the work on the scale model went quite swiftly because there was really no meddling with the work, as sometimes happens in the process.

If you view the images of this scale model, you will see that it clearly said "Javelin" on the rear license plate (AMC fans can smile right here). This was the original intended name of the car as envisioned by Richard Teague. But there were several others at the time who were also thinking of using this name. I tell you more later in Chapter Thirteen when I talk about American Motors' AMX. But for right now, suffice it to say that the beginning of the Javelin name for a Richard Teague–designed car probably started right here.

Bill Schmidt and Dick Teague occasionally drifted in to check up on the progress of Beaubien and Flory's scale model, but they pretty much maintained a hands-off approach. Thus, the model was finished in short order.

According to Tom Beaubien, the contract with Ghia was $60,000. To put this in perspective, a 1956 Caribbean even loaded with factory air and wire wheels would have come in well under $8,000, and that was still a hugely expensive car for the day.

Aside from all of the obvious styling, there was a plan to do some serious engineering that would take the mechanicals beyond the fabulous electronic Torsion-Level suspension that was included on the Clipper chassis under Predictor. One of these ideas, supposedly proposed by Packard engineer John Z. De Lorean, was to move the Ultramatic transmission to the rear of the car to balance weight. The rear suspension would then have instead been independent. This truly was way ahead of the curve.

Some press releases, particularly in Europe, somehow got wind of this plan and publicized it as if the engineering was actually installed on the car. Unfortunately, there was no money to do the rear-mounted transmission and independent rear suspension. But De Lorean got his wish years later as the design appeared on Pontiac Tempest.

From the time Beaubien's scale model and drawings were sent off to Italy until the day the big crate arrived back in the United States, it was approximately six months! And remember, Ghia had other cars such as Plymouth's Plainsman in progress at the same time. Pretty impressive!

Fried wiring and smoking motors repaired and made operational by Creative Industries, Predictor was ready to wow onlookers on display at the 1956 Chicago Auto Show.

The Predictor was already sitting back in Packard styling studios in Detroit by New Year's Day, 1956. Beaubien recalls that it was a Sunday morning, January 1, 1956, when the Predictor was finally uncrated at the Packard Plant on East Grand Boulevard. He said that the uncrating was done on this day because the car had just arrived and because being both a holiday and a Sunday, few people would be around. Doing so at the time also bypassed a union issue.

Tom Beaubien had the incredible foresight to bring an 8-mm movie camera to that uncrating. Although we did not have the absolute best methods, back in the 1990s I was able to resurrect enough of the film to make a digital copy.

On hand were various persons from Packard staff. These included Bill Schmidt, along with his wife, Mary, and son. Of course, on hand were Tom Beaubien, Luigi Segre (the head of Ghia), and his wife, as well as other Ghia and Packard staff members.

As the sides of the crate came off, there were gasps around the room as the gleaming pearlescent white beauty was slowly released from its dark confines. These were real seasoned car people in the room and they had seen lots of incredible machinery in the past. But nobody had ever seen anything like this! It was awe-inspiring.

In the film, Bill Schmidt draws on his pipe a bit and paces around the car as it sits low in the crate base. Schmidt's son appears in a smart red blazer. Beaubien believes the fellow holding the child was Bill Braathen, who was not associated with the project but was a member of Packard styling and friend of

Schmidt's. Also present was Predictor scale modeler Charles Flory and Packard Planner Riley Quarles.

Bill swivels the driver's seat (the front seats swiveled) and opens the hood, which sags from overtaxed springs. There are no names on the car at all at this point. The axles are lashed down on what appear to be 4 x 8 wooden blocks. Quickly, Predictor was out of the crate and up on wheels.

The full-size Predictor was finished in the same pearl-white color applied to the Request, one of the 1954½ Panther updates (the car owned by Creative's Rex Terry) and to the Predictor original scale model. So there is the clear lineage of the Predictor, despite some later controversy in the industry and with historians about its styling and an Edsel connection. The Predictor and its upright center grille and pearl-white color came directly from Creative and the theme of the Request.

And there is an important thing to remember about the Predictor's color. In later years, some people got the odd notion that the Predictor was pale yellow. This has even been reported in magazines and on the Internet. But the color was nothing of the sort. Remember Gary Hutchings' comment about how Creative's specially mixed experimental paint turned yellow over time? I assure you, the Predictor was originally pearl white, no matter how it may have appeared years later.

Yes, Ghia had performed a miracle of building the Predictor in six months and for a relatively reasonable price. But in the rush to complete the Predictor, some areas had not received proper attention. The Predictor was a very complicated dream car and these shortcomings quickly became apparent.

The first surprise came no sooner than a battery was hooked up and Bill Schmidt tried operating the power windows. The passenger side window began to retract, then stopped short with a fizzling sound. Soon after, smoke began seeping out of the door. But this wasn't the end of the electrical maladies.

At least one source claimed there had been unspecified damage that occurred to the roof during the transatlantic shipping. The roof "rolltop" sections shorted too. These interlocking flexible extruded aluminum sections over the driver and front passenger had a dual purpose. They worked like an old rolltop desk.

First, whenever a door was opened the motorized roof section could be set to retract to allow maximum head clearance for ingress/egress. The section then closed with the door.

No mystery where these photos were taken. Rare shot with headlight doors open was taken as part of repair documentation at Creative Industries. Several people the author knew actually did repair work.

Creative Industries photographer took these photos. By now readers should recognize the yellow brick building and famous driveway on East Outer Drive. General Manager Rex Terry had model pose with Predictor after repairs were documented.

Predictor sits with headlight doors open and roof panels retracted in Creative's famous driveway.

Second, the sections could also be retracted for more open-air driving. The resulting look and effect of this design was similar to T-tops that were popular later on American cars of the 1970s.

After a few cycles of opening and closing the doors, one of the roof sections began pouring smoke. The upshot was yet more barbecued wiring.

So when you've got a brand-new dream car malfunctioning and billowing smoke with an auto show debut in Chicago just a few days away, who were you going to call? Who else? Packard hustled the Predictor over to East Outer Drive and Creative got right to work. Creative's people labored day and night on the Predictor.

In the end, Creative quickly eliminated all of the electrical bugs and got Predictor fully operational. With everything solidly functioning, photos of Predictor were taken at Creative Industries' General Offices on East Outer Drive. Here is what it said on Page 61 of the December 1978 issue of *Car Classics*: "Packard Predictor, the car was essentially built by Ghia in Italy, but Creative did the fittings and rewired the complicated electrical systems. Creative also performed all service on the car not handled by Packard engineers. Publicity photos were taken in front of Creative's Outer Drive plant."

Gary Hutchings told me that Creative was under the gun to get the electrical work on Predictor fully functional and working reliably. Not only this, but they were cautioned that any troublesome systems had to be easily diagnosed and repaired in the field in case a malfunction occurred at a show. As a consequence, Creative's crew, laboring on a 24/7 basis, merely bypassed some of the Ghia's wiring and made up their own harnesses. Some of the most critical new sections were actually left uncovered and tagged in tactful locations (see photos). This method allowed Creative's field engineers (who accompanied the car to shows) to make swift diagnoses and additional repairs if needed.

Creative made certain that the Predictor was delivered on time to the Chicago Auto Show, and it was a hit! The Predictor was perhaps the most successful dream car exhibited that year. Spectators stood oftentimes 10 deep around the turntable where Predictor was on display. The crowd went wild over Packard's new dream car, but nobody knew that Creative Industries had made it all possible. Best of all, everything continued to operate with no more smoke or sizzling. But all was not well back home in Detroit.

Upstairs in the offices on Grand Boulevard, Packard execs awaited the great press that was surely to come with the new Predictor. Waiting was about all they could do. When a source that had the purse strings on the 1957 run yanked funding, the Packard coffers suddenly ran dry. There was no money left for a real advertising campaign, so the Predictor would just have to wow the crowds mostly on its own and under the watchful eye of at least one Creative staffer. The trigger had been pulled, but there was no bang and no bullet seemed to be leaving the barrel.

The situation was not good, but those executives must have been more than crushed when they popped open the January 16, 1956, issue of *Newsweek* magazine.

Right next to the illustration and publicity blurb on their new Predictor dream car was a crash-and-burn story about Packard's rather dire business situation. The article pointed out that Packard "had suffered 85 unauthorized strikes and assorted work stoppages." It went on to say that these events and others had contributed to a "$29 million loss in the first nine months of 1955." It was one of the first published hints of the beginning of the end. One calamity built on top of the others until a few months later it was game over.

By some miracle, the Packard Predictor survived the melee that ensued in Detroit at Packard headquarters. As an abandon-ship mentality took over, some vehicles, including Creative-built full-size fiberglass models and the sole running 1957 steel-bodied prototype engineering mule, were cut up for scrap. Others were driven off into the night; some never to be seen again. Thousands of rare photos and paper archives were shoveled into

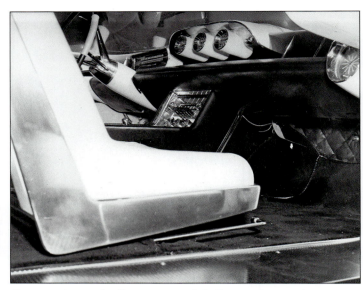

Look closely and you'll see Creative quick-fix repair tag hanging under instrument panel. Creative had to make their own wiring harnesses and bypasses to get Predictor functional after harnesses and motors overheated and burned. Predictor was accompanied by Creative staff members and tags gave information on how to bypass or make quick repairs in case of additional malfunctions. There were none.

Carpeted panel adjacent to quick-fix repair tag shown here had to be altered from Ghia's original so that Creative personnel could easily access electrical bypass harness fabricated at Creative after fire from overheated wiring took place at Packard factory.

the roaring fires of the powerplant furnaces. Then all was quiet.

In the chaos and confusion, somehow the Predictor had managed to be transported to South Bend, Indiana, where the Studebaker-Packard Corporation now called home. For a number of years, this Packard dream car sat rather forgotten under a dusty tarp in a corner of the old Studebaker Plant in South Bend. Predictor was now parented by a company that cared less about Packard and a dreamy luxury future and more about compact economy cars in their present.

Did everybody love the Predictor? No. Some Packard employees were less than enthusiastic about the Predictor. And there were always those who just never got warm and fuzzy over 1950s dream cars. But the best example I can think of was again personal, and yes, again it involved Creative Industries.

Today, the Predictor lives in the Studebaker museum in South Bend, Indiana. Like most dream cars of the 1950s, it is loved and admired by some, misunderstood and criticized by others. But Predictor lives on.

Perhaps the most poignant aspect of Packard Predictor's history will always be a sad reminder of broken dreams. Of what could have been–and perhaps what should have been. But to me, Predictor is also a shining tribute to the men and women who worked so hard to make Packard a name revered around the world. By some incredible fate this dream car has managed to outlive not just Studebaker and Packard Corporation, but the amazing Creative Industries of Detroit as well. So we are indeed lucky to have this fantastic automobile still with us here in a future it so richly deserves to inhabit. At least, that's how I see it. Creative Industries of Detroit helped to save the Predictor, but they couldn't save Packard.

Predictor proposal artwork. Packard was not too overly impressed by Continental Mark II when compared to Predictor. But somebody sure liked those Mark II parking light bumper nacelles! (Photo Courtesy Stuart R. Blond and The Packard Club)

CHAPTER ELEVEN

THE STAINLESS STEEL CARS AND JOHN Z. DE LOREAN'S DREAM

lways on the cutting edge: The four-door hardtop craze, brushed stainless, and silvery finishes swoop onto the automotive scene, and predict the future.

Welding Exotic Metals

Beginning in the 1930s and all through the war years of the 1940s, Creative Industries founder Fred Johnson had explored and perfected welding techniques and welding machines. As I have mentioned earlier, Fred's Progressive Welder continued to broaden the horizons for production welding, accomplishing things that had never been done before. In short, Progressive Welder Company stood at the apex of the technology.

The company's techniques and machines could handle almost any metal or combination thereof. Johnson and his staff at Progressive Welder worked tirelessly to hone these techniques to the point where Progressive became an industry leader in these areas. If you wanted to know how to weld and fabricate designs of special metals, Progressive was the go-to company of the era. One of these new directions involved new welding techniques with aluminum. The other involved stainless steel.

Progressive's cutting-edge welding knowledge was rolled directly into the new company. Ultimately it fell to Creative Industries to take welding of exotic metals to new heights in the automotive realm.

During late 1954/early 1955, Creative Industries actually engineered and cobbled at least one of two prototype four-door hardtops for Packard. This senior car would have been a new version of the model Four Hundred for 1956. The trick here was to make the rear door open suicide style, hinged from the rear. Had there been funds available to produce it, the Packard four-door hardtop would have

Three different prototypes of De Lorean stainless steel sports car. Car on left was built by Creative Industries and was closest to actual production vehicle that was built in Ireland. (Photo Courtesy William Collins Collection)

been a unique sporty luxury four-door hardtop. It would've beat Cadillac's car with similar doors by a year. Packard's hardtop also would have predicted direction for Lincolns for almost the entire decade of the 1960s. But there was no money to squeeze the new model into the already troubled production run. As such, the new four-door hardtop body was postponed until 1957. But, of course, that production also never came.

The Incredible Eldorado Brougham

Rex Terry, the general manager of Creative Industries, could be seen each morning pulling into either the front drive of the East Outer Drive facility or into the staff entrance off Moenart Street. The armed, uniformed gate guard at that entrance, a fel-

Packard four-door hardtop was originally planned for 1956 model year when this body style was the rage. Creative cobbled at least two cars together using 1955 pilot production model Four Hundred two-door hardtop body melded with frameless 1955 Patrician four-door sedan doors. Trick here was reversing rear doors to open suicide style. (Photo Courtesy Richard Teague)

Only known existing photo of Rex Terry (here with daughter Pamela) and his Eldorado Brougham, rumored to be early pilot production. Possibility exists that Terry may have had two Broughams. Stainless steel roof made Rex smile. For anyone inclined to doubt, promo images of USS 1960 stainless steel T-bird were taken at this same location, Terry's home. (Photo Courtesy Pamela Terry Bonk)

Magnificent beauty of stainless steel roof on Eldorado Brougham was incredibly futuristic to 1950s eyes.

low named Hutch who always seemed to have the stub of a half-smoked cigar in his mouth, smiled and tipped his hat as Terry drove past.

In earlier days during nice weather, Rex might have been driving his Packard Panther. But Rex Terry had one of the very first Cadillac Eldorado Broughams rolling on the streets of Detroit. Eldorado was top of the line for Cadillac models. But the Eldorado Brougham was the top Eldorado.

The Eldorado Brougham was a four-door hardtop with a stainless steel roof. At about $13,000 in 1957 to 1958, it easily cost thousands more than a Rolls Royce and even more than Continental Mark II.

Creative's parent company, Progressive, invented countless welding techniques, and even numerous welding machines, that worked especially well with stainless steel. Although it was a difficult process to weld stainless to normal steel, Progressive also perfected almost any mating techniques using stainless by the years of World War II. Much of this was due to their experience in fabricating for the U.S. military and aircraft. So was it any surprise that Rex Terry owned one of the first production cars with a stainless steel roof?

1960 Stainless Steel Thunderbird

The first stainless steel–body cars of any note in the United States were a special set of 1931 Model A Fords. These were ordered by Allegheny Steel Company (prior to their merging with Ludlum Steel). Not much is known about this handful of cars (perhaps three) today, but they set the wheels in motion for the idea of stainless steel car bodies.

Allegheny-Ludlum Steel Corporation (ALS) then formed a joint venture with Ford Motor Company. This project resulted in a set of six 1936 Fords all constructed with stainless steel bodies. I believe that Fred Johnson and his Progressive Welder Company (listed for public knowledge or not) were consultants on this project. These cars were exhibited all over the country and also used by key ALS salesmen.

A short time after the Eldorado Brougham ended, Allegheny-Ludlum Steel was again inspired and determined to reprise their original 1930s promotion of stainless steel–bodied cars.

Just how 'ageless' is Allegheny Ludlum Stainless?

In 1935, Allegheny Ludlum Steel Corporation and Ford Motor Company agreed to build six 1936 model two-door Ford sedans with bodies made of stainless steel. Stainless engineers wanted to find out just how long a stainless steel car would last.

The situation was different then. Commercial stainless was just beginning to outgrow its adolescence. It had been successfully introduced to the automobile industry just five years before, in 1930. Stainless steel car bodies seemed like a good way to demonstrate to automobile people that this metal was easy to work with, once you got the hang of it.

All, except one, of the six original stainless steel Fords have their history known. The company still has two it uses for shows and displays; one is on permanent display at a museum in Cleveland. Another is owned by a stainless steel buff from way back, Dr. Jerome Vlk, a prominent Chicago orthodontist who pio-

Allegheny Ludlum Steel issued brochure about stainless steel in automobiles and their stainless concepts. Their first reference is 1935, although earlier stainless Ford Model A vehicles were known to be built.

Promo photo of 1960 stainless steel–bodied Thunderbird and 1936 Ford. Recognize the house? It's Rex Terry's home. (Photo Courtesy Pamela Terry Bonk)

One of two 1960 stainless steel–bodied Thunderbirds in Rex Terry's driveway with 1930s convertible. Although production T-Birds had rear fender skirts, they were deleted from both stainless steel models. (Photo Courtesy Pamela Terry Bonk)

Ford Motor Company agreed to participate again and this time, two 1960 Ford Thunderbirds were built in stainless. These cars were every bit as striking as their silvery 1936 counterparts. But they were also built at a very opportune moment.

The Thunderbird made the jump from a two-passenger sports car to a four-passenger sports/luxury/personal car with the new 1958 model. With this shrewd move, T-Bird sales exploded and set sales records. So the four-passenger Thunderbird was here to stay.

Stainless steel is a lot harder metal (than normal steel) to press out into a car body. It needs to be hit harder and resists twisting and stretching more than normal steel. Compound bends and curves may not press out faithfully to the shape of a die. Thus any dies used in making conventional steel car bodies could be damaged when switched over to stamping out stainless. So it was determined to use the Thunderbird dies only after the last 1960 steel bodies and extra parts had been stamped.

Today some say that Budd did the cars and needed no input from anyone since they had been making stainless train cars as well. Others identify photos that were obviously taken at Creative and claim they were taken at the Ford Wixom Assembly Plant. No matter who did what and when, the fact remains that Creative Industries indeed was contracted to do these two cars. I was told in no uncertain terms that while Budd supplied the stampings, Creative consulted with Budd and assembled the body using their own engineers and special welding and finishing techniques.

David Margolis gave me a photo in the 1970s of a bare 1960 T-bird body-in-white sitting in Creative's Outer Drive facility. You can see the typical corrugated steel walls of Creative's security areas behind the car body. People who

Many contradictory stories exist today, so judge for yourself. Photos tell the real story. Bare body of 1960 stainless steel–bodied Thunderbird. Recognize the shop and corrugated steel partitions? This was Creative's Outer Drive facility.

Detailed view of Allegheny Ludlum stainless 1967 Lincoln Continental convertible concept pictured in company's promotional brochure. There was no mention of Creative Industries.

Female employees of Union Carbide Corporation pose with 1960 stainless Thunderbird and 1936 stainless Ford.

model. Now, here is the rest of the story.

Two stainless steel cars, a 1960 Thunderbird and a 1936 Ford, were photographed with a model in front of a house with white pillars and shutters. This house was the residence of none other than Creative's general manager, Rex A. Terry. The only photo I could find of Rex with his Brougham was also taken here. As I mentioned earlier, the Eldorado photo includes Rex's young daughter, Pamela. And yes, Pamela confirmed that all of these photos were taken in front of their house in Birmingham, Michigan.

The photo of the Thunderbird taken in front of the Terry house then maintains the stealth disconnect of the car from Creative. Of course, if one knew that house, there is no question about a connection here.

Between Allegheny-Ludlum Steel, Union Carbide, Budd Auto Body, Creative Industries, and Ford Wixom, it may remain unclear for some who did what, and when. And as someone once said, perhaps that is the way "they wanted things to be." And there was more to come.

Ford later participated in three stainless steel 1967 Lincoln Continental convertibles (one trimmed more like a 1966). These beautiful convertibles were built again for

worked there knew these partitions very well, and I saw these partitioned areas many times myself.

At one point in 1961, Union Carbide Corporation also got involved with promoting these cars. UCC released press photos of the car sitting alongside one of the 1936 stainless Fords in front of its corporate headquarters in New York. This building was built with facings made of stainless steel. Two female Union Carbide employees posed with the cars in these later press release photos.

As a final capper on the matter, a photo appeared in the September 5, 1960, issue of the premier car industry trade publication, *Automotive News*. This publication is read by all of the top professionals in the business. But the paper said nothing to reveal Creative's connection here.

In this issue, a blurb appeared with the photo showing the stainless steel T-bird with a model. The caption never mentioned Creative Industries, but a brick house with white pillars and shutters is clearly pictured directly behind the car and

MEET THE LINCOLN CONTINENTAL

Except for the stainless steel body, everything about this distinguished American motorcar is Lincoln Continental equipment.

The car has a 462 cubic inch V-8 engine which develops 340 h.p. at 4,600 r.p.m. Its overall length is 220.9 inches, its wheelbase 126 inches. The automobile weighs 5,680 pounds, almost exactly what it would weigh with a standard Lincoln Continental convertible cold rolled steel body.

The convertible top is completely automatic, fully retractable and self storing beneath the car's rear deck. Equipment includes power side and vent windows, remote control side view mirror, power lock doors, a six-way power adjustable driver's seat, power antenna, and the luxurious interior design for which Lincoln Continental is world famous.

The convertible is a one-of-a-kind special; a source of enduring pride to both Allegheny Ludlum Steel Corporation and Ford Motor Company.

MEET ALLEGHENY LUDLUM STAINLESS

This magnificent all stainless steel car body was made from standard type 304 stainless, a high volume sheet rolled during a normal production run at the corporation's Brackenridge Works near Pittsburgh, Pa.

More than 1,500 standard Lincoln Continental convertible body dies, jigs and fixtures were used to form 18 sub-assemblies and 35 separate pieces of stainless steel which went into the completed body.

Approximately 287 stainless body parts were made. These included individual pieces, sub-assemblies and spare parts for future use.

Stainless steel trim, and wheel covers are standard equipment on all Lincoln Continentals, as are stainless steel mufflers — something every motorist has yearned for at one time or another. No changes were made in this standard equipment.

WHY STAINLESS STEEL IS DIFFERENT

Now give the Continental's satin finished body a closer look. See how it glows with a special metallic splendor. Then touch its hard, smooth surface. Because stainless steel is especially hard, smooth and clean, it reflects light or diffuses light in a special way depending on finish.

THE SECRET OF STAINLESS

The secret of stainless steel's corrosion resistance was discovered at the turn of the century when scientists found that the addition of sufficient amounts of the element chromium to ferretic (iron-based) metals made them almost totally resistant to atmospheric corrosion and much more highly resistant than most other metals to severely corrosive industrial environments. Besides chromium other alloying ingredients often go into stainless steels. This is a family of metals rather than one kind of metal.

YOUR OWN STAINLESS STEEL CAR?

Unfortunately, you will probably never get to own a car with a stainless steel body — although it would be fun and easy to keep clean.

There's something else about stainless steel. It's the next thing to permanent. By the standard of longevity for automobiles, or even for man, Allegheny Ludlum stainless is almost ageless.

Allegheny Ludlum Steel brochure about stainless steel in automobiles and their stainless 1967 Lincoln Continental convertible concepts. Shop and people here appear to be Creative Industries, but there was no mention of Creative.

Early press release composite photo for John Z. De Lorean's masterpiece stainless steel De Lorean sports car.

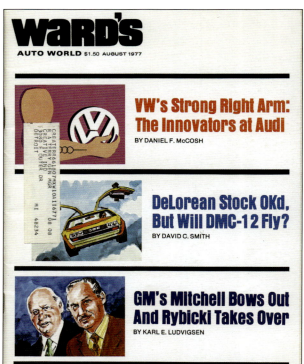

Look closely at mailing label on this Ward's Auto World trade publication from August 1977. Rex Terry gave me his personal copy, which included a story about De Lorean DMC-12 stock sales and launch of company.

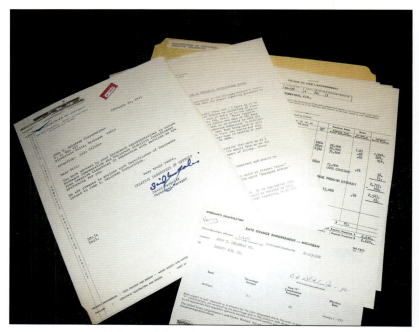

Letter to DMC from Creative's David Margolis, along with workman's compensation insurance papers, from 1977. Letter was addressed to Bill Collins, Jr. who was DMC Chief Engineer. DMC was largely headquartered at Creative Industries prior to their move to Bloomfield Hills, and Collins sometimes drove his Pontiac Banshee concept car to work at Creative!

Allegheny-Ludlum Steel Corporation, again all done with Creative's help.

Today, the 1960 Thunderbirds have indeed survived. The original 1959 Ford sun spiral hubcaps are now missing, replaced over the years by faux wire spoke wheel covers. One Thunderbird remains in the collection of ALS and the other was donated to a historical society that eventually loaned the car to the Crawford Museum Cleveland, Ohio. Crawford also has one of the 1936 Fords and one of the Lincoln Continental convertibles.

De Lorean's Stainless Steel Sportscar Dream

Much has been written about the famous De Lorean sports car, and we won't attempt to tell the whole story here. But few know that a major part of its gestation took place at Creative Industries. Although the earliest prototype (number-1) was built at a company called Triad/Visioneering in a suburb north of Detroit, the actual production feasibility prototype (number-2) was built at Creative Industries on East Outer Drive.

I vividly recall one day back in the 1970s when I came to visit Dave Margolis at Creative. We were walking around in the shop area in the rear where the partitioned client areas were located. Suddenly a door on one of the corrugated metal enclosures flew wide open when someone was walking out, and there it was. I politely did my best not to stare and turned my head. But I could clearly see that the car that was in the enclosure, make no mistake about it, sure looked like brushed stainless steel to me.

I looked over at David and tried to maintain my composure. "It's all stainless, isn't it?" I said.

"Shhhhh!" he said as he put a finger up to his lips. But David knew I wouldn't say anything to outsiders. So after a few minutes, he relented. "They're selling stock and I guess it's not much of a secret anymore, but John De Lorean is making a stainless steel sports car, and we're building the prototype here."

De Lorean engineer Bill Collins would drive his Pontiac Banshee sports car concept to work at Creative during early days of DMC-12 development. Beautiful Vixen motor home in background was designed by Collins. (Photo Courtesy William Collins Collection)

Years later, Creative staffer Joe Ramsay told me a bit more. "During the time they were making the De Lorean prototype in one of the design areas over in the shop, there was this guy who used to come to work driving one of the GM concepts, the Pontiac Banshee. It was white with louvers on the back. He parked it right in our back lot! This would have been just before we moved to the new building."

One of handful of gold De Loreans, this one at National Automotive Museum in Reno, Nevada.

The person who drove the GM Banshee concept to work at Creative was Bill Collins. He was De Lorean's chief engineer. I

De Lorean company paperwork including canceled checks, factory blueprint, and more.

asked Collins about driving the Banshee to work at Creative. "I don't think I drove it every day, but yes, I did drive the Banshee in to work at Creative. That car was the one that Joe Bortz got later. I really don't recall a lot of our time at Creative. We had an office there and there were several of us there. Joe Sahutsky was my chief draftsman.

"Those three photographs, those three DMCs that I sent you, the first car on the left is what I call the number-2 prototype, the one that Creative built. The second one is the one that Triad built. And the last one is the eppo wood model. We really only built one of the prototypes at Creative.

"The first prototype was the one that John [De Lorean] used to go out and line up the dealers. The second one was more representative of production. That first car had a Citroen engine in the back end and it was not representative of what production would be."

From his days at Packard to his time at Pontiac and finally at De Lorean Motor Company, John De Lorean had given the auto industry many things. And he had boldly, fearlessly gone all in, gambling that his stainless steel car would revolutionize automobiles. He lost his fortune, he lost his reputation, he lost his wife, and eventually he lost the De Lorean Motor Company.

But while John Z. De Lorean's dream of making a stainless steel car eventually crashed and burned, nearly 9,000 examples were built. The DMC-12 was real. And it was unforgettable, even if only as a movie icon from the *Back to the Future* trilogy.

The prototype was built at Creative, and what basically served as DMC headquarters was camped out at Creative for years, right up until it was moved north of Detroit to the Bloomfield Hills and Troy areas.

De Lorean had come and gone, but either way, the stainless steel dreams of both Fred Johnson and Rex Terry had also finally come true. Back along the way, the dream had even spread to trucks (another Creative Industries specialty). In 1962, a giant 18-wheel truck tractor known by some as the Yankee Clipper was built for the Autocar brand out of stainless steel. Creative Industries could proudly say it helped make the dream of stainless steel vehicles come true.

Letter from David Margolis of Creative Industries on Creative letterhead to De Lorean chief engineer Bill Collins regarding workman's comp certificates for work on DMC-12. Image on Creative letterhead depicts a planned architectural fascia and second story morph of Outer Drive building that was never fully completed.

CHAPTER TWELVE

FORD MYSTERE AND KIDDIE CARS

*T*his chapter gives the scoop behind the scenes with the magical Mystere and wild high-end junior cars.

The Fabulous Mystere

If you entered via the front door on Outer Drive and then turned right inside the Creative Industries headquarters building, there was a room at the end of the long hallway. This beautiful boardroom was where the big meetings took place with clients.

Now, there had always been revelations in this room, for this is the nature of big business. And there were always secrets in this room; some never discussed outside of those walls. Some were incredible surprises. Others were eyes-only presentations unveiled when the window sheers or drapes were drawn.

But there was one thing that was certainly *not* secret in this wondrous room. It was the very large framed portrait under glass, proudly hanging on the wall to the right as you entered. The fabulous Ford Mystere dream car. What few people outside of the car business knew was that Creative Industries actually built the Mystere for Ford Motor Company.

The Design

As you might imagine, several designers and clay modelers were involved in this futuristic concept, but the principal designer on the Mystere was Ford's Bill Boyer. He was a design genius. Working under Frank Hershey, Bill Boyer is also credited as father of the original Thunderbird that debuted for the 1955 model year.

As concept cars went, the Mystere was one of Ford's crowning glories in their growing portfolio of dream cars. The wild FX-Atmos preceding it had also been constructed by Creative, but only the Mystere and the Lincoln Futura rose to such stellar status.

The mind-set of the 1950s, particularly in North America, was somewhat unique. One of the differences was an almost unbridled enthusiasm for the future. It embraced an immutable faith and optimism that a perfect world of wonder was somehow just right around the corner. In that imagined world of the not-too-distant future, people would live together in harmony. Automobiles would perform incredible feats, serving all our needs and would thus be the living embodiment of that future.

Bill Resztak (cigar) and unknown Creative staffer constructing a motorized juvenile car. Note the Mystere-like side trim sweep molded into body. (Photo Courtesy Jim Resztak Collection)

Framed image of the Ford Mystere hung on boardroom wall at headquarters for Creative Industries of Detroit at 3080 East Outer Drive. No idea where it is today.

Rear view of the Mystere shows rocket-like styling along with "rabbit ears" style antenna, considered futuristic in 1950s and used on many home televisions.

Movie star Clark Gable sits with unidentified passenger in his new 1955 Thunderbird. Car was fitted with special supercharger.

The Mystere shows off its pearlescent Magenta, Raven Black, and pearlescent white colors and the Creative-built large bubble top. Grille pods in the front bumper were claimed to house oil coolers for the gas turbine engine. (Photo Courtesy Ford Motor Company)

Cynicism was something that began to arrive in the 1960s, and became set in concrete by the 1970s. But the 1950s were virtually immune of what developed later, particularly regarding automobiles.

The Mystere was a concept that truly represented the very essence of a dream car. It, in fact, actually got people dreaming.

Although the Mystere was part fantasy, part science fiction, it had another intangible quality that made it endearing. The Ford Mystere was a dream car, but it had features that were just familiar enough to show a lineage from what you saw out on the streets at the time and something you could wrap your mind around as a possibility

The Mystere was a visual masterpiece, all backed up with charts and explanations and press releases that had an almost hypnotic effect on anyone who saw it. Ford even had Mystere photographed with an elegant, sensuous Marilyn Monroe–like model in a pink A-line dress and T-strap heels. Floodlights

didn't merely illuminate the Mystere; they were like glowing hands that caressed the sinuous lines and curves of the car. Every glint and glisten as the car sat on display made a viewer want to possess it. The Mystere story began at Ford Styling in Dearborn, Michigan.

Rarely did a single automotive designer manage to see his ideas on paper transformed into an actual car, but it occasionally happened. One such instance involved a talented visionary in Dearborn who pretty much had that elusive privilege not once, but twice. His name was William P. Boyer and like Creative's Lynn Griffin, he was a graduate of Pratt Institute. After graduation, Boyer went to work for General Motors, but by the early 1950s, he moved to Ford's realm. It was there his talent truly took wing. Working under Frank Hershey, Bill's work at Ford ultimately resulted in this talented designer creating much of what became the new Ford Thunderbird that debuted for the 1955 model year.

Model with 1950s A-line dress and T-strap shoes shows off the Mystere's captivating lines. Some today might refer to rear grille as a "diffuser" but purpose was not racing, it was rather to vent heat imagined from rear-mounted gas turbine engine. (Photo Courtesy Ford Motor Company)

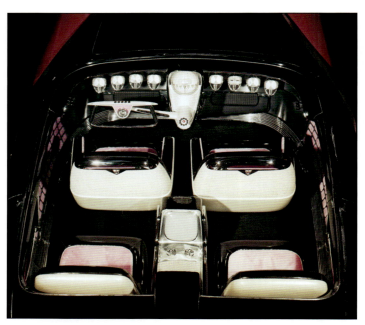

The Mystere interior was as modern as today. Aircraft style steering control could be swapped from left to right. Note pushbuttons on steering wheel. Gauges floated in clear alcohol. Television in rear was way ahead for 1950s and created a sensation. Bucket seats with armrests would not appear in production for decades. Colors and brushed finishes were very trendy. Ribbed curving lower trim would finally appear on 1961–1963 Thunderbird. Involvement of Creative was not mentioned openly. (Photo Courtesy Ford Motor Company)

Build Team

Thunderbird was a hit in sales, but Ford had even more ambitious plans for yet another dream car. Once satisfied with the refined Bill Boyer design, it began to take shape in full-size clay over at the Ford styling studios in Dearborn. Like the FX-Atmos, this new Ford concept was made of fiberglass and Creative Industries also constructed it. But here is where the story gets a bit confused. Some say that a plaster plug was pulled at Ford. Others say that the clay was brought to Creative and plaster molds pulled.

However it happened, the task to build the Mystere was handed over to Creative Industries of Detroit. David Margolis and Gary Hutchings were immediately attached to the project. Dave oversaw the entire project from Creative's end while Gary was immediate supervisor, working in contact with Bill Boyer.

Garriston Hutchings was a hands-on kind of guy and immensely talented. He had worked on virtually every dream car project ever done at Creative in the 1950s. Hutchings thought his name was a tad too formal, so he preferred to be called Gary. He was always enthusiastic about cars and a wonderful encyclopedic source of information about Creative.

Gary loved the car business and felt at his best only when he was knee-deep in the creation of some new automobile or technology. He (along with Hugh Olson who arrived in 1957) was Creative's go-to man for fiberglass and plastics. But Gary also knew his steel and he knew his paints. And Hutchings was there when a lot of key things happened at Creative. He actually worked on projects for Packard, such as Ed Macauley's Phantom/Panther and Pan American. And Dick Teague's Balboa, Panthers, and Request. Gary was one of the crew that resurrected the Packard Predictor when it caught fire and got it operational (and kept it that way) for the auto shows. He had worked on Ford FX-Atmos and when Ford came calling about more dream car projects, of course, Gary was all too eager to help bring these cars to reality.

Back at the Outer Drive facility, a metal chassis of sorts was rigged up for the Mystere in the rear shop where heavy welding took place. This chassis was nothing like a typical automotive frame, but rather it was merely to support the finished car and hold the wheels.

Said Gary, "It didn't have a real suspension and Ford basically just wanted it to be strictly for looks. Dave and I were gung-ho to make it [the Mystere] into a real car. And we had aircraft engineers working for the company who were just itching to put a turbine into that car and make it go, but as with the Atmos, the Ford guys turned us down and Dave said to just keep quiet about it. So we gave up. As I recall, we just welded a steel box frame to put under it and we went to work from there. It was too bad, because you could just look at that thing and imagine a turbine whining out back and whooshing it off down the highway!"

But there is so much irony here because the operable 1955 Thunderbird gas turbine with the Boeing 701 engine was not merely a frivolous, futile exercise.

Creative staffers had suggested a way to put a turbine in the FX-Atmos and they were even more ready to drop one in the Mystere. Dave Margolis noted, "Our aircraft engineer guys drew up a turbine application for the Mystere. If Ford had given us the time and the green light to do it, we could have had the engine in the car. A little more time and money and we could have had it running."

But there was no budget and no staff at Ford to build both a dream car and turbine car all in one. Ford had decided not to chase after General Motors. Meanwhile over at Chrysler, George Huebner was already doing press interviews with his fully operable running 1954 Plymouth Turbine Special. Chrysler had taken a quantum leap ahead of everyone else, so at that point, the buzz about gas turbines in cars was at a fever pitch in Detroit. So just to hedge their bets and cover all bases, Ford PR people continued to indicate that a conventional engine could also be installed.

The grilled pods in the front bumpers were claimed to be oil coolers (again, potential turbine stuff). Out back was what some folks today might call a "diffuser," but again this was thought of at the time as a rear grille to release heat and ventilate a gas turbine engine.

Turbine Engine

Countless newspaper and magazine stories talked about a gas turbine engine in the Mystere. The headline in a feature debut story on the Mystere in *Popular Science* said, "Ford Designs a Body for a Gas Turbine," just like that. So something had to be going on behind the scenes. In 1957, the *Bristol Daily Courier* of Bristol, Pennsylvania, ran a story on Mystere when it was on display in Philadelphia. The headline was, "Dream Car Can Use Turbine or Gas Engines." So what brought that on? A newspaper report on the 1958 Auto Show for St. Paul, Minnesota, referred to the "turbine-powered Ford Mystere" and called the display "a glimpse into the future." As late as the 1960s, the Florida *St. Petersburg Times* referred to the Mystere as an "engineering research vehicle" and stated that it had a gas turbine engine.

Hutchings and his crew were disappointed, but they continued work on the Mystere, pulling molds and laying up sections of the body in fiberglass. According to Gary, all of this work was again done over at Creative's Mt. Elliott facility, where the Dodge Granada and Packard Panther bodies were being fabricated. Gary Hutchings and his crew pressed ahead, working feverishly on the Mystere. Ford (actually Frank Hershey) had set a deadline that Creative was now racing to meet.

You could naturally assume that with all of the systems not needing to hook up and actually function, there would have been some great reduction in electrical work needed. After all, there were no full wiring circuits and fusing. Right? Wrong. It would not be quite that easy. The Mystere was a pushmobile, but it was hardly *all* fake. Those quad headlights as well as the big taillights and interior gauges were 100 percent illuminated.

Gary Hutchings and crew had to hand-build an almost complete automotive type wire harness, complete with bulbs, sockets, connecters, and fuses, to power all this lighting. A wiring harness for an onboard battery had to be devised. And then came the gauges.

The full set of futuristic gauges had to *look* operable; and again, they also had to illuminate. But Gary and his crew quickly discovered the gauges, fake or not, would be no walk in the park.

The gauges were highly unusual in both appearance and function. Each meter other than the speedometer was encased in a plexiglass housing that contained clear liquid. The gauges had to remain legible; and above all, they couldn't leak or cause staining.

There was an array of eight in all (four in front of each front seat). In addition to the usual fuel, ammeter, oil pressure,

PRODUCTION CAR FEATURES

- Inspired design and exterior trim on 1955 through 1957 Fords
- "Oil cooler" pods out on the front bumper inspired the parking light/turn signals of 1956 Fords
- Basket-handle "meeting bar" roll bar inspired 1955–1956 Ford Crown Victoria models, especially those with Skyliner transparent roof panel. Porsche's "Targa bar" was similar years later
- 1958 Thunderbird owed a lot to the Mystere's four-passenger bucket seat interior
- Electronic push-button transmission controls became Edsel Tele-touch
- Electronic push-button ignition with security number operation
- The Mystere's height was the same as that of the 1955 Thunderbird
- Phone with microphone for the driver predicted both phones in cars and "hands-free" safety operation of recent years
- TV in rear of automobiles today
- The rocket-like turbine exhausts and taillights topped by fins were eventually everywhere. From FIAT 8V to 1961–1963 Thunderbird, to the almighty 1959 Cadillac (the early renderings of Mystere even bore ironic, predicting resemblance to the 1959 Cadillac turn signal/parking light/fog light assemblies)
- Just about everybody had quad headlights in the United States by 1958
- Finally, a "rabbit ears" antenna array was mounted on the rear deck. This was considered *very* futuristic and modern at the time. Many people were beginning to buy similar-looking antennas for their television at home, but TV rabbit ears became a very popular automotive accessory from Sony and Panasonic for cars and limos in the 1960s and 1970s

and coolant temperature, there were also bearing temperature, tachometer, inclinometer, and altimeter indicators.

In my December 1978 article for *Car Classics*, Gary said, "I had one heck of a time getting those gauges installed. I think we installed them in an alcohol liquid. They floated, you know!" Years later, someone who worked in the shops at Creative back then told me, "Guess we made Cunningham's happy that day. One of our guys went in and bought ten or fifteen bottles of the stuff!" Cunningham's was a popular old drug store chain well known to Detroiters from the glory days.

Gary was also one who was excited about unusual, new techniques and looks in automotive paints. And Creative was

MYSTERE FEATURES

- Gas turbine engine (proposed)
- Special gauges: bearing temperature, fuel, oil pressure, tachometer, inclinometer, altimeter
- Hands-free radio-telephone with microphone in steering wheel
- Push-button ignition switch operated like a combination lock
- Clear bubble canopy
- Quad headlights
- Roll bar
- Either-or steering (left-hand or right-hand) with rectangular steering wheel
- Electronic push-button transmission selector mounted on steering wheel
- Front and rear swivel bucket seats with armrests
- Rear-mounted television in center console
- Front and rear radio-audio system
- Roof-mounted air conditioning and "flow-through" ventilation
- Overhead console with aircraft-type switches/controls
- Floating gauges
- Rear-mounted "rabbit ears" dual antenna array
- Side quarter intake scoops for turbine engine
- Rear diffuser to release engine heat
- Oil coolers mounted in front bumper
- Tri-tone paint colors
- Height was 52 inches, wheelbase was 121 inches, and width was 80 inches

Bill Resztak sets up welding on chassis for motorized juvenile car built at Creative. (Photo Courtesy Jim Resztak Collection)

a great pioneer in eye-popping paint jobs during the 1950s and 1960s. Creative did a great deal of work with experimental paints, particularly with Rinshed-Mason Company. Creative Industries was one of the first to use mother-of-pearl finishes on show cars they built. Today this kind of paint finish is not a particularly unusual thing, but in the 1950s it was heart stopping! Most people had never seen a car painted that way before.

Over the years, the Mystere was done in three overall color schemes (all had a pearl-white "meeting bar"): Pearlescent magenta and black, iridescent light blue, and metallic dark blue, and iridescent murano pearl white and pearlescent pink.

Steering Mechanism

Some accounts have implied that the steering mechanism in the Mystere was adapted from an airplane. This notion certainly seems very likely. There were those in design at Ford who were aircraft enthusiasts. But at Creative, the influence was even more pronounced. What were the favorite pastimes of the two big honchos at Creative: Fred Johnson and Rex Terry? Both were die-hard pilots. Creative was always involved in aircraft design and actually designed, engineered, and even manufactured numerous aircraft components. This is a little-known fact, but certainly a very important point to remember.

David Margolis once told me that Creative had made several suggestions to Ford's people about various aspects of the Mystere. One of these had to do with the steering wheel and mechanism.

A central pivot allowed the steering to rotate to an "either-or" position. This was one of the first times when a car was instantly adaptable to driving British style with the driver sitting on the right and the car oriented to driving on the left side of the road, or American-style with the driver seated left and driving to the right of the road. In other words, the Mystere could be driven anywhere in the world, at least in theory.

The Mystere was also one of the first cars to take a single hood ornament and split it into two trim pieces atop the fenders. This provided the driver now with a better gauge for the

Creative's Outer Drive facility photo shows Creative's Bill Resztak (left) and Johnny Wilson setting up a juvenile car to be donated to Detroit Zoo for popular Jo Mendi chimp show. (Photo Courtesy Jim Resztak Collection)

Rear of Detroit Zoo's Jo Mendi chimp show car under construction at Creative. Body was aluminum. (Photo Courtesy Jim Resztak Collection)

Creative's Bill Resztak setting up another juvenile car. A two-tone blue version of this model would be built for Rex Terry's daughter, Pamela. Engines were Briggs & Stratton; bodies of this style were fiberglass. (Photo Courtesy Jim Resztak Collection)

Creative's Bill Resztak demonstrates light weight of fiberglass juvenile car bare body. Some think side trim was intended to show off Creative's offset "V" logo in stylized form. Others think it was to mimic Ford Mystere. And yes, Bill worked on the Mystere. (Photo Courtesy Jim Resztak Collection)

Photo taken at rear of Creative's Outer Drive facility shows Creative's Bill Resztak with completed juvenile car and Rex Terry's Packard Panther. Date written on photo is mistaken since Panther has 1954½ update already completed and Buick at left is 1955 model. (Photo Courtesy Jim Resztak Collection)

Rear of Creative's Outer Drive facility shows completed juvenile car and Rex Terry's Packard Panther were originally both painted silver and black. Date written on photo is mistaken since Panther has 1954½ update already completed with 1955 Packard taillights. Note "dual exhaust" ports on juvenile car, along with Mystere-like side trim. (Photo Courtesy Jim Resztak Collection)

fender tips and made the vehicle look wider and lower. And those fender tips would certainly be wider once the industry followed the Mystere and adopted four headlights rather than two. The Mystere's press releases claimed that the extra headlights were actually two sets: one for city and the other for highway driving. Quad headlights are old hat today, but when the Mystere first rolled out in 1955, four headlight beams were considered futuristic!

Press Reviews

Despite the fact that it was inoperable, the Mystere looked incredible, and most newspapers and magazines treated Mystere as if it were a real car.

The *Bristol Daily Courier* newspaper reported in November 1957, "A hinged bubble-type glass canopy forms the roof. The hinged forward section and the fixed rear section meet at the center at a steel meeting bar, which also serves as a roll bar. Mystere is entered by raising the forward half of the glass bubble-type roof, hinged at the hood cowl." *Popular Science* said just the opposite and reported that the Mystere's bubble canopy "hinged at the back, can be pushed up 70 degrees. Passengers get in and out through half doors. The front seats swivel outward to make it easier." In the 1960s, while the Mystere was still making the rounds, *St. Petersburg Times* reported, "The rear canopy is fixed. The front canopy is hinged to the cowl panel and opens for passenger entrance. Simultaneously with the raising of the forward canopy, the doors open to facilitate passenger entry and exit." Numerous news reports claimed that the Mystere doors either swung out or folded down, but the fact is that they were merely outlines in the body. In reality, and like the FX-Atmos, neither the Mystere's doors nor top ever actually worked. It was all just show business.

As was the case with the FX-Atmos. Dave Margolis said that Creative had wanted to make all these features operational, but there was no time and no budget. "We did make a duplicate seating mock-up of the interior for Ford," but this has never been mentioned. Some journalists claimed to have actually sat in the Mystere, but this was either with the top removed and person hoisted in or possibly done in Creative's seating mock-up. *Popular Science* indeed showed men seated in the car with what appears to be either the roof removed or an interior mock-up. One photo showed what looks like Bill Boyer "talking" on a telephone while seated in the rear. Another photo showed two occupants in the front seats swapping the steering controls from one side to the other.

Popular Science went on to say, "A push-button ignition switch works like a combination lock on a safe." Had the switch gone into production, the theory was that each car would have its own unique combination number similar to Ford Motor Company's door-mounted pushbutton keyless entry of recent years.

When it debuted to the press at the magical Ford Rotunda in October 1955, the Mystere was a mind blower. According to Dave Margolis, even the press people who thought they had seen everything were not fully prepared for the incredible Mystere. Although the FX-Atmos had plenty of wow factor, it was so far out that some journalists dismissed it more or less as pure fancy. But the Mystere? Somehow it *seemed* more real, despite the fact that it was only a pushmobile. Whether they believed the Mystere was real or not, unlike FX-Atmos, Mystere was treated as the real thing in the press, even years later.

What Happened to the Mystere?

In short, the Mystere had it all: bubble top, sporty interior with gadgets, the trendiest colors, mystery engine, the most futuristic look and features. But despite its wild popularity, incredible looks, and features, Mystere was still a pushmobile. The fantasy had finally been outrun by the reality.

The Mystere had an unusually long show life for an early concept, especially being a pushmobile. The Mystere was still making the rounds in the 1960s, claiming to be an "engineering research vehicle." It was still in newspapers such as the *St. Petersburg Times* in the 1970s. And over the years, the car morphed into multiple color schemes. Several publications claimed that the Mystere had cost Ford in excess of $225,000 (1950s dollars) to build. So with that kind of money invested, it seemed that the Mystere would be a permanent fixture on the automotive scene.

According the David Margolis, Creative was called upon once again to do some refreshening work on the Mystere, but Dave (as usual) did not specify what that work was. But by 1959, the black areas of the car were repainted white, and that was a bad move. From time to time, photos of the Mystere turn up in this underwhelming color scheme. Looking at these images leaves little wonder why Ford eventually turned its attention away. After that, the Mystere's trail became increasingly obscure. Whatever happened, appreciation for the Mystere had somehow begun to wane.

The life of a show car is only as long as both the public and the corporate heads see it as valuable. Once such a concept car drops off the corporate radar, bad things usually begin to happen. Double that equation if said concept is a pushmobile. Unfortunately, the Mystere fell under all these headings. It was rumored during the 1970s that the Mystere was dusty, damaged, and forgotten, and ignominiously pushed from one storage spot to another in Dearborn. The unforgettable dream car had unfortunately become forgotten.

I finally learned of the Mystere's fate one night years later and thousands of miles away from Detroit. My late friend, designer Herb Grasse, told me an interesting story over dinner one night in the 1980s at a restaurant in Hiroshima, Japan. At the time,

Herb was running design for Ford of Australia and living with his wife on one of the top floors of a very nice Hiroshima hotel (I believe that Bill Boyer preceded Herb in this Ford position).

I asked Herb if he knew the whereabouts of the Mystere. He shook his head and responded, "Sad story. I hear via the Ford grapevine that somebody ordered it cut up." I was mortified and looked at Herb in disbelief, knowing he was a big prankster and hoping it was all a joke. I waited for the laugh, but Herb was dead serious. He assured me it was no joke. "It wasn't too long ago either, it was still hanging around. The Mystere was in pretty bad shape, and they just didn't want to save it anymore. It's gone."

The Creative-Built Mystere-Inspired Junior Car

Rex Terry's daughter, Pamela, was the apple of his eye. During the time that Creative was building the Mystere, they were also under contract to build several small-motorized cars. At least two such cars were donated to the famous Detroit Zoo, to be used by a famous chimpanzee there. The zoo had a hugely popular chimpanzee show (in those days you couldn't have a TV show, movie, or stage show without chimpanzees in it). The chimp show was the hit of the zoo and kids in the Detroit area all begged their parents to go see it.

Named Jo Mendi, this chimp was world famous and was not really just one chimp, but a lineage of chimpanzees given this name. Originally out of New York at least by the 1930s, the Jo Mendi act was known for smoking cigars, driving a car, and even changing a flat tire! So eventually the act and Jo (supposedly one of the long line of descendants) ended up at the Detroit Zoo. Where else would a chimp who drove a car go to live in those days?

Creative built at least two cars for Jo and the chimps to use in the show at the Detroit Zoo. Rex Terry donated these cars on behalf of Creative. Each featured electric headlights and taillights. Power was by Briggs & Stratton motors. They had an accelerator and brake pedals, inflatable tires, and a parking brake. There were chrome bumpers and a beautiful little split windshield. For reasons unknown, a Dodge hood ornament from a full-size automobile was installed on the hoods of these cars.

The very first of these cars was constructed out of aluminum. It is possible that the second was constructed in the same material. However, subsequent versions were built out of fiberglass.

Rex instructed Dave Margolis to set aside an extra chassis like the one built for the Jo Mendi cars. This chassis was used to carry a different body made of fiberglass. It became a motorized miniature car for his daughter Pamela.

The Creative employee who actually constructed these cars was William Resztak, who loved doing this kind of work and actually built numerous juvenile and miniature motorized cars.

Bill Resztak and other Creative staffers admiring completed juvenile car and Rex Terry's newly updated Packard Panther. (Photo Courtesy Jim Resztak Collection)

Bill was a highly skilled staffer who also worked on lots of Creative projects and was the key man who worked on President Eisenhower's bubble-top Lincoln limo. I believe that Bill also constructed the chassis for the Mystere.

Also powered by a Briggs & Stratton gasoline motor, this little car was fully drivable with brakes and electric lighting. The front cross member of this chassis constructed by Resztak had a little red rectangular metal tag riveted on. It said "Creative Industries of Detroit" with a serial number along the bottom.

The body of the cars as used for Jo Mendi was the basis for Pamela's little new car. However, it was made of fiberglass and modernized in appearance, yet basically the same underneath. The flat style split windshield of the Mendi car was deleted in favor of a modern wraparound windshield (a mid-1950s must-have!). The same bumpers, wheels, tires, and hubcaps were carried over. The same Darrin-esque "dip" on the trailing end of the door was retained from the Jo Mendi car. However, the bulging rear fenders were eliminated, along with the side-mounted taillights (someone said these were originally bus clearance lights). The new rear fenders were flush with the body and included mock tailfins. The side-mounted taillights on the Mendi car were then repositioned at the rear of the tailfins and pointed downward, resulting in a kind of modern hooded look.

The styling of the body on this car was inspired by the fabulous Mystere. Like the Mystere, the sweep of the hooded headlight flowed back into the front fender of this little car. And the thin horizontal bars on the front of the Mystere? Translated into a little grille also made of thin horizontal bars. The center crease of the Mystere's hood? That was translated over to the little car, too.

New Mystere-like sweeping side trim was also a kind of stealth send-up of the Creative offset "V" logo. In addition, the thick molding sweep along the side made up for body rigidity lost when the bulge of the rear fenders were removed. The new Mystere trim sweep on the side of Pamela's little motorized car was not merely cosmetic but also functioned now as a side-impact brace. A built-in safety feature!

As time passed and Pamela matured and grew taller, she began telling her dad that she wanted a horse. But where would you find a horse in the Detroit area in the 1950s? Fortunately Rex's friend, Don Mitchell (of Mitchell-Bentley over in Owosso) and his wife, Metta, bred and raised horses as a hobby. They had a lovely farm they called "Donmetta" where their prized horses pranced and grazed in the fields. Don's daughter, Sue, was often featured at shows with one of her prize-winning horses.

So naturally Rex put in a call to Don about a horse for Pamela. By coincidence, it just so happened that Don's granddaughter Kristi was pining away for a little car like the one Pamela had, and Pamela wanted a horse! Well, the upshot of this was that the two powerhouse car biz men traded to make the little girls in their lives smile. Pamela's little car went to Don Mitchell, where it was re-trimmed for his granddaughter, and a beautiful horse came back for Rex's daughter. And all was right with the world.

Pamela's car was renamed "Kristi's car" and was painted silver-gray and medium blue. Like the Jo Mendi car, a real automotive hood ornament was added. When it appeared years later in the Mitchell museum, a logo from a brass-era Mitchell car had also been affixed to the rear quarters

So what happened to this little Creative Industries car? I inspected the Kristi car at the Mitchell auction in late 2014 and sure enough, the little red plate saying Creative Industries of Detroit was still on the front crossmember of the chassis. After the auction, this little car dropped out of sight but was last rumored to be living in Florida. There were more interesting little cars to come from Creative Industries of Detroit.

Pamela Terry sits in her new Creative-built motorized car in Outer Drive shop area about 1954. Motor was Briggs & Stratton. Headlights and brakes all worked! Color here was two-tone blue. (Photo Courtesy Pamela Terry Bonk)

Pamela Terry's car as it looked when last seen by the author in 2014 at a museum auction.

CHAPTER THIRTEEN

EL MOROCCO, FLOATING ON AIR, PLYMOUTH XP-VIP AND JUNIOR PLYMOUTHS TOO!

*H*igh-tech glass, safety, and the invention of Chameleon paint plus how musicians, bright thinking, and Creative led to a car named for a Las Vegas hotel.

When Chevrolets Became Cadillac El Dorados

And now, a little history on a rare custom-built car made in Detroit during the 1950s. And how Chevrolet Bel Airs were transformed (through the magic of Creative Industries) into Cadillac Eldorados, or at least something that looked like them.

A man my father and uncle both knew in the 1950s had a huge fabric warehouse on East Forest Avenue near the big railroad crossing in Detroit. His name was Reuben Allender. My dad often took me to visit with Reuben Allender in his warehouse. There one could spend hours in the inner sanctum looking through all of the amazing items. I recall my father talking endlessly with Allender about cars, and in particular the Cadillac Eldorado.

Allender was originally from Canada and had done very well in his business enterprises. Although my uncle's business was in Detroit, he too had built a house in Canada and lived there since the 1940s. They also both loved Cadillacs. Allender was fascinated by all of this.

Now, to this day, I can't recall all of the details about how Allender and music got connected. But famous jazz musicians from all over the world used to come to visit at my uncle's music shop. Sometimes they just wanted to see the latest instruments or to chat and socialize. Everyone you could imagine from Miles Davis, to Dave Brubeck, to Charlie Parker was a customer, or at least had dropped by once. And those who were doing well (and some who weren't) often pulled up in fancy cars.

Out of these people, one tall, lanky fellow in particular really impressed Reuben Allender. He was a tenor and baritone sax player named Floyd "Candy" Johnson. As far back as the early 1950s, we just knew him as Candy. He had played with all of the greats, including Duke Ellington and Count Basie. Candy was a showman and recording artist and had also done pretty well for himself.

Although Allender probably liked Candy's playing as so many others did, I recall there was something else that also

Photo shows off clean lines of XP-VIP "idea car." Overall body shape reflected Plymouth's new long and low understated production body style for 1965. Stubs of glass (or plexiglass) just peek upward at rear beltline to imply retracted glass roof, which was claimed to be sun reactive. Supposedly, flexible glass roof would slide forward in grooved guides in sides of roof bar.

impressed Allender. Candy was probably the first person I knew to buy a new 1955 Cadillac Eldorado. In those days, this was considered a real spaceship of a design. The rear end of the body was said to be a prediction of future regular Cadillacs, so the Eldorado was really something special. Candy had his Eldorado tricked out just a little with a special paint job. When Allender saw Candy's Eldorado, something must have clicked in his head. I know he went right out and bought one, too.

Many musicians loved flashy cars like Candy's Eldorado. But they could rarely afford one. Ruby had some kind of fantastic idea to convert a Chevrolet over to looking like an Eldorado. He reasoned that he could make serious money selling such customized cars to people who wanted a cool-looking Eldo, but had no prayer of affording one. Allender wondered how and if anyone could do the job.

However it transpired, Reuben Allender indeed somehow connected with Creative Industries and the impressive, unusual El Morocco series was born. The September 1956 issue of *Motor Trend* featured a white El Morocco convertible with Florida license plates on the cover. *Motor Trend* referred to it as a "baby Cadillac."

In an unusual turn, *Motor Trend* actually acknowledged Creative Industries and their involvement with El Morocco. The article by Don MacDonald stated, "The beautifully adapted Fiberglas fins on the El Morocco were prototyped by Detroit's

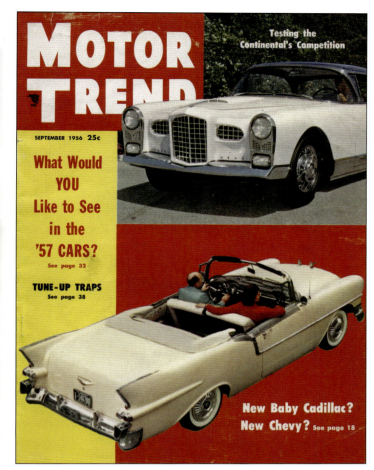

September 1956 cover of Motor Trend *features an early version of the El Morocco based on 1956 Chevrolet, but looking very much like 1956 Cadillac Eldorado. The magazine refers to El Morocco as a "baby Cadillac." Prototype and quarter fins were done by Creative Industries of Detroit.*

New 1957 version of El Morocco was based on 1957 Chevy, but made to look like 1957–58 Cadillac Eldorado Brougham. This original sales literature was given to author by Reuben Allender in the 1950s. Note official name for 1957 was "El Morocco Brougham."

Creative Industries, a firm known for building Ford's Atmos, Packard's Panther and a number of other popular show cars. Creative built molds from the prototype so production is now relatively simple. The spanking new Chevy convertible arrives from one of Detroit's dealers with whom Allender has contractual arrangements. A large chunk of the rear fender is cut away and the laminated Fiberglas fins are bolted in place. Epoxy resin is used to bond the laminates as well as the plastic to the metal in an invisible joint."

The magazine listed Allender's actual R. Allender & Company fabric warehouse address at 1966 East Forest Avenue, Detroit, Michigan.

El Morocco was more purely ingenious handiwork from Creative. The taillights were adapted from the current Dodge. Dagmars were converted from old surplus headlight buckets. List price was $3,250, including a 265-ci Chevy Powerpak engine. This was less than half the price of a new Cadillac Eldorado convertible, so Allender envisioned a bunch of buyers would result. Of course, this rush of buyers never happened. Sales never reached more than a trickle, but he was in business.

Allender eventually set up a kind of makeshift assembly line in a building not far from Detroit's Belle Isle Park. Conversions of Chevrolets took place there.

When the new, even wilder 1957 Eldorado Brougham debuted and Creative's Rex Terry had one right away, Reuben Allender made a new decision. There would be a new El Morocco, but this next model would look like the Brougham instead of just a regular Eldorado. With more help from Creative and more clever parts swapping, Allender wound up with a 1957 Chevrolet that looked for all the world like an Eldo Brougham, at 30 feet away. But not many of these new El Morocco customs found homes either.

With the radical body change for the 1958 Chevy, Allender finally threw in the towel on El Morocco. A rather forlorn El Morocco often continued to sit out front of R. Allender & Company on East Forest Avenue. I last saw it in the dead of a winter, parked at the curb on Forest with plowed snow piled high all around it. The car apparently had not moved in a while. And then it was gone.

Years later, one of the guys I knew at Creative told me they had worked up another El Morocco prototype based on a newer

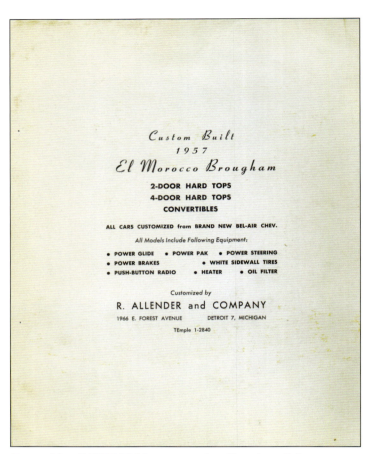

Rear side of 1957 El Morocco sales literature lists specs and give address for R. Allender and Company on East Forest Avenue in Detroit. But no mention of Creative Industries.

Dr. Bertleson's futuristic air car went by several names. Taking shape here in full-size clay in Creative Industries shop on Outer Drive. Note raised precision plate appears to be identical to one used later for AMX. Corrugated metal partition in background was one of Creative's locked security enclosures.

Chevy. This new El Morocco would have had a space-age modern look with fins. But I never saw the car.

The Ford Levacar and Creative's Air Car

At the beginning of the 1960s, one Detroit newspaper ran an article in their Sunday magazine that showed Detroit's expressways of the future all paved in green grass. After all, environmentalism was emerging, and if there was no reason to pave roadways in a future of floating, hovering cars, why not pave the freeways in grass? Anyway, it was one of those ideas that was talked about very seriously in the 1960s.

Along this theme, Ford introduced its single-passenger Mach I Levacar concept. It was right in step with what were then thought to be directions for the future. Levacar drew large crowds for regular demonstrations at the Ford Rotunda.

The Levacar floated on a cushion of air and could literally be pushed forward or backward by a simple nudge. Nobody quite explained how it would brake, but Levacar was talked about as capable of moving along special roadways at high speed. At the time, this notion was completely believable. It was an amazing idea and so very futuristic to our eyes back then. Levacar's theme also had serious impact on the industry. And the magazines were filled with floating and hovering cars. In fact, *Popular Mechanics* ran a rather extensive story on hover cars and hovercraft in its June 1960 issue.

Although Creative Industries was rumored to have had some involvement with Ford's Levacar, there is no hard evidence of a direct connection, as usual, with Creative. But there were some circumstantial clues that could suggest at least a

Futuristic 1960s trade exhibition in Japan featured Bertleson hovering/floating air car, referred to here as "Aeromobile." Creative head Rex Terry attended exhibition and gave talks with Dr. Bertleson as car was demonstrated. "Creative Industries" sign spun in breezes. (Photo Courtesy Pamela Terry Bonk)

Actual demonstration of Creative-built Bertleson Aeromobile in U.S. trade exhibition held in 1961 at Zagreb in Europe. Huge crowds squeezed in to demonstrations, thrilled to watch vehicle glide on air cushion.

common ground. For one thing, a Levacar-looking graphic was used on the backboard display for Creative's booth at industry trade shows. I also saw lots of artwork for Levacar-looking wheel-less hovering vehicles in Creative's files.

And then came Creative's involvement with Dr. William R. Bertleson of Illinois. Dr. Bertleson invented his own hovercar and was featured in the 1960 *Popular Mechanics* article. Dr. Bertleson, who I met at an SAE conference, was reportedly a surgeon, but he was seriously interested in manufacturing. Here is where Creative Industries again enters the picture.

One way or another, funding was put together that made a version of Dr. Bertleson's hovering car a reality. Creative built a full-size clay model, pulled molds, built a mechanical understructure, and completed a working car of sorts. This vehicle

Rear cover of impressive XP-VIP brochure shows off futuristic full-width taillight. Design actually located illumination protected in steel crossbar (indirect, reflected off pressed metal array). Note license plate here reads "XP-VIP."

was put on world tour with U.S. trade exhibitions and went to Japan and Europe, among other areas. It was quite famous during the early 1960s.

The 1965 Plymouth XP-VIP

By 1965, Chrysler's Plymouth Division was seriously devoted to increasing their market share. The new designs for Plymouths were downright beautiful. Skin of the new bodies had the appearance of being stretched taught over a powerful block. Ornamentation was minimal and linear. The Fury series now looked more luxurious with all of the customary descriptive terms: longer, lower, wider, if not in measurement, certainly in appearance.

And to announce Plymouth's new styling direction and modern philosophies, what better way to do so than with a new concept car based on the production body? This concept was a "strut your stuff" dramatic departure for Plymouth and contained almost every futuristic technology and system imaginable at the time. And who better to build this new concept than Creative Industries? Of course.

And so it was that Creative received the assignment to build what was first known as "XP-VIP" and later, simply "VIP." It represented a whole new level of sophistication for Plymouth. And, at least at the time, took the marque outside of both the dowdy economy image and street racer box and placed it squarely in new territory; someplace the name had never quite gone before. XP-VIP is severely overlooked in histories, but it was a milestone when it first hit the auto shows for the 1965 model year. Here is a little history that has been largely forgotten.

The American car industry at the time was toying with converting their standard production faire into luxury highline models. The opening salvo was probably fired when Ford introduced the new LTD series in 1965. As incredible as it may seem, Ford pitted an LTD against luxury icon Rolls-Royce in a comparison of interior quietness. After all, magazines had pitted the Pontiac GTO and 2+2 up against Ferraris! Why not a Ford against a Rolls?

The amazing LTD was reported to be quieter inside than a Rolls-Royce. Ford ran a commercial showing the test results to an amazed viewing audience that had never heard of Ford LTD before. From that point forward, the old model names were lost in the shuffle and soon forgotten. The LTD remained the top of the Ford line for decades to follow. Chevrolet followed suit with the upgraded new Caprice line, released as a luxurious four-door hardtop for 1965½. Plymouth eventually entered the foray with a production of luxurious series named VIP for 1966. But in Plymouth's case, the concept car came first, and it was a hottie. All were built by Creative Industries.

Original composite press photo shows extremely clean lines of XP-VIP front. Rectangular headlights were illegal in the United States but considered very futuristic in 1965. Although originally named "XP-VIP," license plate here hints toward name of upscale production model that would appear in 1966. Roof was actually longitudinal roll bar.

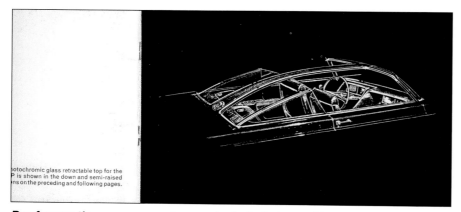

Roof operation was never demonstrated at shows. No actual photos of roof were distributed. XP-VIP brochure illustration was artist's depiction of roof, partially extended here.

I remember seeing the XP-VIP at the Detroit auto show. It was on a turntable with lots of floodlights. People jostled to get a better look at the slowly revolving beauty. And as they did, you could hear folks struggling to describe the color. But there was no single color. Aside from the very clean lines and interesting design, the color, or better yet, colors were one of the most amazing features of this "idea car" (as Chrysler Corporation called it).

As the sleek body turned in the lights, the color transformed from a deep iridescent burgundy, to brown, to iridescent chartreuse, to nail polish pink, to goldish tones, to almost bluish, and then back again. It was one of the few concepts I saw that was positively hypnotic on the stand. People stood slack-jawed, trying to decide what color the car would be in the next second and what to call it. Somebody, somewhere had really done some clever thinking.

Creative's Gary Hutchings told me years later, "The VIP was done with a whole new kind of paint. We called it 'chameleon.' But it drove our painter crazy trying to keep up with it when he was spraying the body. It kept changing colors!"

Safety was finally beginning to catch on with the public after years of almost fruitless promotion by the auto industry. XP-VIP was a very sleek embodiment of a convertible with built-in rollover safety.

From the time of a terrible accident on the Detroit expressway in the 1960s, rollover protection for convertibles was becoming a priority with both the industry and the public. However, most of the roll bars were awful-looking affairs, either welded tubing or things that looked like a giant basket handle. XP-VIP probably had the sleekest looking safety solution anyone had seen up until that time for a convertible: a built-in longitudinal roll bar. It was basically invisible as part of the design and imparted a kind of clever calming sensation to viewers at the time.

The central roll bar featured slotted guideways on both sides. These guideways claimed to be for a special "photochromic glass" that (at least according to the show explanation) allowed a sun-reactive flexible glass to slide up out of the trunk. Brochures handed out at the show talked about the glass roof under a title of "While Waiting for Tomorrow." As the brochure stated, "Working closely with the experts at a leading glass company, we learned about a remarkable new product called photochromic glass. This glass has the amazing quality of 'squinting' to shut out bright sunlight and 'opening up' when natural light fades. We feel it may someday be the perfect substitute for tinted windshields." Of course, only stubs of either glass or plexiglass could be seen on the actual car, suggesting there was something to slide out of the trunk. However, a full glass roof was never installed but was only shown in artist's concepts.

The 1965 Buick Electra hit the scene with a full-width taillight. The 1966 Charger and others followed. The XP-VIP featured a very unusual take on the fad. This one was illuminated indirectly with lighting that bounced rearward out of a large reflector array. Inside was a refreshment bar, tape recorder, and "hi-fi" stereo. Instead of a rearview mirror, there was an electronic monitor by camera, way ahead of its time. Power-operated headrests in the front buckets were a novel feature. But power reclining rear seats were the ultimate. A friend from Creative told me this idea was Creative's suggestion from their experience with the "Queen seat" (see Chapter Five) in the rear of the Eisenhower parade Lincoln. Finally came the customary dream car features: telephone and television.

The XP-VIP was a hit at the shows, but it seems to have disappeared by 1967. Today, no one seems to know the fate of this interesting car built by Creative Industries.

Juvi Plymouths

Creative's Bill Resztak had done some incredible work with motorized juvenile cars at Creative since the early 1950s. He built little motorized cars for his son and neighborhood kids. He also built cars for the children of the famous Briggs family. And as discussed earlier, Bill constructed amazing little cars for

A spectacular new way to attract attention to your Dealership

Plymouth Fury Go-Karts

These are miniature Plymouth Fury Go-Karts. Seventy similar models are now on order for use by Avis Rent-A-Cars in their New York World's Fair display. They are well-built, attractively colored, capable of speeds up to 28 mph, and will hold one person, ranging in size from a juvenile to a full-grown adult. These Go-Karts give you an excellent way to reach new Plymouth prospects by attracting their youngsters.
See details on reverse side.

Original literature advertising Creative-built Plymouth Fury Go-Karts. Note mention that it would fit any driver ranging from juvenile to adult. Flip side of sheet had ordering instructions.

Creative Industries. Many of Bill's masterpieces were executed in steel and aluminum, but the multiples were increasingly done in fiberglass.

Creative turned out some amazingly detailed motorized juvenile Mopar cars during the 1950s. Although a beautiful little 1958 De Soto convertible is credited to and was marketed by Robel Corporation of Pennsylvania, clay models about the same size were constructed at Creative. There were photos in the files. Whether these clay models were for Robel or just a coincidence may never be known, but Robel did indeed market little motorized 1958 De Soto cars. Of course, the little "Firemites" (instead of Fireflite as on the real car) were basically ad hoc promotionals. There were no real economies of scale because the cars were not sold in large numbers at the time. Nobody knew how to get the word out and put some solid marketing behind these clever little cars.

By the early 1960s, the new Go-Kart phenomenon had exploded on the scene. Everybody wanted one. Kids were begging their parents to buy one. Even adults were buying karts. There were clubs, newsletters, and magazine coverage. Some people began racing Go-Karts on small tracks

Original image of the Robel Firemite motorized juvenile car next to a real De Soto Fireflite convertible.

You can use them many ways!

There are countless ways in which you could use these unique attention-getters to build showroom traffic, as well as to promote your Dealership. The secret is to make their use meaningful and result-producing for you. In the adjoining column is a "Starter List." Your individual list need be limited only by your imagination.

You can use these miniature Plymouth Furys as:
Golf Karts—with your advertising on them—for use at your local Golf or Country Club.
A Kiddie Ride on your Used Car or Parking Lot.
A Major Prize in a kids-accompanied-by-parents Contest—especially fine involving a car purchase.
A Traveling Billboard for your special events—Cleanup Sales, New-Car Announcements, etc.
A Junior "Driver Education Car", complete with your emblem—for sub-teen youngsters.
A "Bullpen Car" at Little League baseball games.

These miniature Plymouth Fury Go-Karts are not toys. They will attract the attention of the grown-ups as well as the junior members of your community. Plan your Go-Kart program now—and place your order today. All orders must be in by July 15, 1965, and each order must be accompanied by your check in full payment.

Plymouth Fury Go-Kart Specifications:
- Wheelbase—44¼ inches
- Overall Length—81 inches
- 4-hp, 4-cycle Gasoline Engine
- Recoil Starter ■ Friction Brake
- Metal Bumpers ■ Fiberglass Body
- 11-inch Pneumatic Tires
- Light Blue or Gold Color
- Speed—25 to 28 MPH (Governed down for juvenile use)

PLYMOUTH DIVISION ◆ CHRYSLER MOTORS CORPORATION   *Plymouth*

Order Blank

Rear of original Plymouth Go-Kart information included specs, colors, and order form. Also suggested uses. Note payment was to be made out to Creative Industries. Price was $495, a lot of money for mid-1960s, about the same as real used car.

As usual, Creative Industries saw the phenomenon in a whole new way. Why not put a realistic-looking body on a motorized chassis and call it a Go-Kart, a buzzword everyone knew? Then market the little car alongside its big brother? The notion got Plymouth's attention and Creative made a serious agreement to market their little cars via Plymouth dealers. Avis Car Rentals ordered a bunch for use at their New York World's Fair exhibition area.

Payment for the little cars was sent to Chrysler's marketing office on East Jefferson Avenue, but actual checks were made payable directly to Creative Industries. It stated so on the order form.

A mere handful of the 1965 Plymouths survive today. How many of the little cars (Plymouth and otherwise) did Creative make? Good question, but I was told at least a few hundred. How many brands of junior cars did Creative make? Nobody knows. In fact, nobody seems to know exactly when Creative stopped. But Bill Resztak left for a position at General Motors about 1968. Although production was possible without Bill's involvement, he was the real spark plug behind it all.

One more time, Creative Industries had made a lot of people very happy. And here is yet another vivid example of how Detroit and the automotive industry were back then. It was an incredible time and place filled with amazing, talented, visionary, caring people. Anyone who was there was lucky indeed.

and empty shopping mall lots on weekends (yes, as incredible as it may seem today, shopping malls used to close on Sundays). Of course, Go-Karts were utilitarian. Most consisted of little more than a bare frame, seat, steering wheel, motor, and four wheels.

Creative's Bill Resztak started building motorized cars for his kids and neighborhood kids in early 1950s. Also built some for kids of famous Detroit Briggs family. This one built for son James was made of metal and was electric. Many more were gasoline powered. (Photo Courtesy Jim Resztak Collection)

CHAPTER FOURTEEN

THE OIL CRISIS, ELECTRIC CARS AND AUTOCYCLES

Some very "Creative" reactions to weathering the oil storm in the automotive world of the 1970s are uncovered here.

The Oil Embargo

I stopped by to see my old friend Dave Margolis at Creative Industries on one of my frequent visits from California to Detroit. It was 1975 and a lot had changed in the car business.

The oil embargo crisis that hit in 1973 sent shockwaves throughout the industry and the American economy. The upshot of several developments in the Middle East resulted in an embargo of oil shipments to the west and suddenly gasoline that previously was cheap and plentiful in the United States became almost unobtainable.

In the near panic that ensued, Creative was approached to engineer or develop nearly every kind of stopgap vehicle imaginable. From pedal-powered adult vehicles to propane and electric conversion kits, would-be oil crisis heroes presented a never-ending stream of ideas to Creative Industries. According to Creative's people, few of these ideas had any hope of reaching the prototype stage, much less production. But there was one idea that held promise.

Resurrecting the Electric Car

Even in the best of times, there was always something new going on at Creative. So with the ongoing oil crisis and Creative's knack for being on the cutting edge of all things automotive, one could only expect a quick and interesting response to the situation at hand. In an automotive wasteland, Creative Industries was still promising a brighter future.

I asked Dave what they were working on to combat the gas crunch and he pointed out of the window at what looked like a red late-model 1975 Chevy Malibu. So while I couldn't see much of the car, I knew whatever it was, it had to be special.

Transformer I

Dave gave me a quick overview on the odd Malibu. "We're making a limited run of a new electric car. Now these don't have

This early Transformer I appearing in the completion area in Creative's shops has the rare red color with white vinyl roof. The electric car was based on the Chevy Malibu. Actor Lloyd Bridges of Sea Hunt *and* Tucker *movie fame owned one.*

Mid-1970s view of Creative's driveway leading off East Outer Drive. This much-transformed driveway was once the main entrance to Fred Johnson's Industrial City and Progressive Welder Company. Just peeking out of Creative's roll-up shop door is an early Transformer I prototype electric car in rare white color.

Transformer I prototype sits inside Creative's main shop in mid-1970s. More detailed view of Creative's driveway leading off East Outer Drive. Location of building at right was always in dispute. If windows were tilted open, Creative's trucks could not pass. Due to security reasons, Creative altered the shop building to have door facing Outer Drive so interior could not be easily viewed from next door.

the wild styling like the dream cars you love, but you can drive right past the gas pumps and smile with one of these! And you can get one with all the same goodies they sell on any Malibu, just no gasoline required to run it. The company we're working with to make these is marketing them as the 'Transformer I.'"

Just to illustrate how the passage of time changes perceptions, the mental image of "transformer" in those days was synonymous with meaning something electric. A transformer was something you used to operate your electric train. Today? It might just as easily be envisioned as a movie monster or superhero. Perhaps as a car that morphs into a giant robot.

Most Transformer I cars had a bench front seat. However, the Malibu Dave showed me had swivel bucket seats, the same as those offered for a while by General Motors.

Dave continued, "Some of the movie crowd out in Hollywood are getting into these, and we've already built one specially for Lloyd Bridges."

Lloyd Bridges again. When Creative did the 1965 Plymouth XP-VIP concept (more on this car later), it had a small television showing the TV logo for Lloyd's very popular show, *Sea Hunt*.

Now in the 2000s, this may draw the sound of crickets, but back in the 1950s and 1960s, the show's storyline with scuba diving was considered mega-cool. AMT even made model kits with little scuba tanks you could pose in an open trunk! It was the buzz of the day. So the Lloyd Bridges connection was still alive and well at Creative. And now it was linked to a new electric car.

I asked Joe Ramsay, who worked for Creative Industries in the 1970s to 1980s, about his recollections of the electric

Malibu. "The main shop there on Outer Drive wasn't all that big. So they really had to manage their usage of the space. It wasn't the kind of place where you'd walk in and go, man, this is huge! So they had to organize whatever they had pretty closely to get everything to fit. I just remember all those Chevelles and Malibus lined up in there for the electric car program. They were everywhere in there; they were all stacked up. We made them all right there on Outer Drive.

"Creative had to do a lot of engineering on those cars and it wasn't just the cap over the grille. Those cars were just loaded with very heavy batteries and the weight alone was a problem. A lot of things had to be beefed-up just to carry all that weight around; and that was even counting that they had pulled the heavy V-8 engine out of the cars. They had this little electric motor and a lot of batteries.

"There was a guy who was really smart on all that stuff. His name was Tony Brohl. He was, I think, the project engineer on the Lloyd Bridges car. They were really working away on those cars for a while and then all of a sudden they stopped. I don't know whether they just ran out of funds or what but they just stopped.

"Most of the ones I remember were dark blue with a white vinyl top. But you have a photo of red ones and a white one. I know they made one in a special color for Lloyd Bridges. I think it might have been the first one."

No one seems to know for sure but the rumor was that Bridges was a moneyman in the project, possibly funding some or most of it to try to get the electric cars off the ground again in Detroit.

This notion is not at all a stretch because Lloyd Bridges was a known environmentalist, long before it became fashionable. According to an article in the *New York Times* upon his death in 1998, Lloyd Bridges was a major spokesman for environmental causes.

As the newspapers announced in 1975 when the Transformer I commenced production, it was the first electric car built in Detroit since the 1930s. With all due respect to John Travolta's Oldsmobile Silhouette in the movie, *Get Shorty*, some were calling the Transformer "the Cadillac of electric cars."

The parent company of the Transformer I was known as Electric Fuel Propulsion Corporation (EFP). The company referred to their location as "Greater Detroit." But the address was Robbins Executive Park East, 2237 Elliott Avenue, Troy,

1977 TRANSFORMER I Electric Car

Later version (1977) of Transformer I as pictured in press kits and customer handouts. Note two-tone paint and new driving lights in front cap. Electric car was still based on Chevy Malibu.

Detailed view of 1977 Transformer I front as pictured in press kits and customer handouts. Note new driving lights in front cap. Electric car was still based on Chevy Malibu.

Michigan, just north of Detroit. Actual production of these converted Chevy Malibus took place at Creative's East Outer Drive facility, right behind their headquarters and general offices.

And despite the claims of more recent times that General Motors didn't want electric cars, the big corporation certainly gave their tacit blessing to Transformer I and Electric Fuel Propulsion Corporation.

The Transformer I was claimed to be good for up to 100 miles of driving, but that range turned out to be more like 50 to 90, depending on how and where you did your driving. But however you drove it, this was no hybrid. The lead-cobalt batteries had to be kept charged or it was adios muchachos on your electric driving.

However, perhaps the wildest aspect to this driving range was the addition of an optional trailer with gasoline generator installed. Some accounts boasted it was possible to drive in a range up to 1,000 miles with the generator trailer bobbing around out back, cranking out voltage! Of course, then the driver was back to using gasoline. And from the environmental standpoint, there was the added pollution from the generator. In many cases, this was all a moot point. During the fuel crisis of the 1970s, it didn't matter whether you were buying gas for your generator or your car, you were still buying gas and subject to all the same frustrations.

Side view of 1977 Transformer I as pictured in press kits and customer handouts showing new two-tone paint and vinyl roof treatment. (Electric car was still based on Chevy Malibu.)

Detailed view of 1977 Transformer I rear showing lightning bolt logo and bulging trunk lid to accommodate batteries stuffed into vehicle. Note Michigan red, white, and blue 1976 Bicentennial license plate.

Plush interior of 1977 Transformer I featured power windows and power door locks, tilt steering, and premium stereo sound system. Very luxurious for a mid-size Chevy, more so for an electric car of the time.

The theory behind these cars and most electrics of the modern era was that people would only use them for short errands and limited periods of time. Unfortunately, up until very recent years, some rather unrealistic/idealistic principles have been envisioned. The upshot of these miscalculations has often been disappointing.

By 1977, fancy two-tone paint, AM/FM stereo tape audio system, driving/fog lights, and sunroof were available. Top speed (with the caveat of "for passing") was now listed as 70 mph. Cruising speed was boosted from 50 to 55 mph with a cautionary note of "on level roads with at least 25% battery charge." Acceleration was listed as 0 to 30 mph in 8 seconds, hardly muscle car territory.

Who Killed the Electric Transformer?

Price for the Transformer I was originally listed in newspapers as $8,580 in 1975. But by 1977, that price tag had reportedly ballooned to a whopping $36,000. Not exactly extreme for today, but back then? *Immense* would be one word. As electric cars went, the Transformer I was plush. But at $36,000, "plush" was not enough to translate into serious sales.

ELECTRIC FUEL PROPULSION CORP.
Robbins Executive Park East
2237 Elliott Avenue
Troy (Greater Detroit), Michigan 48084
U.S.A.
313/588-0250

1977 TRANSFORMER I Electric Car

Description & Specifications

DESCRIPTION. 2-Door Coupe, 4-Passenger, International Size, Electrically Powered, with a wide range of luxury equipment available such as Electric Sky Roof, Semi-Automatic Transmission, Power Steering, Power Brakes, Power Windows, Swivel Bucket Seats, Power Door Locks, Six-Way Power Seats, Tinted Glass, AM/FM Stereo Radio and Tape System, and many more.

RECOMMENDED USES. For Professional and Business people in towns, cities or large metropolitan areas who drive 50 to 100 miles a day (10,000-20,000 miles per year).

PERFORMANCE. (On level roads with batteries at least 25% charged.)

    Top Speed (for passing): 70 mph

    Cruising Speed on Motorways: 55 mph.

    Acceleration: 0 to 30 mph in 8 seconds.

DRIVING RANGE.

    Commuting between Suburbs and City: Up to 100 miles (assuming 90% driving on open Expressways, 10% driving in city traffic and with some supplemental charge while car is parked and not in use).

RECHARGING TIME CAPABILITY.

    Using an External Fast Charger: 45 minutes for an 80% charge. EFP gasoline fueled Mobile Power Plants or electrically powered Charge Stations, which will be located at Petrol Stations, Motels and Shopping Centres, are considered External Fast Chargers. A 10-minute charge would result in 15 miles of added driving range; a 30-minute charge would give 45 miles of added driving range.

    Using the Car's On-Board Slow Charger: Approximately 8 hours when plugged into a 240-volt, single phase, 50 amp. circuit at home or office, assuming the battery is fully discharged; or, 4 hours if battery is only half discharged. (A supplemental charge can be had anywhere by plugging into an ordinary 110 volt, 15 amp. circuit.)

Jan/1977

The 1977 Transformer I specifications now stated top speed of 70 mph. Lists two methods of charging but no longer mentions trailer-mounted generator. Not optimistic statement of "professional people who drive 50 to 100 miles a day."

1977 TRANSFORMER I Electric Car

Description & Specifications

PHYSICAL SPECIFICATIONS.

Dimensions in Inches:	Wheelbase	112.0
	Length	212.3
	Width	76.6
	Front Tread	61.5
	Rear Tread	60.7
Exterior and Interior:	All-Welded body on perimeter frame	
	Deep-Dip Rust-Proofing	
	Moulded full foam seating, front and rear	
	Armrests, front and rear	
	Cut-pile nylon carpeting	
	Soft-rim steering wheel	
Mechanical:	Full Coil suspension system, 4 wheels	
	Front disc brakes	
	Rear drum brakes	
	Front and rear ride stabilizer bars	
	Dual cylinder, 4-wheel hydraulic brakes	
Cooling and Defrosting:	EFP Battery Powered Air Conditioner	
	Flow-through Power Ventilation	
	Liquid fuel heater and defroster	
Seating:	Front – Swivel Bucket or Bench Seat	
	Rear – Bench Seat	
Motor:	32 H.P. Direct Current	
Propulsion Battery:	180 Volt Tri-Polar, Lead-Cobalt Power Unit	
Accessory Battery:	12 Volts	
Controller:	Solid State Electronic Control	
Tires:	HR78-15D Load Range Steel Belted Radial, White Sidewall	
Charger:	On-Board Slow Charger, Multi-Voltage: Input 208, 220 or 240 Volts AC, Single Phase, 50 amp. or 110 Volts, 15 amps.	
Price:	Transformer I de luxe model $36,000	
	Prices FOB Factory, Detroit, Michigan, State and Local taxes excluded.	

Jan/1977

Second page of 1977 Transformer I specifications now stated a price of $36,000, which was more than many average household's income in 1977.

Smiling Larry O'Dowd, boss of Creative's sheet metal and casting prototyping, proudly poses with GM electric prototype in Creative's shop. Creative made many of the components for this vehicle. (Photo Courtesy Larry O'Dowd)

TRANSFORMER I

Special Features as Standard Equipment

Deluxe Interior — crushed velour upholstery and special carpeting
Deluxe Two-Tone Exterior
Swivel Bucket Seats (or 6-way Power Bench Seat)
Custom Deluxe Bucket Seat Belts
Power Brakes
Deluxe Bumpers
Bumper Guards
Electric Clock
Litter Container
Rear Window Demister
Electric Door Locks
61-amp. Generator
Heater/Defroster (except for Hawaii and Puerto Rico)
Tinted Glass, all windows
Battery Compartment Heater (except for Hawaii and Puerto Rico)
Dual Horns
Hydrocaps for Batteries
Propulsion Battery Ammeter and Voltmeter and Instrumentation
Auxiliary Lighting
Twin Sport Mirrors, remote controlled
Vanity Visor
Body Side Mouldings
Door Edge Guard
AM/FM Radio
Padded Landau Roof
Power Steering
Sky Roof, Electrically Operated
Steel Belted Radial Whitewall Tires
Rear Towing Package
Deluxe Wheel Covers
Power Windows
Intermittent Windshield Wiper System

Jan/1977

Amazing third page of 1977 Transformer I specifications with long list of features, but note heater and defroster were unavailable in Hawaii and Puerto Rico!

Rear of GM electric prototype in Creative's shop. Creative made many of the components for this vehicle. Note the manufacturer's license plate. (Photo Courtesy Larry O'Dowd)

With a top speed of 50 to 55 mph and a 50- to 100-mile range, the performance capabilities narrowed the Transformer I's appeal to a trickle and EFP finally pulled the plug on production.

Americans tend to like heat in the winter and air conditioning in the summer. These systems alone can soak up gobs of power. And the specter of being caught in heavy urban traffic merely compounds the drain of power. These factors, along with price, eventually combined to doom the Transformer I.

Boss of Creative's wood, plastics, and prototyping, Hugh Olson (blue shirt and tie) stands behind a modernistic three-wheel creation posed with unknown clients (possible Onan). Although some countries outside of the United States had them, rectangular headlights were still considered futuristic in 1960s and 1970s in the United States. Photo was taken at Creative's viewing area on East Outer Drive.

All things considered, EFP (via Creative) had made a valiant effort. Several Transformers were in rental car fleets around the country. Avis ordered 12 of the first cars built and reportedly added more later.

Initial production was announced at 1 car per week, and although it was envisioned that production would eventually reach 25 cars per day, it just never happened.

Following the Transformer I, Creative was also involved in other electric car projects. One such project was intended to produce electrified Chevy Chevette compacts. But it is unclear what ever happened with this effort. Of course, in all the hubbub about GM's EV-1 electric car, nobody ever mentioned (you guessed it) that none other than Creative Industries made at least 25 of the components for the GM electric.

Big Trucks and Motor Homes

There was once an ashtray that sat on Rex Terry's desk. In the center of the personalized, engraved circular silver base was a gold-plated dog, a famous OEM ornament from a Mack truck. It was there in gratitude to Rex and Creative from the company.

Cross-country trucking was always a huge business in the United States. And with the completion of the nation's superhighway system, 18-wheel trucking exploded throughout North America. Little by little, the roads got wider, the drives got longer, and the trucks got bigger. Creative recognized a niche market here and by the mid-1950s had already begun to work with various long-haul truck manufacturers to help in design and engineering.

One of the areas that needed attention most was driver comfort. Since drivers were now spending ever-increasing time out on the road, Creative turned its attention to developing

If only these walls could talk. Workman completes cleanup on specially trimmed Ford tractor for 18-wheel show rig built by Creative Industries being done at the same time as Transformer I cars. Note Michigan Bicentennial license plate. (Photo Courtesy Hugh Olson)

new and ever more luxurious sleeper cab accommodations. And while all this was taking place, there were new considerations for the driver during time not spent behind the wheel. Creative began including features no one had ever seen before. Televisions, refrigerators, and hi-fi stereos all began making their way into 18-wheel trucks, courtesy of Creative. And when the Citizen's Band (CB) radio craze hit in the 1970s, Creative was already there, installing bigger, better, and more powerful units than anyone had considered. So a long-haul trucker might be driving coast to coast, but that driver could now bring along all the comforts of home.

And for the ever-increasing number of driver-owned rigs, Creative turned out custom orders with flashy paint jobs, graphics, and chrome. Today this is a widespread business, but in the 1960s and 1970s, Creative turned out some very trick trucks that were way ahead of their time!

The famous Creative driveway and infamous building next door (note the whited-out windows to prevent gawking at Creative projects). Front view of specially trimmed Ford tractor for 18-wheel show rig built by Creative Industries being done at the same time as Transformer I cars. Paint jobs like this today on trucks are not unusual, but in 1977 a treatment like this was a head-turner! (Photo Courtesy Hugh Olson)

Gift ashtray to Creative's Rex Terry from Mack Truck Company. Gold-plated famous bulldog ornament of Mack trucks. Creative built a few special trucks for Mack, including an early sleeper cab with advanced features. (Photo Courtesy Pamela Terry Bonk)

Another area that Creative delved deeply into was motor homes. In the early 1970s the back lot on Creative's East Outer Drive location was overrun with van conversions and motor homes. You could see them from the street behind buildings and a chain link fence as you drove by on Moenart Avenue. There was everything from custom-built Dodge vans, to Winnebagos, to compact foreign campers built on Asian import truck chassis. Creative did them all.

And by the late 1970s, De Lorean's Chief Engineer Bill Collins was working at the facility and he had designed the impressive, amazingly versatile Vixen motor home.

Joe Ramsay, who was working at Creative back then, sums up the whole story. "When the oil crisis hit, the bottom just dropped out of the motor home business. Creative's business with the motor homes almost disappeared overnight."

But according to Joe and others who worked for Creative in those days and later, countless motor homes were supplied by (and many engineered by) Creative Industries. Some of the work was directly for big manufacturers; other work was done

Development Engineering, Inc. a division of Creative as viewed from Moenart Street, behind 3080 East Outer Drive, was remnant from Fred Johnson's Industrial City era. Trucks, motor homes, even buses were either built or converted or designed here. Business died quickly during the oil crisis of 1970s. (Photo Courtesy Steve Koppin)

for suppliers and aftermarket accessory firms. In the period of the oil embargo and the years that followed when business was low, Creative continued, ever flexible in other areas.

Cyclecars and Wild Airplanes

For the most part, it appeared that motorcycle-based cars that emerged during the oil crisis eventually faded from the scene. Or did they? Actually motorcycle-based or motorcycle-powered cars that had cropped up during the oil crisis somehow stubbornly managed to persist, even if hanging on by a thread. Some were now labeled "commuter vehicles" and others eventually revived the old terms "cyclecar" and "autocycle." However, there was one rather interesting exception.

Jim Bede was a gifted designer and engineer who originally came up with the amazing and beautiful BD-5 aircraft. This gorgeous little pusher prop plane was intended to be a futuristic, yet affordable kit plane that any pilots could build for themselves. Eventually the BD-5 gave way to the jet-powered BD-5J aircraft. Both planes were works of art in themselves.

The stunning looks and performance of the BD-5J were evidenced up on the big movie screens in the James Bond film *Octopussy*. In that movie, there were some rather miraculous flying stunts. During one in particular, a BD-5J was flown right through an airplane hangar and landed on a road! But it was not the first or last time that a BD fuselage glided down a paved highway.

By the 1980s there was an offshoot of these aircraft that ended up on American highways. Bede fashioned his new motor vehicle off the fuselage of the BD-5 airplanes and initially dubbed it BD-200. It was designed to carry two passengers seated in tandem and claimed to be capable of speeds in excess of 100 mph. These vehicles were powered by a succession of various motorcycle engines ranging from Honda to Yamaha and were also claimed to have fuel economy of 100 mpg!

Eventually the automotive namesakes of Bede's aircraft went by many titles due to business issues. However, these land-locked vehicles may best be known by two brands: first Litestar and then Pulse. The latter was built by Owosso Motor Car Company and referred to as a GCRV (ground-cruising recreational vehicle). Creative Industries assisted Jim Bede in the aircraft and car engineering, prototyping, and possibly more.

However, no one at Creative ever revealed specifics of their involvement. As usual, such business was strictly confidential. But nearly everyone at the company knew that Creative was involved in both the BD-5 aircraft and the Litestar/Pulse cyclecars. In fact, there were several newspaper and industry announcements that Creative Industries would produce the BD5-J. References called it a "poor man's jet" and listed prices around $29,000. Assembly of the aircraft was actually scheduled to begin, not in Detroit, but in Newton, Kansas. But parts would be made in Detroit. Whatever happened, the story stopped there.

And without giving away any deep details, Hugh Olson's project board that hung on the wall next to his desk at Creative on East Outer Drive revealed a very important, yet silent admission. This corkboard was always covered with pushpin postings featuring snippets of dozens upon dozens of his team's projects, from Boeing 757/767 aircraft, to Sikorsky helicopters, to various automobiles. Without any words, there was a simple cutout photo of a brightly colored Pulse cyclecar at the bottom center of that posting board. You know the rest of the story.

Again, if only these walls could talk. Hugh Olson's desk and project board at Creative Industries. How many fascinating images do you see? Creative worked on them all. From rocket launchers, to Boeing passenger airliners, to 18-wheel trucks, to helicopters, to (look in lower center) the Pulse cycle car. Creative Industries did it all! (Photo Courtesy Hugh Olson)

CHAPTER FIFTEEN

THE DODGE CHARGER AND MOPAR WING CARS

As told throughout this book, Creative's ancestral history leads very strongly back to Chrysler, despite Creative's links with so many other companies. Of course, the Chrysler Corporation relationship was only just beginning and the connection with Dodge Division was a long and very productive one. Most of it, you may have never heard before.

Charger I

The Dodge connection had remained strong with Creative Industries' General Manager Rex Terry since his Mopar tenure in the 1940s. Although Dodge Division had not done any big project with Creative that was visible to the public since the 1954 Granada, there was still a continuing business relationship. From time to time, Creative had turned out runs of small parts for the division anonymously. Castings, brackets, even some racing parts. But by 1962, things were changing all around. Creative was bigger than ever and Dodge was getting increasingly serious again about their public persona as a performance brand. Although Virgil Exner was now out of the picture, Dodge wanted to continue promoting the division as having great style. It wanted something completely new, something that was eye-popping, yet dripping with a performance look. And with De Soto now gone, Dodge wanted to edge even more upscale, perhaps filling any niche left behind by its defunct sister division.

And rather than a "you can't buy one of these" kind of dream concept, Dodge wanted the entire package based on a production type body. Something that customers could see and quickly identify with cars they could actually buy. So this new concept would have a strong kinship with the 1964 Dodge. Indeed the Charger I started life as a standard production Dodge Polara.

Who Did the Styling?

It is important to understand the mind-set of both the industry and the American public at that time, at least from a car enthusiast point of view. During this era, several standard production cars were transformed into sporty two-passenger roadsters with minimal cut-down windshields; more like what you find on a European Grand Prix racer or Indy car of the day. Most of these wild cars didn't even have a provision for a folding top or roof of any kind. The formula went something

Front view was considered striking in mid-1960s. Rectangular headlights are nothing special today but considered futuristic then.

like this: little windshield, big engine, two passengers, flashy wheels, headrests, no roof.

Inspiration likely came from the George Barris TV Batmobile penned by Herb Grasse. But regardless of its origins, the sporty two-passenger theme was very trendy. Like the others of the genre, Charger I was based on a production full-size Dodge and had all of the expected features. As you might suspect, Creative Industries was very much involved in this new Charger project. Here is what is known, courtesy of Gary Hutchings who was there when it happened.

Creative-built Charger I. Note height of front end and general stance. Also note unblocked side exhaust cutouts in quarter panels.

Charger I side view. Note height of front end and general stance. Also note finned blocking plate with wing nut over cutouts in quarter panels. Talbot racing mirror was common in Europe on racing cars.

Charger I interior was considered very futuristic and plush. Deep pleats in buckets were for extra venting. High bolsters and shoulder padding were claimed to provide "extra support for high-speed driving." Note floor-mounted Torqueflite shifter. Tach aimed at driver in brushed metal housing was similar to the production unit.

Affectionately known as "Hugh's Crew" seen here at lunch break. These guys worked on the Charger I and numerous other projects. Creative had an on-site kitchen left over from the Progressive Welder days and operated at this point by an outside vendor named Ray. Employees referred to it as "Chez Ray" (pronounced "shay-ray"). He served special sausages and sandwiches.

"We received basically a stock car from Dodge division, but with unfinished interior. I don't remember whether it was a convertible or not, but I do remember that we had to do some torching before one of Hugh's guys got working on it. Everything was stripped and set aside, and that's how it started."

According to Gary, Hugh Olson's crew worked directly from styling illustrations and did clay on the car until they had it right where they wanted it. From there, actual pieces were fabricated. Dodge people stopped by a few times to check on the progress, but according to Hutchings, Creative was pretty much left on their own to do the work.

Hugh Olson was in charge of clay work, plastics, prototyping, woodwork, and probably got any sheet metal work done that was needed. Olson had been with Creative since at least 1957 and knew all of the ins and outs of setting up the clay work to get any necessary templates, dies, or molds done. He was also a top plastics man.

Most said that Hugh was a very precise and demanding boss, but he was well loved by his very loyal crew. Olson got the very best out of his people and he would have been the first to be there working with them side-by-side, putting in long hours.

Luckily, the Charger I still exists today and has made appearances in recent years in magazines and on the auction circuit. However, over the years the Charger I has managed to acquire a Hemi engine and other slight modifications.

426 Wedge or 426 Hemi

The numbers "426" on the front fenders and hood scoop didn't refer to "Hemi" in the early 1960s. And the Charger I never had the word "Hemi" anywhere to be seen on the car. The numbers "426" actually meant the almighty max-wedge 426 cubic-inch V-8, the one in the Ramcharger Dodges. Ramchargers were *the* cars at the drag strip during those days. And with all due respect to the Hemi and how it is viewed today, the max-wedge was considered an awesome, screaming deal of an engine back then.

So, yes, the Hemi was and is a fantastic engine, but the Charger I brochure neither mentioned nor showed it, and the engineers at Dodge were still cooking the new Hemi at the time. But the brochure very well does mention and show the max-wedge engine. The brochure stated very clearly that the Charger was equipped with a "426-cu.-in., 365 horsepower V-8 engine featuring a single four-barrel carburetor." It then went on to say, "The drag-strip Ramcharger engine (415-425 horsepower with twin four-barrel carburetors) can be accommodated by modifying the Charger's lower hood panel."

There are also slight visual differences in the car as it appears today. The Charger I as it sits now is squatting low in the front and high in the rear. But that wasn't the trend of the time and the Charger I certainly wasn't sitting this way when

A specialty show car—the youthfully styled Charger by Dodge is none-the-less a "get-up-and-go" car, reflecting in its styling the outstanding competitive performance records established by Dodge cars in recent years. Using basic Dodge body panels, the Charger's close kinship to standard-production Dodge cars is easy to see. Special Charger features include an airscoop, a unique combination headrest-rollbar, and a "competition-height" windshield, which deflects the flow of air over the driver.

Charger I brochure front and rear views. Note taillight spacing is not as seen today. Also note blocking plates installed over both exhaust cutouts.

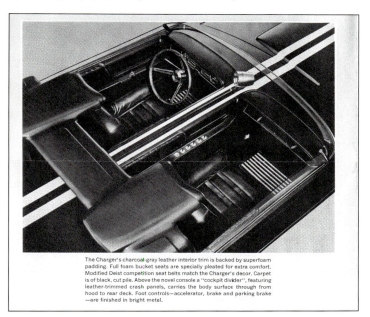

The Charger's charcoal-gray leather interior trim is backed by superfoam padding. Full foam bucket seats are specially pleated for extra comfort. Modified Deist competition seat belts match the Charger's decor. Carpet is of black, cut pile. Above the novel console a "cockpit divider", featuring leather-trimmed crash panels, carries the body surface through from hood to rear deck. Foot controls—accelerator, brake and parking brake—are finished in bright metal.

Charger I brochure overhead view. Floor treatment was similar to Oldsmobile Starfire.

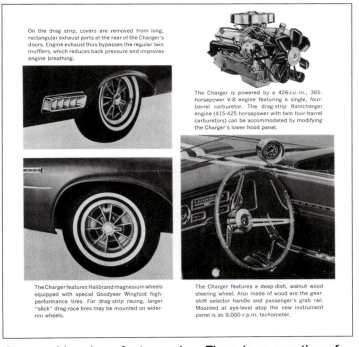

On the drag strip, covers are removed from long, rectangular exhaust ports at the rear of the Charger's doors. Engine exhaust thus bypasses the regular twin mufflers, which reduces back pressure and improves engine breathing.

The Charger is powered by a 426-cu.-in., 365-horsepower V-8 engine featuring a single, four-barrel carburetor. The drag-strip Ramcharger engine (415-425 horsepower with twin four-barrel carburetors) can be accommodated by modifying the Charger's lower hood panel.

The Charger features Halibrand magnesium wheels equipped with special Goodyear Wingfoot high-performance tires. For drag-strip racing, larger "slick" drag-race tires may be mounted on wider-rim wheels.

The Charger features a deep-dish, walnut wood steering wheel. Also made of wood are the gear-shift selector handle and passenger's grab rail. Mounted at eye-level atop the new instrument panel is an 8,000-r.p.m. tachometer.

Charger I brochure features view. There is no mention of hemi, but there is a detailed reference to Mopar 426 max-wedge engines.

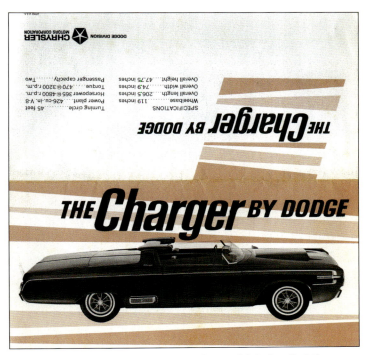

CHRYSLER MOTORS CORPORATION / DODGE DIVISION

THE Charger BY DODGE

SPECIFICATIONS
Wheelbase .... 119 inches
Overall length .... 206.5 inches
Overall width .... 74.9 inches
Overall height .... 47.75 inches

Power plant 426-cu.-in. V-8
Horsepower ... 365 @ 4800 r.p.m.
Torque .... 470 @ 3200 r.p.m.
Passenger capacity .... Two
Turning circle .... 45 feet

THE *Charger* BY DODGE

Charger I brochure cover. Note that vehicle is slightly raked with front higher than rear.

The Charger features Halibrand magnesium wheels equipped with special Goodyear Wingfoot high-performance tires. For drag-strip racing, larger "slick" drag-race tires may be mounted on wider-rim wheels.

Halibrand magnesium wheels, most likely the origin of the rodding term "mag wheel."

On the drag strip, covers are removed from long, rectangular exhaust ports at the rear of the Charger's doors. Engine exhaust thus bypasses the regular twin mufflers, which reduces back pressure and improves engine breathing.

Detail view and explanation of the Charger I's exhaust as shown in brochure.

first seen at Creative. Nor was it this way in the press photos or brochure.

And there are some other differences that have worked their way in over the years. For instance, somewhere along the way the six lights on the rear of the Charger were repositioned. As they are now, the light bezels are spaced wider apart. But they weren't that way when the car was originally at Creative. And they were not that way in the original press photos, or in the original brochure. Somehow over the years, the rear light placements have changed. But either way, the car survives and is still beautiful.

At Creative the front and rear bumpers were removed and "rolled pans" (1960s term for custom curved, tucked-under valance panels) replaced the chrome bumpers. Chrome and rubber bumperettes sometimes mistakenly referred to today as "nerf bars" were installed on the pans. These bumperettes were either adapted from or inspired by similar units used on 1957–1960 Mopar station wagon tailgates. When folded down, these tailgates rested on the rear bumper, cushioned by a rubber bumperette in a chrome bezel.

A European Talbot racing mirror (as commonly used on 1960s Formula One race cars) was mounted on the left front fender and appears to remain there today.

The original wheels installed by Creative were listed as Halibrands. These were made of real magnesium. Ultra-light, very expensive, and actually capable of catching fire and burning.

But magnesium wheels were so ultra cool that even some 1960s Cox slot cars came with real magnesium wheels!

Of course, Halibrand magnesium wheels were such a big deal back then that they were most likely the source of the slang term "mag" or "mag wheels" based on their metal. So although later cast and forged wheels were usually made of either pressed steel or aluminum, the term "mag" stuck forever.

As a further note of interest, Creative folks also had a serious fondness for Rader wheels (yes, the correct spelling) made in Long Beach, California, in connection with famous racer, Mickey Thompson. According to one of my friends, a set of Raders was originally considered for the Charger at one point, but Halibrands won out. Raders came in many different designs and were very trendy around Detroit in the 1960s, as were most things California back then.

It remains unclear whether the exhaust ports on the lower quarter panels just aft of the doors actually worked. However, they were originally intended to be another popular 1960s custom and racing feature known as cutouts.

These so-called cutouts simply bypassed the stock mufflers and (the theory was) thus boosting horsepower by reducing engine backpressure. This was a de rigueur feature for anyone wanting to be cool on the strip back in the Woodward Avenue days.

Original press release photos from Creative's files showed straight side view with rectangular blocking plates attached over the cutouts. However, photos taken from an angle showed the blocking plates removed. If you look at the original Charger brochure, blocking plates with a single large acorn wing nut are attached in all views except a detail shot where they actually took the time and space to explain the function of the cut-outs. The kids and the racers and cruisers back then already understood all this and didn't need the explanation. The show-and-tell was all just for the squares, grown-ups, and general public.

Charger II

With the success of the Charger I at the auto shows, Dodge didn't waste any time and quickly had Creative get busy assembling a successor to the first Charger. This time out, the Charger II was a prediction of the all-new 1966 production Charger. It was Dodge's way of saying, save your pennies, guys, because look what's coming in the pipeline!

The Charger II was a complete departure from its predecessor because there was really no existing production car on which to base it. The design itself took precedence over the rather understated silvery-gray colors in and out. At the auto shows the car seemed to be moving even while standing still, and there were subtle design touches everywhere, from the European look of the grille to the rolled edges of the rear deck. Although they would hardly be noticed today, the rectangular headlights in those days were unusual for the United States and considered very futuristic.

The Charger II's sweeping overall design was a fastback configuration that was very much in vogue at the time. Plymouth's Barracuda, AMC's Marlin, and others were adopting fastback roofs on sporty cars with bucket seat interiors. Thin-shell bucket seats featured backrests ventilated by open slots. This time the interior was designed strictly for four occupants with a full-length console. The rear buckets and panel behind them were all designed to fold flat and resulted in a very large, flat cargo area all the way to the rear of the vehicle.

A novel feature for the day was no side vents at the B-pillar. This was because of another item in vogue at the time: flow-

Quarter front view of the Charger II shows off sleek fast-back that was all the rage in the 1960s.

Rear view of the Charger II shows off flowing fastback roof best. Also note full-width taillight (another trendy 1960s theme). Backlight window was concave on ends.

through ventilation. Because air conditioning was the norm of the future and because ventless side windows have a cleaner, longer look, vents were deleted. Windows were all power operated.

I never got a chance to interview anyone at Creative about II, except that I did mention it once to Dave Margolis, who responded with one of his "we did it, but no elaboration" smiles.

Designer Bill Brownlie, who had done work for everybody from Briggs Manufacturing, Packard Motor Car Company, and ultimately Chrysler Corporation, was unusually complimentary about Charger II, but no names came up for who might have fathered the design.

As I said earlier, much ado has been made in recent years regarding the engine for the Charger I. A further point of curiosity was the engine for the Charger II. This time, the brochure vaguely avoided any mention of a specific engine for this concept. The brochure stated as follows: "Under the sleek hood of Charger II, there's room for any of Dodge's high performance V-8 engines." Period. This should have been a serious clue. Why was Dodge being so mysteriously noncommittal about the Charger II engine? And if the new Hemi was such a big deal on the minds of Dodge execs, why didn't they shove one into the Charger II? Because they were waiting for something far more special.

History tends to distort over time. Although the Hemi is viewed today as the Holy of Holies in engines, back in the 1950s and 1960s, the talk on the street was all about the engine of the future. And it wasn't a Max-Wedge or Hemi. Chrysler had it, but it wasn't even a V-8. And by golly, it was coming, any day, pretty darn soon.

Chrysler Turbine

My Chrysler turbine history was published in the June 1980 issue of *Hemmings Motor News' Special-Interest Autos* magazine.

Charger II interior shows off new vented seats, thin-shell buckets, full gauges, and twin armrests.

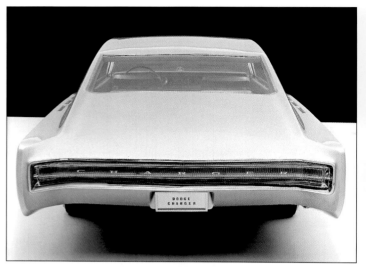

Full-width taillight created lower and wider look. Note sculpting in roof and venting on rear fender tops.

In that history I related a conversation I had with Bill Brownlie, who was in Chrysler's design section. Here is what Bill said:

"Lynn Townsend called Elwood Engel, myself, and others into a meeting during the time of the 50-car program, and we discussed actually offering a new turbine car on a limited basis to what would have been virtually hand-picked customers as a test of public acceptance. In that meeting it was decided to build a limited number of special-bodied turbines. That body became the '66 Charger fastback."

As I understood it from Brownlie, the Charger II was not just another concept follow-up. It was actually intended to *predict* the 1966 Charger but not the 1966 Charger that people know today. Had it been built the way it was originally intended, the Charger II would have had a new generation of Chrysler's famed gas turbine engine under the hood, and so would the production model.

The "50-car program" Bill Brownlie referred to was the original Chrysler Ghia Turbine Car evaluation wherein 203 "typical American drivers" were selected to drive and evaluate special Ghia-built Chrysler Gas Turbine cars.

Here is an excerpt of what I wrote in that 1980 history:

"The engineering boys did a few more tricks in this first production turbine car. The power package was cradled in a cushioned quick-change unit, which also incorporated the transmission and front suspension. One pump served the engine, transmission, power steering, etc. but no motor oil as such was used since transmission fluid performed all necessary lubrication functions. One very interesting point is that there was no torque converter in the three-speed gearbox. The function of the converter was taken over by the rotating blades of the engine itself. Remember that the gas turbine was not unlike

Father of Chrysler's gas turbine program with 1960 Plymouth Turbine Special, ramping up to the Turbine Charger. George Heubner dispels silly, persistent rumors that gas turbine exhaust was overly hot and melted things. Heubner holds a handkerchief in exhaust with no ill effects. Chrysler's advanced regeneration system reused exhaust heat and lowered tailpipe exit temps to below conventional engine exhaust temps.

one big torque converter in principle with hot compressed air (instead of fluid) turning the second set of vanes."

"Chrysler purposely left the exhaust wail a little louder than necessary to draw attention to the car, and auto show pamphlets alerted people to 'listen to it. The exciting new sound of the Chrysler Corporation Turbine Car.'"

Those CGT cars were painted Turbine Bronze and were about the size of an early 1960s Thunderbird. The sporty interiors were designed to accommodate four passengers separated by a full-length console. Sound familiar?

Turbine Chargers

Bill Brownlie's bombshell statement about the 1966 Dodge Charger in my article (by the way, the actual official name was "Turbinecharger" and was sometimes listed simply as "Turbine Charger") said everything.

The Turbine Charger in effect would have been the limited production replacement for the 1963 Chrysler Ghia Gas Turbine Car. Here is more of what I wrote about the Turbine

George Heubner at Chrysler Engineering Headquarters in Highland Park. Car is 1960 Plymouth Turbine Special. It is rumored that Creative supplied some parts for and built two Turbine Specials. (Photo Courtesy Richard Padovini)

Two of 55 Ghia-built Chrysler Gas Turbine (CGT) cars from consumer test program. Author wrote one of the first magazine histories and drove two of these cars. There would have been direct ancestors to production Chargers had things gone as originally planned.

Charger in 1980. "Tom Golec, supervisor of car development, recalls that low-volume tooling was ordered and approximately 500 Turbine Chargers were planned for the initial run. Golec points out that a special no-slip clutch unit was developed for the 1966 Turbine Charger, but was never used due to very high cost. Supposedly two 1966 Turbine Chargers with the special clutch were built, but they were never shown to the public. The Charger became a sporty Dodge with a conventional engine and slightly different trim (the Turbine job had a grille opening much like the 1970 Challenger). The project was stillborn.

"What killed the project? The mid-1960s produced a variety of rumblings out of Washington. Insurance companies clamped down on supercars, safety laws were written, and smog laws took effect. Once the Clean Air Act became reality, it specified control of NOX emissions and, according to George Huebner, it was not known at that time if the turbine would meet future NOX requirements. The first direct result was to shelve the 1966 Turbine Charger. The government was now in the car-making business and Chrysler was out of the turbine car business, at least on any mass scale. Regulations on conventional engines took on very high priorities, and although a sixth-generation engine was developed to meet NOX standards, little was done with it; engineers were largely occupied with the emissions problems of piston engines."

Now. If you were paying attention, there were two 1966 Turbinechargers built. So who built them? What happened to them? Where are they today? And why weren't they ever displayed? All good questions, but by now you ought to have an idea about some of the answers.

At least some of the low-volume tooling mentioned by Golec was indeed ordered. Much (and perhaps all) was from Creative Industries. From the days of Fred Johnson's Industrial City, there was also a heritage of expertise with metallurgy and casting. As I have mentioned earlier regarding Ford's 1950s concept cars, Creative had expertise in gas turbines and had once been prepared to install such engines in Ford's concepts had Ford wanted.

Turbine Charger Prototypes

Another unknown factor is that Creative's graphics department and what became known as Creative Universal had already been doing some of the turbine manuals for Chrysler. But even more unknown was the fact that Creative Universal division was also handling manuals, training materials, and training for Ford's Gas Turbine truck program. I have photos of these training programs that were held at Creative's division on East Outer Drive and elsewhere. And

Chrysler CGT displayed with various generations of Chrysler gas turbine engines. Item displayed closest to driver's headlight may have been special limited-slip engine clutch for Turbinecharger. (Photo Courtesy Richard Padovini)

Turbinecharger grille strongly resembled 1970 Dodge Challenger, still years away in design pipeline.

Turbinecharger rear would have been cross between Charger II and production Charger. Door mirrors mimicked Charger I tachometer housing. Grilles in fender ends provided extra air to gulping turbine.

Creative had all kinds of aircraft engineers on staff and had been working with gas turbine helicopters and other aircraft for quite some time. One thing was for sure: Creative Industries knew the turbine business.

Dave Margolis told me, "We were all set to do the complete prototypes (Turbine Chargers), even ready to do training materials and assist with the user program if necessary. We started off with a bang and then suddenly, nothing."

My understanding is that two Turbine Chargers were built, completed (except for engines), and made ready. But theses cars were never shown to the public. A quick-change engine cradle system either identical to or similar to the Ghia cars was built by Creative (this same cradle system would have been used in reverse on the Typhoon). But it is unclear whether the new generation turbine engines were actually installed in these two Turbine Chargers. Furthermore, it is unknown if the Turbine Chargers were ever completely finished and driven. Rumor went on to say that Creative was told to ship the cars to an undisclosed location where they were kept hidden. Whatever happened after that is a mystery, but Dave Margolis let another piece of the puzzle slip when he mentioned that he later heard the cars had been "cut up." The Charger went on to become a successful conventional sporty performance car for the 1966 model year, and the turbine engine idea was soon forgotten.

In the end, a wild Charger III was constructed by a company other than Creative. And while that concept was quite popular, the raison d'être for the Charger series had somewhat evaporated as the gas turbine engine mover further and further into obscurity. So, sadly, the engine was never officially linked with the Charger as it had originally been envisioned, and ultimately faded from the automotive scene. This history is unknown today.

Mopar Wing Cars

Yes, Dodge Daytonas were indeed an off-line assembly done by Creative Industries. But more important is the fact that Creative actually manufactured the parts *as well as* doing the conversion assemblies on Daytonas. Creative also prototyped and manufactured the parts for the Plymouth Superbird that arrived after the Daytona. But they did not assemble the Superbirds. That job was left to Plymouth Division.

Charger 500
But first I asked Steve Koppin about the very limited production Charger 500 that preceded the Daytona. Creative Industries did the conversion work to produce these performance models that led ultimately to the Daytona wing cars.

The Incredible Typhoon Sports Car

Something else learned in my research was never publicized. There were also supposedly at least two gas turbine sports cars built based on the Elwood Engle–designed car made by Ghia. These were in addition to the two turbine-powered Chargers. The difference was that these turbine sports cars were two-passenger mid-engined roadsters! Yes. The design was to include a removable hardtop, and there were headrest fairings behind the front seats that looked similar to Ford's Thunderbird Sports Roadster. One of these cars was a non-running mock-up supported on jack stands. The other reportedly was an operable (or potentially so) engineering feasibility car. This was an extremely hush-hush project and that Huebner's people provided drawings to Creative in hopes of getting an engineering feas car actually built. Indeed, I saw illustrations of these cars at Creative's Outer Drive facility in the 1970s.

The sports car would not have been named Turbine Charger, but instead would have been called Typhoon. The Typhoon had air intakes just aft of the doors and a shorter wheelbase than the Ghia-built four-passenger cars. Can you imagine a genuine two-passenger, mid-engined gas turbine sports car with a lock-up clutch screaming down the highway? Had it been a success, Typhoon would have been the Viper of its day, and it would have been a world sensation.

Richard "Wing-King" Padovini was involved with Chrysler gas turbine program from beginning to end. He would later purchase a Charger Daytona new and he still owns it today!

What happened to the Typhoon? No one could recall. There was a rumor that Creative had begun engineering layout work on the Typhoon feas car. But sadly, that work was also abruptly canceled with no reason given. As far as I know, all that survives of Typhoon are a couple of photos of the static mock-up.

I asked Richard Padovini, who was a point man for Chrysler's Turbine Car program, about the Typhoon. Padovini went on nearly every exhibition of Chrysler's gas turbine cars and often was a point man that interfaced with journalists and the general public. His memory of the car was as a static model, but he could not recall any details on the engineering feas cars or anything related to Creative on these cars. But he knew of Creative's involvement with Chrysler. I call Padovini the "Wing King" because not only is he an authority on Chrysler's gas turbine cars, but he also bought a brand-new Dodge Daytona, which he still owns to this day.

The original two-passenger Typhoon sports model of the Chrysler Ghia gas turbine car was reportedly planned as a mid-engine. The early full-size model was painted Turbine Bronze. By the New York World's Fair another Typhoon was shown described as Pearlescent White (guess whose specialty). It had large side vents, chrome trim, different front bumper, and no grille. (Randy Treadway Photo)

Young Richard Padovini shows Chrysler turbine component next to testing equipment for gas turbines.

Very young Steve Koppin and his pet dog standing next to one of three Creative Industries courtesy cars in mid-1950s, in this case a Ford wagon. Steve would later work personally on the Dodge Daytona wing cars. Steve's father, Verne, would later become co-owner of Creative Industries. (Photo Courtesy Steve Koppin)

All grown up, Steve Koppin poses in recent times with his retired father, Verne, who was president and co-owner of Creative Industries. (Photo Courtesy Steve Koppin)

For those who don't know, this was Dodge's first attempt at refining the aerodynamics of the 1968–1970 Charger body for NASCAR and big track racing. Although the 500 differed little in appearance from regular Chargers of its day, the two most notable visual cues were a flush-fitting Dodge Coronet grille and flush backlight window. But these were not styling modifications for appearance's sake. The changes were an effort to reduce wind drag at high speeds.

The normal production Charger for 1968–1970 had a recessed grille and hidden headlights. This wide-mouth air-scoop type of recessed grille design was yet another throwback

to the stillborn Turbine Charger design we've discussed.

The new recessed grille may have looked beautiful, but it was problematic aerodynamically. The new recessed 1968 Charger grille created a roller dam of air in front of the car. This condition wreaked havoc on handling at high speeds. Although the aerodynamic condition wasn't objectionable to the normal driver on regular highways, it was a thorn in the side of high-speed race driving such as NASCAR. And there was another problem. In their beautiful 1968 Charger re-styling, Dodge had adopted a flying buttress roof design that recessed the backlight window glass. This roof design had already been wildly popular in the day and was originally seen on GM's 1966–1967 mid-size cars. It looked even better on the sleek new Dodge Charger, but it wasn't aerodynamic.

The roof design was quite handsome on the Charger body, but at high speeds it created a mass of dirty air around the backlight and again affected the streamlining. Neither of these points meant much in everyday driving, but at high speeds on the track, the Charger just couldn't slip though the air at its true potential.

Chrysler's racing people got to work on ways to improve the body for racing. The upshot of this situation was to modify both the grille and rear window to fit flush. A standard Coronet grille with exposed headlights was positioned at the very edge of the grille opening. This flush-fitting change got rid of the recess and roller dam of air at high speeds. A new flush backlight window was also installed that eliminated the flying buttress roof profile.

Hugh Olson's team was responsible for performing the prototype configuration and determining the steps needed to convert a normal Charger into a Charger 500. Anything that wasn't a stock off-the-shelf component was Creative's responsibility. Any parts that needed to be fabricated were determined, engineered, and fabricated by Creative's people. Conversions were done at Creative's Outer Drive facility and at least one other unnamed building.

Meanwhile, Ford had already been experimenting with their mid-size model and likewise discovered they could squeeze more speed out of their Fairlane on the tracks by extending and rolling the end of the nose and by installing a flush grille. The result of their research resulted in the new Torino Talladega edition (and Mercury's corresponding Spoiler II edition). Like the Mopars, 500 of these cars had to be built and available for sale to the public in order to make them eligible for NASCAR racing. So Ford quickly jumped into the battle and produced the requisite number of cars. So it was game on!

Despite all the 500 aero tweaks, it just wasn't enough to get the Charger up to its full potential speed on the NASCAR circuit tracks. So, this competition thus led to the Charger 500 becoming the basis for the even wilder Daytona series that arrived in 1969.

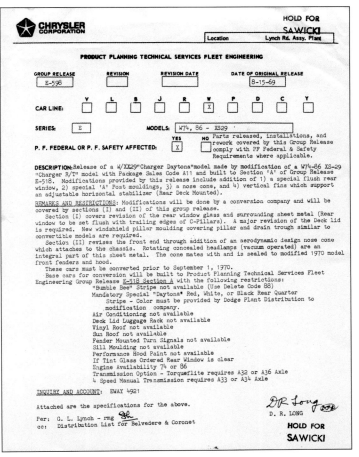

Left memo (No. 1042):

ENGINEERING SPECIAL EQUIPMENT APPLICATION
CONCURRENCE MEMO   No. 1042

DATE 5-22-69

TO: J. Benedict   LOCATION: Technical Information H.P.
FROM: J. Lake   LOCATION: Fleet Engineering   Lynch Rd.

INQUIRY NO. EWAY 4921
Grp.Rel. E-518 Sect.A
CAR LINE & MODEL Charger R/T W 74, 86, XS29

OPTIONAL EQUIPMENT – LIST ALL PERTINENT INFORMATION
All except vinyl roof or rear deck luggage rack

PF SAFETY YES X NO
PF FED   YES X NO
REMARKS
TELEPHONE APPROVAL GIVEN

CONFIRMING THE TELEPHONE CONVERSATION OF _____ DATE
FROM _____ TO _____   YES ___ NO X

APPROVAL IS REQUESTED FOR THE BELOW LISTED SPECIAL ORDER EQUIPMENT TO BE USED ON THE ABOVE VEHICLES.
Modification into Charger "Daytona" XX29 model by outside conversion company as follows:
1. Special 18" nose cone added to 'F' Series Charger front end sheet metal incorporating swivelling hideaway headlamps and special turn signal lamps in place of standard 'E' Series charger R/T front end.
2. Revised rear window glass and surrounding sheet metal, including revised deck lid, so that rear window is flush with trailing edges of C-pillars.
3. Windshield pillar outside mouldings similar to convertible to be added.
4. Adjustable airfoil section to be mounted on the rear deck.
Reference attached correspondence Product Planning Letter 3-17-69; Meeting Minutes 1-14-69
P. M. Rothwell; Dodge Product Information Bulletin #17 4-15-69.

ORIGINATOR – DO NOT WRITE BELOW THIS LINE.   SIGNED: J. B. Lake

REPLY (LIST ALL RESTRICTIONS IF ANY)
Assurance of design compliance to the 27 Federal Motor Vehicle Safety Standards applicable to 1969 passenger cars has been secured for the vehicle described above. Signed statements confirming design compliance are on file in the Engineering Standards and Data Department of the Engineering Office. Included in the design compliance file are copies of the items of correspondence identified above, and Engineering Office Action Letter (File #2337) dated 3-28-69.

NOTE: MUST BE SIGNED BY CHIEF ENGINEER OR AUTHORIZED AGENT FOR PF SAFETY OR PF FEDERAL ITEMS.
SIGNED J. T. Benedict
DATE: 8-14-69

RETURN THIS COPY TO THE ORIGINATOR   REPLY COPY   Sheet 119 of 119

Right memo:

CHRYSLER CORPORATION
HOLD FOR SAWICKI
Location Lynch Rd. Assy. Plant

PRODUCT PLANNING TECHNICAL SERVICES FLEET ENGINEERING

GROUP RELEASE E-598
REVISION
REVISION DATE
DATE OF ORIGINAL RELEASE 8-15-69

CAR LINE: V L B J R W[X] P D C Y
SERIES: E   MODELS: W74, 86 - XS29

P. F. FEDERAL OR P. F. SAFETY AFFECTED: YES [X] NO
Parts released, installations, and rework covered by this Group Release comply with PF Federal & Safety Requirements where applicable.

DESCRIPTION: Release of a W/XX29 "Charger Daytona" model made by modification of a W74-86 XS-29 "Charger R/T" model with Package Sales Code A11 and built to Section 'A' of Group Release E-518. Modifications provided by this release include addition of 1) a special flush rear window, 2) special 'A' Post mouldings, 3) a nose cone, and 4) vertical fins which support an adjustable horizontal stabilizer (Rear Deck Mounted).

REMARKS AND RESTRICTIONS: Modifications will be done by a conversion company and will be covered by sections (I) and (II) of this group release.
    Section (I) covers revision of the rear window glass and surrounding sheet metal (Rear window to be set flush with trailing edges of C-Pillars). A major revision of the Deck Lid is required. New windshield pillar moulding covering pillar and drain trough similar to convertible models are required.
    Section (II) revises the front end through addition of an aerodynamic design nose cone which attaches to the chassis. Rotating concealed headlamps (vacuum operated) are an integral part of this sheet metal. The cone mates with and is sealed to modified 1970 model front fenders and hood.
    These cars must be converted prior to September 1, 1970.
    Base cars for conversion will be built to Product Planning Technical Services Fleet Engineering Group Release E-518 Section A with the following restrictions:
        "Bumble Bee" Stripe not available (Use Delete Code 88).
        Mandatory Special "Daytona" Red, White, or Black Rear Quarter Stripe - Color must be provided by Dodge Plant Distribution to modification company.
        Air Conditioning not available
        Deck Lid Luggage Rack not available
        Vinyl Roof not available
        Sun Roof not available
        Fender Mounted Turn Signals not available
        Sill Moulding not available
        Performance Hood Paint not available
        If Tint Glass Ordered Rear Window is clear
        Engine Availability 74 or 86
        Transmission Option - Torqueflite requires A32 or A36 Axle
        4 Speed Manual Transmission requires A33 or A34 Axle

INQUIRY AND ACCOUNT: EWAY 4921
Attached are the specifications for the above.
Per: G. L. Lynch - rmg
cc: Distribution List for Belvedere & Coronet
D. R. Long
HOLD FOR SAWICKI

Chrysler memo regarding Dodge Charger Daytona construction and protocols. "Outside conversion company" referenced was Creative Industries.

Another Chrysler memo regarding Dodge Charger Daytona (code-named W/XX29) lists what is and is not available as equipment, options, etc. "Outside conversion company" referenced was Creative Industries.

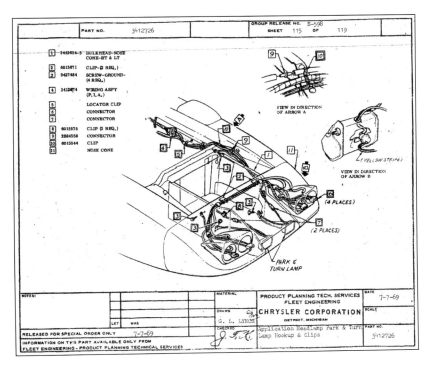

PART NO. 3412726
GROUP RELEASE NO. E-598
SHEET 115 OF 119

1 3412624-3 BULKHEAD-NOSE CONE-RT & LT
2 6015071 CLIP (2 REQ.)
3 9427484 SCREW-GROUND- (4 REQ.)
4 3412474 WIRING ASSY (P.I.A.)
5   LOCATOR CLIP
6   CONNECTOR
7   CONNECTOR
8 6015575 CLIP (2 REQ.)
9 2884558 CONNECTOR
10 6015644 CLIP
11   NOSE CONE

VIEW IN DIRECTION OF ARROW A
VIEW IN DIRECTION OF ARROW B
(YELLOW STRIPE)
(4 PLACES)
(2 PLACES)
PARK & TURN LAMP

NOTES:
MATERIAL
PRODUCT PLANNING TECH. SERVICES FLEET ENGINEERING
CHRYSLER CORPORATION DETROIT, MICHIGAN
DRAWN G. L. LYNCH
CHECKED
Application Headlamp Park & Turn Lamp Hookup & Clips
DATE 7-7-69
SCALE
PART NO. 3412726
RELEASED FOR SPECIAL ORDER ONLY 7-7-69
INFORMATION ON THIS PART AVAILABLE ONLY FROM FLEET ENGINEERING - PRODUCT PLANNING TECHNICAL SERVICES

Extensive wind tunnel testing by Wichita State University, Lockeed/Martin Marietta, racing people, and Creative revealed the final solution for Dodge: take the Charger 500 modified rear window and add a slippery nose cone in front and a high wing on the rear. Problem solved. The result was known as the Dodge Charger Daytona.

Of course, in order to run such features on a car in a NASCAR race, they had to be based on a car being sold to the public. And the rub was there had to be at least 500 of these cars produced and for sale at dealerships before the Daytona could legally be raced. Dodge didn't have the capacity to set aside a line for such a special car. Therefore, it was quickly deter-

Another Chrysler memo (Product Planning Tech Services Fleet Engineering) regarding electrical and mechanical components for Daytona front clip, including modified power headlights.

mined such a specialized production would have to be what the industry refers to as an "off-line" project.

In the end it was all farmed out to Creative Industries. Various divisions of Creative engineered and fabricated the parts. Actual prototype and clay work were done at Creative's East Outer Drive facility. But by the time a contract was awarded for Daytona production, Creative quickly determined that such work had to take place elsewhere geographically. Creative already owned or leased buildings all over the Detroit area, but this project required a dedicated facility. There could be no delays since there was a deadline looming to meet the NASCAR requirements.

Here is what Chrysler's Fleet Engineering Division Concurrence Memo dated May 22, 1969, stated: Modification into Charger "Daytona" XX29 model by outside conversion company as follows:

Special 18-inch nose cone added to 'F' Series Charger front end sheet metal incorporating swiveling hideaway headlamps and special turn signal lamps in place of standard 'E' Series Charger R/Y front end.

Revised rear window glass and surrounding sheet metal, including revised rear deck lid so that window is flush with trailing edges of C-pillars.

Windshield pillar outside mouldings similar to convertible to be added.

Adjustable airfoil section to be mounted on the rear deck.

Of course the "outside conversion company" mentioned here was Creative Industries.

A further Chrysler Product Planning Technical Services Fleet Engineering memo dated August 15, 1969, stated as follows: "DESCRIPTION: Release of a W/XX29 'Charger Daytona' model made by modification of a W74-86 XS-29 'Charger R/T'

model with Package Sales Code A11 and built to Section A of Group Release E-518. Modifications provided by this release include addition of 1) a special flush rear window, 2) special 'A' Post mouldings, 3) a nose cone, and 4) vertical fins which support an adjustable horizontal stabilizer (Rear deck mounted) . . . REMARKS AND RESTRICTIONS: Modifications will be done by a conversion company and will be covered by Sections (I) and (II) of this group release. These cars must be converted by September 1, 1970." The memo goes on to list what option codes would and would not be available. It stated that the Bumble Bee stripe would not be available, but that in its place would be a "mandatory special 'Daytona' stripe in a coordinating color to the body." Again, the unnamed "conversion company" was Creative Industries. And so the work began in earnest.

Steve Koppin Connection

I talked with Steve Koppin, son of Verne Koppin, who became one of the co-owners of Creative upon Rex Terry's retirement. Steve is quite modest, but he has owned his fair share of incredible cars over the years. And Steve grew up around Creative. He was regularly around Creative Industries facilities since he was a young boy, so Steve knew every nook and cranny of the buildings and many of the people who worked there. And Steve was very familiar with most of the projects and ultimately became Manager of Special Vehicles Division at Creative Industries.

Although his family is steeped in Mopar history and lineage in both love and work, Steve has always been an avid car man, no matter the brand. There are still stories circulating all over Detroit about the beautiful Shelby Mustangs that Steve owned years ago. These included a 1968½ Shelby 500 KR and a 1969 Shelby 500.

Being yet another kid who grew up in Detroit's glory years, Steve couldn't wait to go to work for his dad's company. There

Creative Industries Dodge Daytona assembly/conversion facility building at 10 Mile Road and Brittany north of Detroit as it looks today. Of course, Creative is long gone and there is nothing for Mopar fans in the building today. (Photo Courtesy Steve Koppin)

Creative Industries gets award from Boeing. Don Merzoian, who oversaw Charger 500 and Daytona conversions, is seated with glasses on the left of table. Larry O'Dowd stands in dark suit holding award on right. Larry oversaw sheet metal forming of Daytona nose cones and components. (Photo Courtesy Larry O'Dowd)

With Charger Daytona hood and 1970-style front side marker light (early Daytona had reflectors mounted farther forward) placement in place, early clay modeling to lay out Plymouth Superbird at Creative Industries in Hugh Olson's area on Outer Drive. (Photo Courtesy Richard Padovini)

Note illuminated 1970-style side-marker location here. Vehicle here is early clay modeling to lay out Plymouth Superbird at Creative Industries. Also note reverse scoops (actually for tire clearance) not yet installed on fender tops. (Photo Courtesy Richard Padovini)

he could see all the action at American automotive ground zero and play with real cars 24/7.

He helped out around Creative since his very early years, but Steve dived in for his first full-time automotive work during a summer assignment in 1969. It was then that he became involved with hands-on work on the wild Dodge Daytona cars.

Steve Koppin said, "I worked there directly on the Charger Daytonas. This was the whole reason we got the plant on 10 Mile in East Detroit, which is now known as Eastpointe. That's a fact.

"The Daytona project was my first real job at Creative. I worked there the whole summer before I started up the Special Vehicles Division with Dave Margolis. Don Merzoian was our plant manager and he's passed, as you know. Don was a fountain of information with everything he worked on. He was the manager of the program.

"These were the Charger Daytonas that we built at the plant at 10 Mile Road and Brittany. Actually I had more than one function originally. I was helping out wherever I could, doing a little bit of everything. I watched the cars come off the carrier trucks and drove them in and parked them.

"Of course the parts and cars were coming in so fast that we ran out of space to stack the stock fenders. There was a separate office inside the building with its own roof. Once we discovered that the roof over that office section was designed in a way that it could handle the weight, we began stacking fenders up on the inside roof. They were safe and out of the weather. We got those fenders in (the Daytona parts built at another Creative division) and nose cones and we put them on top of the inside office area. It was one of my jobs to do so.

"It was a huge office inside the building and the roof of that office area was really pretty heavy duty. It had to be because of all the weight we put up there. I had two or three guys helping me just sitting the parts up there. We stacked everything and we organized the parts up there nicely in rows.

"You asked if we had any special racks to hold the parts. No. We just sat them up there bare. There was enough room so we just put them up there bare, no racks."

To get an idea of turnover time, I asked Steve how long the fenders and front clip parts stayed up there.

"Not very long! We were taking them down and putting them on the cars we were modifying. And Don (Mirzoian) kept the schedule rolling along so the parts never sat around long. These were fenders, nose cones, and the back windows."

I continued by asking, "So the fenders and parts you put up on the inside roof over the office section were all new parts fabricated by Creative. What about the parts you removed from the new production Chargers that had just come in?"

Steve responded, "It just wasn't worth it for Chrysler to pick up those original painted production fenders. So they just told us to get rid of them. We gave so many bump shops a great deal! Some of the stuff we just gave away, just to get rid of it all. And that was okay with Chrysler. It just wasn't worth the aggravation of trying to put all these parts back into production because you know, the parts had already been painted on the cars and now they were used parts. Chrysler couldn't put them back into the production system and they couldn't be sold as new."

Many stories were floating around Detroit about brand-new Charger front fenders being stacked on the outside roof of a building on East 10 Mile Road not far from Gratiot Avenue. Joe Ramsay, who worked at Creative, even remembers that you could actually see Charger fenders stacked on the roof of one building on 10 Mile as you drove by. Many have assumed this

was yet another Creative Industries building. To clarify this point, I asked Steve about the fenders on the outside roof and wondered if these were the ones he was stacking and storing.

Steve responded, "No. But I also remember driving along 10 Mile and seeing those fenders up on the roof. My dad even noticed them. But that was not our place. It was one of the bump shops we had gifted with fenders. It was a small place just a few blocks from our facility at 10 Mile and Brittany. That little shop ran out of room and we gave him so many fenders he decided to stack them up on his roof. And yes, it is true they could be seen while driving by, but that was not our facility. Those fenders were just ones we had given away.

"I remember the painters too. You know, we had a bunch of body men and painters. You know, when we modified that back window area and made it flush, we had to spot that all in. And, of course, we had to paint the nose cones. It was quite an area to do, so we had to put in a full spray booth and hire several painters so that they could go in there and paint the cars and parts. These all had to be nice jobs because the cars were going direct to the dealers to be sold.

"Now going out, they could put maybe three or four cars on one of these carriers. On a normal car without the long nose and the big wing on the back they could fit maybe six or seven cars on a carrier. But these wing cars could only be shipped out about three at a time. The carrier communicated with Chrysler and picked them up there and deliver to us. These were complete, finished production Chargers that we had to tear apart and convert over. Once we finished the conversions, we communicated with the carrier and they picked the cars up and took them away the very next day. It went like this: Pick up this serial number, this serial number, and this serial number. The carrier truck arrived and they hauled the cars off to their

Front view shows Charger hood recesses filled in with clay, covered by tape. Reverse scoops now installed on fender tops. Early clay modeling to lay out Plymouth Superbird at Creative Industries on Outer Drive. Vehicle being used here was Plymouth Road Runner. (Photo Courtesy Richard Padovini)

Early version of wing. Also note rear backlight window filled in with clay, preparing for streamlining. (Photo Courtesy Richard Padovini)

Canted vertical struts support wing, similar to some unlimited racing class powerboats. Idea was dropped in favor of straight vertical supports similar to Daytona. (Photo Courtesy Richard Padovini)

Thin straight vertical wing supports and altered Charger-style hood recesses. Front marker light recess here is completely filled in. Note two extra vertical struts in wing. (Photo Courtesy Richard Padovini)

Nose details of early clay modeling to lay out Plymouth Superbird at Creative Industries. Note side marker completely filled in, still experimenting with type and location. Also note disguised hood. (Photo Courtesy Richard Padovini)

Front clip early clay modeling to adapt Plymouth Superbird at Creative Industries in Hugh Olson's area on Outer Drive. Note additional nose cone designs sitting next to wall. (Photo Courtesy Richard Padovini)

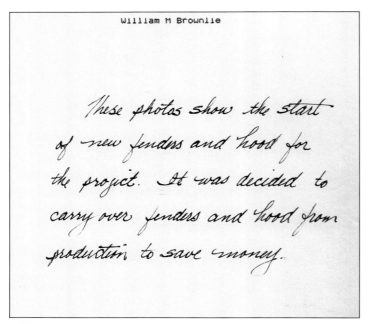

William M Brownlie

These photos show the start of new fenders and hood for the project. It was decided to carry over fenders and hood from production to save money.

Bill Brownlie's note to author about ill-fated 1972 Challenger with Daytona-influenced nose.

destinations, back to a lot, or sometimes right to a dealership. This was done as quickly as possible to get the cars back into the sales channel." Steve revealed a lot of previously unknown information.

Unfortunately, while I also knew Don Mirzoian from many years ago, I never asked him for photos. Don at one time had worked for the Ionia Division of Mitchell-Bentley. He came directly to Creative from Mitchell-Bentley. Sadly, Don passed in 2010 and his daughter Janet (who also worked for both Creative and Mitchell-Bentley) said they never kept much of anything from her dad's career at Creative after moving a few times. Most of it got tossed.

Likewise, Steve Koppin said, "Looking back, I'm so sorry I didn't take photos of all these things. We were all so busy working and having fun with all of the projects and trying to meet deadlines, I guess if it hadn't been for Dave Margolis taking pictures, all that would be lost today."

I asked Steve a few more questions about the Daytona project.

"I have photos taken by Creative's photographer of a Plymouth Road Runner being set up with a wing, clay, and a nose cone to become the Superbird. Did you do any of the work on this prototype?"

"No. That would have been Hugh Olson's boys. But I can tell you exactly where that was all done: inside Outer Drive. Out back. I remember. I've seen the pictures and I was there where they did the mock-up. I recognize it all. I was in all those different buildings over on East Outer Drive. There were about three of those sections where we were so flexible back

then at that location and would change rooms or buildings around for various projects, contracts, or changes in the needs of the company. We had engineers and then someone might say, oh, we need this room now, get rid of the engineers in here because we just took on a new company or project. Those rooms were used for Hugh Olson's mock-ups, where the clay guys were doing their stuff and making tooling. Yes, all that stuff was done over there."

"And Hugh Olson was definitely involved in the wing cars?"

"Absolutely. Any time there was clay, wood, plastics, or modeling, Hugh Olson was involved in it. That was his baby! You asked earlier about Bill Reeker. He was the man who worked for Chrysler on the project."

"A lot of people would like to know what happened to the prototype Superbird that Creative built out of a Road Runner?"

"That's a good question. Hugh would probably know, but he's no longer with us. I wouldn't be surprised if they just put all the old parts back on once they had the dies and molds made, and sent it back to Chrysler. We sure didn't keep it around the shop."

Creative Industries did the entire Dodge Daytona. However, by the time Plymouth decided to do the 1970 Superbird, Creative only did the prototyping and manufactured all of the parts to create the car. Actual assembly of these winged cars was left to Plymouth Division and reportedly was performed at their plant on Lynch Road.

The Final Dodge Long-Nose

By 1971, the Daytona and Superbird programs were over, but their legacy with Dodge continued. And the memory of knowledge gained about reducing coefficient of drag and increasing down force had a lasting influence on design. And there was one final car that almost resulted out of the wing car legacy.

Chrysler's Bill Brownlie occasionally leased space at Creative's building on East Outer Drive and elsewhere. Here, experimental and pet projects were tackled. One of these turned out to be the next generation of Dodge Challenger that was originally intended to debut in 1972. Bill said, "We were trying to do away with the scoop effect of the Challenger grille opening. It just wasn't very efficient in the air at high speed and we figured we could do better."

The theory was that a more slippery front-end design would accomplish several positives for Challenger: better handling at speed, potential fuel savings and a whole new look. Brownlie said he wanted to get the nose a little longer and sloped down; a lesson learned from the Daytona. Headlights would be changed to pop-ups and the rest of the old E-Body structure could pretty much be carried over for a Challenger that would have looked very different.

According to Bill, clay work was being done in at least two locations, one of which was Creative Industries. The clays were well along when Chrysler again suddenly pulled the plug. Bill said the Challenger series was falling alarmingly in sales. The oil embargo and huge fees for performance car insurance dealt it a one-two punch. The muscle car handwriting was on the wall and all of the spoilers and fancy paint jobs couldn't undo the reality. It was feared that E-Bodies (Challenger and Barracuda) might not even survive.

Even worse, Chrysler was so busy struggling to meet new safety and emissions requirements for engines that there was just no money left to upgrade the production Challenger. So the features originally destined for the 1972 Challenger were instead used to morph the short-lived 1970 Challenger Yellow Jacket concept into the Diamante concept. And it all ended there.

Dodge Challenger with proposed nose intended for 1972 in clay. Design change was nixed at last minute due to budget cuts.

Dodge Challenger frontal view with proposed nose intended for 1972 in clay. Lessons learned from airflow, engine cooling, lift, and other issues were attempted to be resolved here. Understructure service as armature was 1971 Challenger convertible.

New headlight placement was not yet decided but would have been pop-up similar to what eventually appeared on Diamante concept car. This design was original inspiration for Diamante front end.

CHAPTER SIXTEEN

VIRGIL EXNER'S STUTZ BLACKHAWK AND FIRESTONE'S LXX TIRES

A lot of interesting automotive artwork once hung on the walls at Creative's Outer Drive offices, such as the famed Ford Mystere. But there was another item of car art on that wall. In fact, there were two of them. One was sized about 8 x 10 and was in a frame. The other was much larger. But aside from the dimensions, both images appeared identical. They were the work of famed designer Virgil M. Exner.

Virgil Exner

As the man largely behind Chrysler Corporation's "Forward Look" of the 1950s when Mopars grew fins and went futuristic, Exner was one of the most iconic designers of the era. His designs were so far ahead of the curve that when GM designers got a peek at Exner's upcoming offerings at Chrysler for the 1957–1959 model years, they were floored. The upshot was a complete paradigm shift out on Mound Road.

There were deep connections between Creative and Chrysler. Virgil Exner had friends at Creative Industries. Both Fred Johnson and Rex Terry also knew Exner even before he had joined Chrysler in 1949. It was around this time that plans were jelling about the opening of Creative. Those connections proved valuable as there continued to be stealth contract assignments to Creative while the years rolled by. But nothing remained static.

As of 1956, Exner had a serious heart attack and Chrysler's design future was suddenly in question. About that time, Packard was on the ropes and an abandon ship call went out as designers such as Bill Schmidt and George Krispinsky were forced to look for work elsewhere. Now remember, both of these men were also very familiar with Creative and indeed had worked there, either at Packard's satellite studio or directly for Creative. So for a while, Messrs. Schmidt and Krispinsky moved over to Chrysler in Highland Park.

Exner already had some plans in place for a new Euro-look compact car line that appeared in the early 1960s. These jaunty designs were sporty with radiused rear wheels, long hoods, and a very lightweight, modern feel about them. Ultimately these lines were marketed as Plymouth Valiant and Dodge Lancer.

Engineering dimensional model for die setup of Exner's 1960 Plymouth Valiant body. Photo was taken 1956–1957 in Creative's shop on East Outer Drive.

Creative did much of the engineering on these cars. As evidence, I managed to find files during the 1970s. One photo shows a body engineering dimensional model for a Plymouth Valiant, sitting in Creative's Outer Drive facility. The photos had been made somewhere between 1957 and 1958. If you look

A 1963 Plymouth Valiant body in clay on precision plate, photographed 9/27/1960 in Creative's Outer Drive shops. By now readers of this book should recognize corrugated steel partitions used at Creative to create locked security rooms.

closely behind the model you can clearly see "Creative" written on a cardboard box. Need I say more?

Yet another glossy photo was also in the same files. This one dated "9-27-60" was of a 1963 Valiant with the all-new bigger body in clay. Just past the clay, which sits on a precision plate, is another one of those corrugated metal partitions you have seen by now throughout this book. You already know where this photo was taken.

Exner eventually recovered from the heart attack and was back in the saddle again, at work for Chrysler. However, a number of things took place in the early 1960s resulting in Exner's departure from Chrysler Corporation. By 1962, he left Highland Park and struck out on his own, continuing design work with his son, Virgil Jr.

The new generation of people around at that time had either mostly forgotten or never knew the era of the true classics. As Exner apparently saw it, the old designs and forgotten names from the past deserved to be revived for another audience. He designed a handful of so-called neoclassic revivals of old brands. Among these were Mercer Cobra, Stutz Blackhawk, Jordan Playboy, Bugatti, Pierce-Arrow, Packard, and Duesenberg. Most of Exner's revival designs were made into scale model kits under the Renwal brand of the mid-1960s. But a lucky few of these designs were actually built as real automobiles. And that's where Creative Industries of Detroit comes into the picture.

Virgil Exner's art proposals for a new Stutz Blackhawk coupe (background) and new Stutz Bearcat convertible. Although Ghia is solely credited for work on Exner-designed Stutz cars, this image hung on the walls at Creative's HQ. Creative was involved. What they did, nobody would say. (Photo Courtesy Pamela Terry Bonk)

Stutz Blackhawk

Conventional histories insist that Ghia of Italy did the Stutz Blackhawk prototype (one price claimed to be more than $300,000) and the Duesenberg prototype sedan (at $60,000). But no history mentions Creative Industries. As usual, it is probably the way Creative and the clients preferred it.

On a visit with Dave Margolis in the late 1970s, I looked through piles of photos and was awestruck by renderings of both the Exner Stutz Blackhawk and something else I had no idea Creative did. There were dozens of renderings of some very handsome but unusual wheels. I recognized some of the wheels instantly. Others I did not. Some were on the Blackhawk illustrations; others were pictured alone. But these were not just any wheels. The rims were extremely large in diameter for the day; I estimated at least seventeen or eighteen inches in diameter. As if that were not amazing enough, the width (cross-section) of

the rim was extremely narrow, perhaps half of normal. I asked Dave about these wheels and he gave me the usual smile. All at once it dawned on me that here was yet another stealth project that amazing Creative Industries had done with no one the wiser. Apparently Creative did some design work, modeling, and possibly some engineering on the radical Firestone LXX wheel and tire combo series.

Firestone's LXX Tires

In Creative's files were photos of full-size plaster mock-ups and resin castings of the wheels. There were even what looked like fiberglass mock-ups of the wild Firestone LXX tires. But I was not allowed to take any artwork or photos. Of course, I was also not allowed to shoot photography inside of the facility.

However, Dave was kind enough to give me a number for a Firestone public relations rep who I called and that person sent me several glossies of the tires and wheels, along with press release information. But there was no mention of Creative Industries and I did not press the issue.

The name LXX was merely Firestone's interpretation of Roman numerals for the number "70." It was the time the tires and wheels appeared and the decade for which they were intended.

The engineering principle of the LXX seemed sound, if not intriguing. A very narrow 3-1/2-inch rim and a bulging tire in an extra-large (for the time) diameter (16-, 17-, or 18-inch)

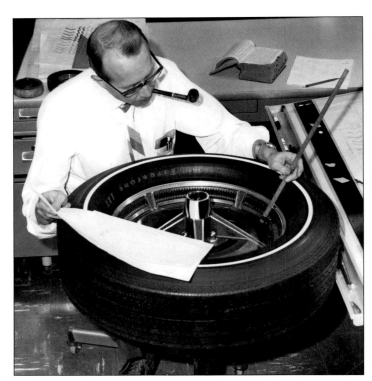

Although different from Exner's renderings, futuristic Firestone LXX tire and wheel system was adopted for Series I Stutz Blackhawk. Firestone engineer measures deep-dish offset for rim. Creative made original design models and possibly tooling for wheels but was never mentioned. (Photo Courtesy Firestone Tire and Rubber Company)

Firestone's manager of advanced tire engineering, John D. Kelly, compares LXX wheel 3½-inch rim to standard rim's 5½-inch width. Bias-ply LXX tire bulging sidewalls were intended to flex, thus improve handling, etc. (Photo Courtesy Firestone Tire and Rubber Company)

wheel was claimed to improve road handling. In theory, such a design could even provide run-flat capability. In the event of deflation, the rim was envisioned to be sandwiched against the bead and tire sidewall.

Of course, the beauty of the complicated forged aluminum wheels and tires was undeniable. Wheel centers were finished in a rough argent with brushed bright edges and a forged five-spoke design. Rim edges were deep-dished and designed in harmony with the tire sidewall. Fine grooving in the rim was so precise it matched similar ribbing on the tire sidewall.

The resulting combination was so startling that it was used as a visual component. The wheel and tire were originally left exposed and recessed into the deck lid of the Blackhawk.

Later versions of the Stutz deleted the classic look of the split-V windshield and the LXX wheels/tires. With a smaller wheel and tire set dropped into the deck recess and neither quite filling it or the fender wells, the look was never quite the same.

There was also another piece of art on the wall. It was also in two sizes and was yet another Exner classic revival. This one

Early Exner Stutz Blackhawk rear deck included exposed LXX wheel/tire. Later Stutz versions deleted LXX, which ceased production. Early taillights were also used on at least one Ferrari. (Photo Courtesy Firestone Tire and Rubber Company)

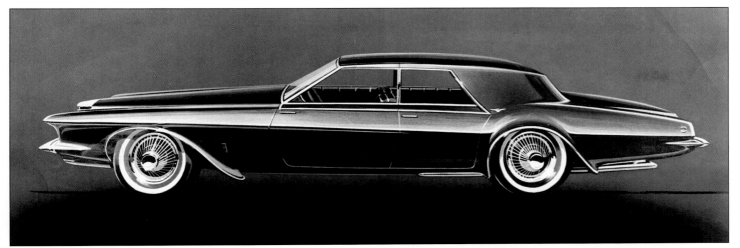

The Exner Duesenberg also built for 1966 was credited solely to Ghia. But this rendering hung on Creative's wall.

was a modern version of a Duesenberg in sedan form. Like the Stutz, the Duesie actually got built into a real automobile. Mounted on a Chrysler Imperial chassis, the sedan was stunningly sleek. Although it did away with traditional Duesenberg cues like an aluminum nostril exhaust tip and "mustache" bumpers, Exner's Duesenberg looked like it was moving, even when parked.

Of course, the big question was, why was the artwork for these cars so proudly hung on the walls in Creative's headquarters? And with all of the material on the Firestone LXX wheels and tires, how could there not have been some engineering interface regarding the Stutz? And with Creative (at the very least) mocking up the wheels, why would, and how could, engineering to mate all of this hardware somehow be done all the way over in Italy at Ghia?

All I can tell you for sure is that Creative did the wheels. Beyond that, the interplay of Exner, Firestone, Ghia, and even Chrysler (remember, they supplied the Duesie chassis) is almost anybody's guess. But no matter who did what, you just can't remove Creative Industries from the equation.

There was one more friendship that should not go unmentioned. This was John Z. De Lorean who, for a while, was a big guy at GM's Pontiac Division. He was one of the people responsible for the Pontiac GTO muscle car. And De Lorean had numerous friends at Creative, among them, Rex Terry. Also, if you read Chapter Eleven, you know that his stainless steel De Lorean DMC-12 sports car prototype number-2 was built at Creative. So guess what chassis and engine was under the Stutz Blackhawk? Pontiac Grand Prix.

For a brief period, the Stutz name found new glory. Elvis Presley bought the first one, then another. He was quickly followed by other celebrities, including members of Hollywood's "Rat Pack" of Frank Sinatra, Dean Martin, Sammy Davis Jr., etc. Lucille Ball, and Liberace even had one.

Early Exner Stutz Blackhawk as debuted at New York's Waldorf Astoria hotel. James O'Donnell was president of revived Stutz Motor Car Company. The $22,500 price made it the most expensive car sold in the United States.

As for the Firestone LXX tire and wheel of the 1970s and the future? They were phased out after a few years. The wheels could only be used with the tires and vice versa. Eventually the tires were just old and expensive, despite their advanced technology.

As the years clicked by, the proud Exner-designed neo-classic era Stutz even found itself on the receiving end of harsh styling critiques using today's mind-set to critique yesterday's design work. But if an automobile can only survive long enough in the world, it usually comes full circle. After all, streamlined Delahayes and 12-cylinder Packards were once just big, old, unloved clunkers. One thing was for sure: nobody poked fun at the Exner Stutz artwork when it was on the walls at Creative Industries.

As for Exner? Although he lived to see his Duesenberg built as a one-off in 1966 and the Stutz went into production in the early 1970s, we lost this great designer in 1973.

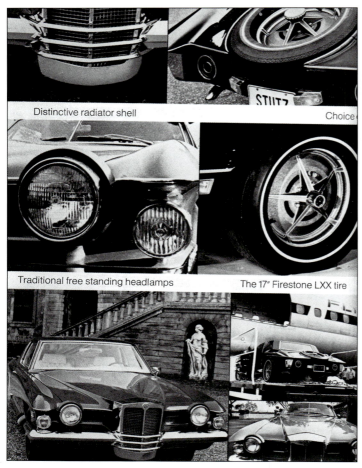

Design features of Series I and II Stutz Blackhawk. Series I had split windshield, 17-inch Firestone LXX tires and wheels.

According to Steve Koppin, who headed Special Vehicles Division for several years, Creative built special vehicles that were sent to the Middle East. Only these were no ordinary special vehicles. Many were equipped with bulletproof glass, weaponry, armor, heavy-duty tires, and other features, along with all the comfort items such as air conditioning and stereo. All were based on American-made vehicles.

According to reports, guess what one part of Stutz Motor Company (the new one making the Exner Blackhawk, etc.) was also selling to the Middle East? A vehicle called the "Bear," not Bearcat, but simply Bear. There were other names as well, such as "Defender," but all were based on Chevy Suburbans. These vehicles underwent huge conversions at Creative and apparently were re-branded Stutz.

Photos show some vehicles came with a large sunroof that allowed a man to stand and look out. According to these same photos, a 50-caliber machine gun was also included on a fully retractable arm. The machine gun could be fired on a roll right out of the open roof of the vehicle!

According to Steve Koppin, Creative Industries indeed did make vehicles so equipped bound for unnamed customers in the Middle East. Several were made, but again, the name of the client selling was unknown. As fantastic as it all may seem and according to those who were around during those times, these things actually happened.

The Stutz bravely, stubbornly held on for several years before finally throwing in the towel. The most expensive car in America had eventually saturated its own market. Even after adding various new models including a convertible, there were only so many buyers out there who could afford such a toy. After a few short years, everyone who wanted a new Stutz had already bought one. But as one automotive sales guru once told me, "There's always tomorrow!"

Lucille Ball's (I Love Lucy TV show) Series I Stutz Blackhawk in Las Vegas museum. The Series I had split windshield. The 17-inch Firestone LXX tires and wheels have been replaced here with regular wheels and tires. Interior was reportedly ostrich skin.

CHAPTER SEVENTEEN

AMX/3, AM-GENERAL, BUSES, THE MIGHTY HUMMER AND PEOPLE MOVERS

*P*ackard's loss had been American Motors' gain. When Richard Teague arrived at AMC in the late 1950s, along with other former Packard design and engineering alums, it meant good things were ahead in terms of AMC styling. It also meant that things were about to change on AMC's engineering front as well. Furthermore, something was going on between AMC and Creative Industries' engineering division, but nobody knew exactly what that "something" was.

Dick wisely held onto his relationship with Creative Industries. With Packard gone as a company, their stealth styling annex at Creative was left without a tenant. However, Richard continued to operate in another area of the Outer Drive general offices building. This fact does not appear to be in AMC histories, but it is a fact nonetheless.

It was only a short time before Dick passed away when he called me to talk cars. I was frankly surprised because I knew he was in such poor health and suffering with the condition that eventually took his life.

We talked about the "impossibilium" 1955 Caribbean hardtops that were made at Creative Industries and Modern Engineering, Inc. We talked about how so much of Packard's work toward the end was subcontracted, with bunches of it going to Creative. And then I mentioned AMX and we were off again.

The AMX/3

Teague admitted that a lot of work had been done at Creative. I asked why everything hadn't been done out at AMC on Plymouth Road. Dick never really elaborated except to say that security was much better at Creative.

According to Creative staffers such as Joe Ramsey, Dick had a good point. Joe said that Teague's area was known as "the Dick Teague" studio early on, but later was known among Creative's employees as "the AMC studio." It was a locked room and nobody but Dick Teague and his staff knew exactly what was going on in there.

Ultimately the topic got to the mid-engined AMX/3. I told Dick that I once noticed a beautiful illustration of a red AMX/3 trimmed in black up on the wall on one of my visits to Creative. I thought everything had been done on this car in Italy. It wouldn't be the first time.

AMX version debuted in 1966. No A-pillars imply "concept" rather than "prototype" category. Rectangular headlights were illegal in the United States. Doorframes were "C"-shaped. Much confusion continues about who did what, where, when. Vignale of Italy is credited with construction, but photos, negatives, and artwork were once at Creative. Taillight "lenses" were made of transparent stainless steel, exactly like Creative did for USS Innovari. Wheels and Talbot racing mirrors (see Dodge Charge I) were also Creative favorites. Two actual vehicles were done in fiberglass; at least one was an operable car. Creative employee claimed they made fiberglass AMXs.

Mid-engine AMX/3 was ultimate in advanced technology and design. Former Packard exterior designer George Krispinsky did some original art for front end. A handful were built but never went to production. (Photo Courtesy George Krispinsky)

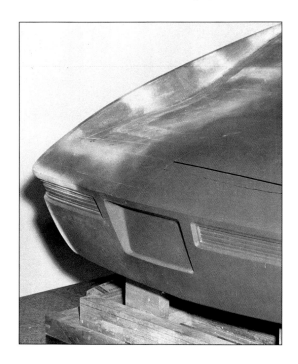

From Creative's negatives, this photo shows an AMX early concept/prototype in clay. White spray bursts are an aid to finding high and low spots before applying color film.

This photo from a Creative negative shows AMX early concept/prototype in clay. Black graphics contrast back-light window and side louvers. Note modeler's inspection notes written in black marker.

AMX/3 Factory Production

Of course, when I asked about the picture on the wall at Creative; all Dick would say was, "Creative, uh, helped us out a bit with that project." No specifics. He went on to say, "There were 26 transaxles left over in Italy." He continued by mentioning that he either owned or had access to 5 more transaxles here in the United States. Dick lamented on the reasons the car never made it to market, but in the end it all boiled down to mainly money. There just wasn't enough of it to bring the car to market under actual mass production. And the profit potential just couldn't be demonstrated. "The numbers just weren't there, but I think we had some good engineering." Dick was right. There was a lot going on at AMC in engineering as well as design in the late 1960s.

I asked Dick about some of AMC's high-performance cars of the late 1960s/early 1970s. I also asked about early street experimentation. He said that he didn't know much about the details since that was another part of AMC. But then he followed with a brief mention that there were "a couple of cars" at Creative during one time or another. He also said that he knew via the grapevine that AMC cars were indeed out on the streets of Detroit being "evaluated." Ahhh. Another mysterious case of Creative and who did what, how, and when?

During one memorable visit to Creative in the 1970s, David Margolis had allowed me to pack up piles of old 8 x 10 glossy photos in their files. These images were dating back to the 1940s and were fast becoming obsolete, at least in the thinking of the 1970s. Many had not been touched in years.

I quickly filled two orange crate-sized boxes with photos and old illustrations. I was told that most of these were already

Photo from Creative's negatives shows AMX early concept/prototype in clay. Precision table, wood substructure, and floor appear same or similar to that used to make Bertleson Aeromobile clay (see Chapter Thirteen).

Image from Creative's file negatives shows early AMX concept/ prototype in clay in two stages of development. Passenger side in evaluation phase, driver's side in refinement stage.

destined for the trash, so I was excited to be rescuing these precious treasures.

I got the first box into the trunk of my car out in the driveway. I was on my way back out with the second box when somebody in the hierarchy noticed me. I was just about to close the trunk lid when Dave, accompanied by another fellow, came trotting up behind me with worried looks on their faces. Dave looked at me, clearly embarrassed and looking for a way to ease the pain. "I'm sorry, but somebody thought it might be a bad idea to let all of these photos out, maybe a violation of our agreements. As much as I think it won't be a problem, I'll need to stop you and ask for the boxes back. I'll try to make it up to you later, but right now, my hands are tied." And that was that. We silently carted the two boxes back inside to a fate unknown. I estimate there had to be several thousand photographs in those boxes, along with beautiful artwork I had picked out. Now, it was all gone.

After some time had passed and on another visit, Dave said, "Remember all those photos? Well, I can't get them back for you, but I thought you might appreciate these." He handed me a manila folder and said, "Put these in your briefcase and look at them later." And with that, Dave handed me not photos but original negatives of AMX clays in brown paper sleeves.

Some of these same photos have been identified in recent years as supposedly having been taken in Ionia, Michigan, at A.O. Smith-Inland Ionia, yet another descendant of good ol' Mitchell-Bentley. So what were these box-camera negatives doing in Creative's files if Creative had no connection with the project?

If you've read the earlier chapters, you already know the relationship of Mitchell-Bentley, their Ionia Manufacturing body division, and ultimately A.O. Smith-Inland Ionia. The latter was involved in making the special 1967–1968 Shelby

Mustangs and at least one ancestral member of Creative's staff was involved here. And we're also back to discussing the Creative specialty of fiberglass bodies.

There were two known fiberglass AMX bodies reportedly produced from the clay. The story was five in number. But what happened to the three additional bodies, if they existed? Good question. One way or another, Creative Industries was quite obviously involved. But we won't speculate details.

For anyone wanting to delve deeper into the mystery, I do offer some final clues. Creative liked using European Talbot racing mirrors on their concept cars of the 1960s. If you remember Dodge Charger I, you may recall it was fitted with a Talbot racing mirror. You may also recall Creative's taste in wheels. They liked Raders and Halibrands. They also liked Dayton radial-laced wire spoke wheels. At least one fiberglass AMX was fitted with Raders and Talbot mirrors. At least one version of the metal AMX concept and another fiberglass bodied version both had radial-laced Daytons.

AM-General, the Trans-Bus and the Mighty HUMMER

You won't see the name of Creative Industries mentioned anywhere in modern histories of AM-General, but it should be. When American Motors bought Jeep at the beginning of the 1970s, the company was descended from the old Willys Motor Company and then into Kaiser-Fraser, then simply Jeep Corporation. A number of things happened over the years. First, the Jeep and General Products division of AMC became known as AM-General.

Mock-up of AM-General postal vehicle proposal at Creative Industries. (Photo Courtesy Larry O'Dowd)

Hugh Olson's crew shown here with sporty Hummer prototype at Creative's East Outer Drive compound. (Photo Courtesy Hugh Olson)

Creative had much experience building four-wheel-drive vehicles. They built this prototype Falcon Ranchero as test-bed for Ford Bronco. Photo taken in Creative's driveway on Outer Drive. Tonneau over bed covered test equipment used to evaluate vehicle performance.

As AMC and Jeep fans know, Jeep continued production in one way or another. But the most important developments happened with government contracts. Eventually a major effort was made to make the company profitable via U.S. federal contracts and transportation projects. The upshot of this branching out led to three general areas of vehicle production: U.S. postal delivery vehicles, buses, and military vehicles. But ironically you won't see one mention of Creative Industries, despite participation in all three.

One logical direction was to furnish vehicles for the United States post office, where Jeeps had often been over the decades. Guess who they called to make prototypes?

Next was mass transportation. With federal funds up for grabs, AM-General decided to dive in to what was proposed as the national "TransBus" program. In this program the company able to meet a set of very rigid guidelines could win a contract to produce a new generation of special buses. These TransBus buses had to meet certain power, carrying capacities, handicapped and wheelchair requirements, all at a price.

AM-General went up against Pennsylvania bus maker, Rohrer, and the king at the time, GM's GMC Truck and Bus division. Eventually three less-than-attractive but operable prototypes emerged, one each per company.

In the end, AM-General made lots of buses, but not based on the TransBus prototype. The TransBus requirements would have resulted in very expensive, complicated, feature-laden vehicles that urban bus lines just could not easily afford. It may have seemed like a nice idea on paper, but the program was doomed. The TransBus prototypes received little more than boutique showings around the country before the program reportedly slipped into obscurity and was quietly dropped.

Histories repeatedly claim that a Canadian bus company made the AM-General TransBus prototype. But you already know who really did it, don't you?

Large version of prototype ambulance conversion cap mounted on Hummer prototype variation built by Creative. (Photo Courtesy Hugh Olson)

Of course, the best known of all the vehicles that came out of AM-General were out of the military branch. Of these designated "HMMWV" (high mobility multipurpose wheeled vehicle) was better known as "Humvee" or eventually, "Hummer." Because the history of these relatively recent vehicles is well known, we won't repeat it here. But Creative's participation in the Hummer development is apparently *not* known. Thus, we humbly offer you some views of prototypes built by Creative Industries.

Production of the civilian version was eventually acquired and continued for several years under General Motors until its bankruptcy. But original prototypes for the military were put together by Creative.

Ford's ACT People Movers

We've talked about the oil crisis of the 1970s and how it affected the auto industry. Nobody knew for sure how long the oil spigots would remain shut off or when disaster would return again. So public transportation became a hot button issue in governments, especially at the federal level and in states with large urban areas.

So even before the time that Creative was struggling to make magic bus prototypes that would meet unrealistic requirements, Ford wisely began scanning the horizon for other possibilities. Ford had no desire to end up a casualty in the potentially oil-less world of the near future. They had one possible solution.

Henry Ford II was quoted in a smooth Ford Motor Company promotional: "First, we are confident that the automobile will continue to be the preferred mode of travel for most people for most trips. Second, we want to share in the market for modes of travel that will be better than the automobile for some purposes. And finally, we believe that a better urban environment will be good for our company and our customers as well as all other Americans." The proposed system would be fully electric, emit no exhaust, and would be very quiet (it would roll on foam-filled tires). Furthermore the system would have no driver.

Driverless vehicles are all the latest buzz of recent times, but Ford and Creative directed the principle to mass transportation. In 1972 a prototype Automatically-Controlled Transport (ACT) people mover line was installed and operated in "Transpo 72" demonstration. Ford claimed more than 25,000 users were transported by its system.

Another Ford ACT was installed at Bradley International Airport outside of Hartford, Connecticut. In the mid-1970s still another line was installed in Michigan between a Dearborn Hyatt hotel and a shopping mall near the site of Henry Ford's old estate known as Fairlane. This line was originally intended to connect to Ford World Headquarters building, but

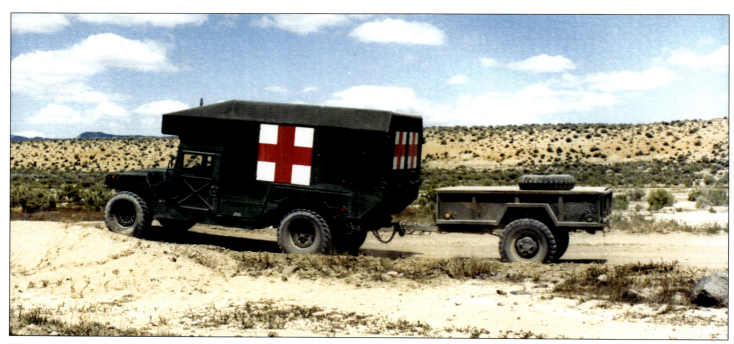

Hummer ambulance prototype variation built by Creative undergoes shakedown run in desert climate for testing and evaluation. (Photo Courtesy Hugh Olson)

HUMMVEE prototype variation built by Creative undergoes winter climate testing. Fully enclosed all-weather capability demonstrated. (Photo Courtesy Larry O'Dowd)

reportedly legal hassles and expenses involved in crossing the freeway were prohibitive.

Some insisted upon calling the Ford ACT a "monorail," which it wasn't because it ran on rubber tires. The ride was quiet and very smooth. It was an interesting, modern-looking system.

Although the Dearborn Fairlane ACT people mover was very well received and even loved by many, sadly, it ceased operation in more recent years. The reason given was due to maintenance costs. Of course, the oil crisis was forgotten and Ford's dream of expanding the ACT system to other locations never took wing. Like so many dream cars, the Fairlane ACT people mover was eventually dismantled and removed. As Alex Tremulis used to say, "I wonder if the future will ever catch up to the past."

Of course by now, surely you know that the Fairlane and Ford ACT vehicles were prototyped and built by Creative Industries.

Late Hugh Olson directed stages of many projects. Shown here with sporty Hummer prototype. Curved wall of glass blocks was originally Fred Johnson's office on Creative's East Outer Drive compound. Later became Verne Koppin's office. (Photo Courtesy Hugh Olson)

Front view of people mover car Ford's ATC system for Fairlane Mall. Shot was taken after completion at Creative Industries. (Photo Courtesy Gary Smythe)

Verne Koppin of Creative Industries stands at far right of Ford's ATC system side view of people mover car for Fairlane Mall. (Photo Courtesy Larry O'Dowd)

During construction at Creative Industries of Ford's ATC system people mover car for Fairlane Mall. (Photo Courtesy Steve Koppin)

Construction at Creative Industries reveals complicated wiring inside vehicle. Ford's ATC system. (Photo Courtesy Steve Koppin)

Floor of ATC system car was aluminum extrusions. Seat frames were tubular steel with fiberglass bucket overlay and replaceable fabric inserts. Steve Koppin recalls that Creative often got calls for replacement seat inserts, which they provided to Ford. (Photo Courtesy Steve Koppin)

CHAPTER EIGHTEEN

CREATIVE'S MANY LOCATIONS AND A LAST LOOK AT MUSTANG PROTOTYPES AND CONCEPTS

Secrecy and flexibility required lots of locations all over Detroit and its suburbs, but wonders still flowed out of Mt. Elliott even at the end.

Creative's Many Locations

One of the first questions about Creative Industries today is, what happened to Creative and where was the original headquarters?

Creative eventually disappeared as a stand-alone company, but it still remains in a rather ancestral way. As for the original headquarters building? This is another story. But it is also important to consider that Creative was never lodged in just one or two buildings. It was all over the Detroit area and ultimately around the globe.

The building at 3080 East Outer Drive was originally constructed in the 1930s to house Fred Johnson's Progressive Welder Company. The front offices were beautiful and made of yellow brick in rather industrial art moderne style architecture. The main entryway and portico were constructed of fluted sandstone and granite.

The corners of the building were rounded and windows were all framed in sturdy metal. Out back was a large attached main shop, accompanied by a series of separate outbuildings. These changed in shape, structure, and number over the years.

Toward the center of this complex was Johnson's beautiful office. It was a separate stand-alone structure. Inside, the art moderne office featured a stunning, sweeping wall of curved glass blocks. It also had what was considered a luxury for those days: wall-to-wall carpet. The adjacent waiting room floor was a glistening tiled checkerboard pattern that was all the rage back then.

The ceiling was vaulted, and beautiful Egyptian urn-shaped sconces in a brushed metal finish enhanced the whole experience. Trendy leather chairs and the decorator colors completed the look.

People today don't know what a Murphy Bed was, but there was a grand one here. It could be pulled down, out of the

Taken in 1955, David Margolis sits in Rex Terry's Packard Panther in front of 3080 East Outer Drive. And yes, "of Detroit" was originally part of the official company name. Look closely and you see that the offset "V" symbol on the building is repeated on the rear of the Panther.

wall, in the room just off Fred's office. Here he could nap and recover from the stress of running his businesses. In the other direction was Fred's personal kitchen where he could grab a snack or full meal anytime. Elsewhere in the compound was yet a larger kitchen and the dining room where Fred Johnson once had daily lunch with his managers and the heads of Industrial City's allied companies.

Progressive remained (reduced in size) in the main building at the founding of Creative Industries in 1950. However, much of the five-acre facility site that had once been known as Progressive Welder Company and Industrial City was quickly renamed Creative Industries of Detroit. Some of the semi-separate companies that were once Fred's Industrial City (such as Development Engineering Incorporated) now became either parts of Creative or continued in an alliance with Creative. I believe the wood company (American Wood Products) that was once allied with or owned by Fred Johnson was somehow spun off and otherwise lost in the sands of time. Some of it remained in different locations all around Michigan.

By the early 1950s, Progressive eventually took up a new residence in Pontiac, Michigan. Johnson passed on in November 1954, but Creative continued to grow with his friend Rex Terry at the helm. Those in positions of responsibility had been chosen well. Creative never looked back and always seemed to have an even brighter future ahead. As one employee told me, "We all thought it would never end!"

As Creative continued to expand and prosper, Outer Drive was quickly outgrown. The speed of this growth was phenomenal. The mere signing of a new contract with a client could instantly require thousands of new square feet for workspace. The upshot of this situation was ongoing rental and acquisition of remote buildings.

As mentioned earlier, one of the early outbuildings was located on Mt. Elliott just off 6 Mile Road. About that same time, sheet metal prototyping had outgrown the space at East Outer Drive.

The original Industrial City allied metal stamping company named Hydro Manufacturing was one of the first to outgrow its environs. Under Creative Industries and now officially "Experimental Sheet Metal Division," this branch was moved to a building at 14325 East 9 Mile Road. The area then was known as East Detroit and is now known as Eastpointe. And

yes, some Mopar wing car parts were fabricated there.

In July 1976, Volkswagen Manufacturing Corporation (VW's American production company) established headquarters in space rented from Creative Industries. By the end of the year, VW moved to larger quarters in Warren, Michigan, but De Lorean (see Chapter Twelve) was still hanging out at Outer Drive.

The long-haul truck business Creative dabbled in at Outer Drive finally began to explode and a facility was established off North Telegraph Road adjacent to a shopping center. Limited production truck runs and customizing or upgrades to 18-wheelers were done there.

When a major union shop dispute arose in the 1980s, Development Engineering Incorporated (DEI) was eventually shut down after a strike. Ironically, another long time company and with similar initials (DIE for Detroit Industrial Engineering) was adopted as a subcontractor. They began performing the work formerly done by DEI. Still with me? DIE eventually became a wholly owned subsidiary of Creative as of 1986 and remained an integral part of the company. DI did a lot of work over many years on Corvette.

As the years rolled by and the contracts continued to roll in, Rex Terry's lieutenants, Verne Koppin and Richard Leasia, took over an increasing amount of responsibilities and ultimately

Floor of Fred Johnson's office and waiting room as it looks today. Grid where floor tiles were laid out is still visible. View is looking toward intersection of Moenart Street and East Outer Drive. Fenced lot across Moenart was formerly Creative employees' parking lot. Location is now a church.

Fred Johnson sits at the head of a luncheon table in the headquarters of his nine-partnered companies known as Industrial City. He is surrounded by managers of the companies who had lunch together daily.

Driveway of contention as photographed by author in 1970s. Building on right was supposedly built on top of property line and so close to Creative's shop that trucks entering from Outer Drive could not pass if building had windows flipped open. In one 1950s incident, a box truck took out an entire row of open windows. Creative also had to change the shop to face roll-up door toward Outer Drive to prevent security breaches.

Driveway remains today, but Creative's buildings are all gone. Building on right has suffered significant damage from scrappers and taggers.

Early remote location of Development Engineering Incorporated (DEI).

Larry O'Dowd and crew pour Kirksite mold at Development Engineering Incorporated (DEI). Larry moved on to other areas under different divisional/company names, but he was guru of sheet metal prototyping, stamping. (Photo Courtesy Larry O'Dowd)

Business flyer for Detroit Industrial Engineering (DIE), which picked up where DEI left off. (Photo Courtesy Ron Pachella)

became owners. With Terry's retirement and ultimate passing, Messrs. Koppin and Leasia first bought out the remaining interest of the Johnson family. As co-owners of Creative, the Koppin and Leasia duo eventually struck a deal with automotive powerhouse, Masco-Tech, for a 50-percent buy-in of Creative's ownership. That amount was later increased to 100 percent and Creative, then known as Creative Industries Group or simply Creative Group, became a wholly owned component of Masco.

In 1986, Creative headquarters left Outer Drive and moved north to Auburn Hills, under its new name of Creative Industries Group, Incorporated. Business cards now adopted a new "CG" logo and the old offset "V" symbol disappeared. The area was booming in those days with Chrysler's relocated operations and many other businesses. Chrysler even opened a lovely

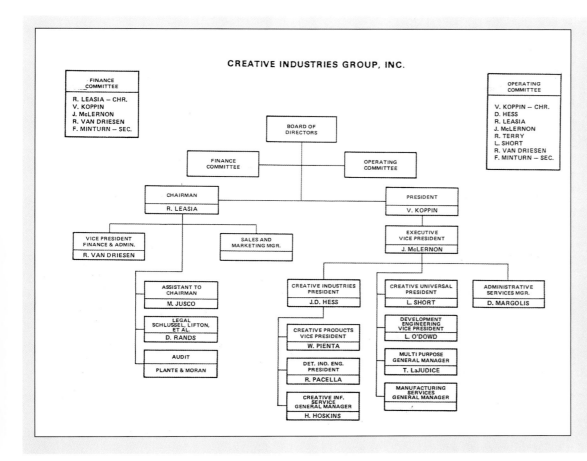

CREATIVE INDUSTRIES GROUP, INC.

FINANCE COMMITTEE
R. LEASIA – CHR.
V. KOPPIN
J. McLERNON
R. VAN DRIESEN
F. MINTURN – SEC.

OPERATING COMMITTEE
V. KOPPIN – CHR.
D. HESS
R. LEASIA
J. McLERNON
R. TERRY
L. SHORT
R. VAN DRIESEN
F. MINTURN – SEC.

BOARD OF DIRECTORS

FINANCE COMMITTEE

OPERATING COMMITTEE

CHAIRMAN
R. LEASIA

PRESIDENT
V. KOPPIN

VICE PRESIDENT FINANCE & ADMIN.
R. VAN DRIESEN

SALES AND MARKETING MGR.

EXECUTIVE VICE PRESIDENT
J. McLERNON

ASSISTANT TO CHAIRMAN
M. JUSCO

CREATIVE INDUSTRIES PRESIDENT
J.D. HESS

CREATIVE UNIVERSAL PRESIDENT
L. SHORT

ADMINISTRATIVE SERVICES MGR.
D. MARGOLIS

LEGAL SCHLUSSEL, LIFTON, ET AL.
D. RANDS

CREATIVE PRODUCTS VICE PRESIDENT
W. PIENTA

DEVELOPMENT ENGINEERING VICE PRESIDENT
L. O'DOWD

AUDIT
PLANTE & MORAN

DET. IND. ENG. PRESIDENT
R. PACELLA

MULTI PURPOSE GENERAL MANAGER
T. LaJUDICE

CREATIVE INF. SERVICE GENERAL MANAGER
H. HOSKINS

MANUFACTURING SERVICES GENERAL MANAGER

New 1985 organizational chart of Creative Industries as under ownership by Verne Koppin and Richard Leasia. Rex Terry continues to be listed. At this point it became The Creative Group and was moving toward eventual ownership under Masco-Tech company. President J. D. Hess was related to famous Hess & Eisenhardt Limousine Company. F. Minturn of Finance Committee is now CEO of MSX International in 2016. (Photo Courtesy Steve Koppin)

museum there. Even the Detroit Lions football team had moved to the "Silverdome," an all-weather facility close by. The future seemed rosy.

Creative's new headquarters was now located at 275 Rex Boulevard, named after Rex Terry, of course. Dave Margolis called me to let me know everyone had moved and invited me to come see "my model" of the Ford FX-Atmos. Dave said it was still sitting on his desk, waiting for retirement. But I had already been living in California for many years then, so visits to Creative were few and far between. I was also knee-deep in my work for Mazda Corporation.

Once Creative morphed so much and people either left or retired, it became a real ordeal just to keep track of everyone. Dave suddenly became ill and we lost touch. Eventually the letters from Gary Hutchings stopped too.

A Final Look at the Ford Mustang

The automotive world of the late 1970s and into the 1980s was still reeling from the effects of the 1970s fuel crises. Performance cars were still hanging on during the roller-coaster ride of the 1980s, but there was always the concern, both in and out of Ford, of what might happen to Mustang. One direction considered during this period came to light when Mazda and

Ford decided to open an assembly plant at Flat Rock, Michigan.

The plan was that Mazda would produce their FWD 626 sedan and MX-6 coupe and, at least for a while, Ford would have built an MX-6-based Mustang successor. But Front Wheel Drive and six cylinders? Mustang's loyal fans just weren't having any of this. Clubs and enthusiasts in magazines recoiled in horror at what might become of their beloved Mustang.

Thankfully cooler heads prevailed and in the end, the RWD V-8 Mustang continued, come hell or high water. The Ford car built at Flat Rock was introduced as the spectacular new Probe coupe. But I need to back up a bit to give you a better perspective on Creative Industries and Mustang.

As I mentioned earlier, Ford was certainly no stranger to Creative Industries. And from the time Mustang first appeared, there were numerous rumors of Mustang involvement at Creative. However, a few instances of Creative Industries' involvement with Mustang are no longer secret, as we will share with you here.

SVO Mustang

By the late 1970s, Ford's brilliance was once again at work on the marque. One upshot was a radical departure in engines and overall Mustang model. It became known as the SVO, which stood for Special Vehicle Operations. This was an

Mustang SVO. (Photo Courtesy Bob McClurg)

Mustang SVO. (Photo Courtesy Bob McClurg)

"outside-of-the-box" Ford department and this radically new Mustang adopted its name. But what most people never knew is that Creative Industries was also involved in this development and program.

Some say it was merely a case of pressure brought to bear from new federally mandated Corporate Average Fleet Economy (CAFÉ) regulations. Others say it was Ford's techie people trying to pump some sunshine into the Mustang. But whatever the reason, the Mustang SVO was a remarkable car and remains one of the most unusual, innovative production/performance cars ever offered. With a mere four cylinders, Mustang SVO pumped out between 175 to 205 horsepower during its model run from 1984 to 1986. Not a noteworthy figure today, but in SVO's era, it was darned impressive. Mustang SVO was as fast as (some say faster) than a Mustang equipped with a 302-ci V-8. Yet SVO had driving performance and handling that bordered on a track racer. It was light, it was agile, and it had go.

The SVO's look was also unique with a nose featuring built-in driving lights, filled-in grille, and a hood with a scoop similar to a NACA duct. The taillights received a special smoked look treatment and striping. But the real differences were far beyond cosmetics.

Virtually everything a serious driver could ask for was either standard or available. Ample four-wheel disc brakes, larger wheels and tires, intercooled turbo, Koni shocks, rack-and-pinion steering, anti-hop rear suspension, Hurst shifter, performance transmission and gauges, bi-wing rear spoiler, special high-bolster

seats with pump-up lumbar support; the list seemed endless. All powered by a turbocharged 2.3 liter SOHC 4-cylinder. In an era of uncertainty about gasoline, there was even a neat little switch that allowed the driver to select between high-octane or regular fuel. A similar switch feature appeared years later on a Mustang concept that I discuss talk shortly.

According to former Creative staffer Gary Smythe, Ford had contracted Creative to do certain work on the Mustang SVO program. Gary said, "The Ford project manager was John Rundles. We had a kind of 'skunk works' going on there at Creative and we ended up building a prototype SVO Mustang! John later went on to Chrysler and I worked again with him years later when I was at Metalcrafters in California doing Chrysler prototypes."

The ideas that poured into the SVO beyond the engine were largely jelled at Creative Industries. Ford had its own project manager on-site, but the SVO was again one of those hush-hush projects secreted away behind the corrugated metal partition walls at Creative. Of course, in typical fashion, precisely whatever Creative did or supplied to SVO will likely never be known in detail.

The Mustang SVO was a masterpiece. But it just didn't have the brute torque and amazing sound of a V-8 that Mustang fans adored and expected in a muscle car. And frankly, SVO cost more to buy even if it cost less to operate. So the Mustang SVO went away after 1986, at least for a while.

Creative Industries executed two Lincoln show cars in 1982 and 1983. These were the Concept 90 and the Concept 100, respectively. These highly electronic showcases introduced features such as onboard computer games, infotainment, and new-age onboard navigation.

But it took until 1992 before another stunning Mustang development took place at Creative. But by then the entire company had undergone a major transformation.

With Creative Group now merely a division of Masco-Tech, there was a rollover in personnel (non-transition, retirement, and death). Few who were with the old regime became part of the new regime. There were now so many players and so many directions one almost needed a scorecard to keep up with it all. The Creative Group had morphed so far past the original company, at this point they were in talks with the Chinese (PANDA) regarding possible production of a car in the United States or China.

History gets confused here, as those looking back today are unaware of the Creative Industries lineage. Reference is usually not even to Creative Group, but rather to the parent company, Masco-Tech. And the parent company itself morphed into yet another name, MSX International. Thus, products and vehicles that resulted under these transitions are now looked back upon as having been made by three different companies!

Mach III Concept Car

Under the Creative Group name, two of the last big projects were particularly noteworthy. One was a production vehicle: the 1993–1994 Oldsmobile Cutlass Supreme convertibles. But these Oldsmobiles were not built in Detroit or even Michigan. Instead, the line was set up just outside Atlanta, Georgia.

But the other project was the beautiful 1993 Mustang Mach III roadster concept. The Mach III was yet another amazing Detroit story and here is just a bit more that you may not have known.

The Mach III was actually a side effect of the Ford Probe episode we have discussed. Author and official Ford Enthusiasts Communication Manager John Clor looks back today at Mach III and points out what a crucial period this was in the brand. Says Clor, "The juncture in that time was a pretty important one for Mustang. There was much consternation over continuing the brand. A lot of marketers just didn't believe that the car had any legs left. There was just no doubt that the entire sport coupe segment was leaning toward front wheel drive, small engines, the Honda Civics of the world. There were just not many people at the company who believed they could keep a rear-wheel-drive V-8 pony car and make it competitive in the market. And the Fox body that came out in 1979 was, at one point, the longest running platform of its time. By the time it reached 1989 and was 10 years running, the feeling among some was that the Mazda-stang would be the perfect replacement."

But there were a handful of those who fiercely opposed this direction. Several names come to mind, but Clor believes Bob Rewey, who was vice president at the time and ran Ford marketing, was the key champion of retaining Mustang as a rear-wheel-drive V-8. According to Clor, this Ford marketing man said he just couldn't sell a smaller FWD drive coupe and call it a Mustang.

John Coletti, who was a Ford product planning manager during this period, was another of those who just couldn't see the Mustang name marketed on a foreign-based front-wheel-drive coupe. The very idea was something to dread; and then there was the old rivalry with GM's Camaro. No way was a FWD import chassis going to do battle on American streets with the likes of Camaro. So as Coletti saw it, the path ahead was clear. He only needed to find allies and convince them of his vision.

According to Mustang expert and author Bob McClurg, Coletti began to dream of an ultimate Camaro-killer car, powered by a gnarly V-8 and rear wheel drive. Ultimately Coletti's dream began to take shape first as a concept car that predicted the exciting directions of the Mustang that followed. This concept reassured Mustang fans they needn't worry about losing the car and the format they loved. And the idea was so nice, they decided to do it twice.

According to McClurg, two project code designation SN95 prototype cars were scrapped out to become the basic building platforms for two Mach III concepts.

Under Masco-Tech's ownership, what was once Creative's Special Vehicles division passed from Steve Koppin's leader-

Final inspection of Mach III ready for show. (Photo Courtesy Richard Rinke)

Two Mach III Mustang concepts ready for show. (Photo Courtesy Richard Rinke)

Creative Group staffers build body of Mach III in plaster molds. (Photo Courtesy Richard Rinke)

Bare carbon fiber body of Mach III mounted on precision plate at Creative Group Mt. Elliott facility. (Photo Courtesy Richard Rinke)

Body of Mach III in primer mounted on floorpan/chassis. Note supercharged ending installed and stock Mustang wheels. (Photo Courtesy Richard Rinke)

View of supercharged engine with wild side stacks during construction of Mach III at Creative Group Mt. Elliott facility. (Photo Courtesy Richard Rinke)

ship to J. Paul Snyder, who served as vice president and general Manager. The construction of the Mach III concepts was overseen by Kevin Vercauteren and preceded swiftly. The two concepts were built, one after the other, with the first construction completed in early November 1992.

The SN95 understructures and chassis were upgraded and stiffened to make them strong enough to handle stresses that could occur from an open cockpit roadster powered by a big stump-pulling 450-hp V-8.

Meanwhile, the blue oval engineering boys went to work on the 4.6 powerplant and beefed it up as well. A steel billet crank was added on the bottom end. And there were some exciting changes up top. Unlike turbocharged engines that use exhaust to drive a mini-turbine to incredible speeds and really need an intercooler to function optimally, intake temperature in the case of a supercharger was not the same issue. However, colder air is normally denser air and thus a boost to horsepower. So, to raise maximum horsepower of the custom supercharged engines, the intakes received a special system

fed by engine coolant to lower temperatures. Think of it as an advanced "cold-air package."

Then came the look of the concept. Bob McClurg says that two-passenger roadster styling had already been dialed in under Ford's Bud Magaldi, who was design manager, and Darryl Behmer, Ford design executive. Many of Behmer's ideas went into the overall design, and Ford's people pushed clay in their studios.

Once the full-size clay model was completed, it was delivered to what Bob describes as Masco-Tech's (think Creative) Mt. Elliott facility (as far back as the 1950s Creative had been pulling molds from clays and molding fiberglass bodies at a Mt. Elliott location). And what was Creative's specialty when they did fiberglass? One-piece molded bodies. So? Mach III got a one-piece molded body, but this time, not fiberglass, but rather state-of-the-art carbon-fiber material.

Richard Rinke (yes, of the famous car dealership family) was representing Creative Group/Masco and according to Bob McClurg was instrumental in snaring the contract to do the

Mach III rolls out of Creative Group Mt. Elliott facility for a drive. (Photo Courtesy Richard Rinke)

Press and display people were told to drive Mach III no faster than "courtyard cruise" low speeds. Of course, wild car with wild engine was too much to resist trying burnout. (Photo Courtesy Richard Rinke)

Preparation for press photos and preview in Arizona, just arrived from Detroit. Mach III wheels are on rear, stock Mustang wheels are up front. Note "Creative Group" jacket being worn by one staffer. (Photo Courtesy Richard Rinke)

MACH III SPECS

Engine: 4.6 DOHC modular with steel billet crank
Aspiration: Supercharged with intake manifold cooler system (using coolant)
Fuel: Unleaded gasoline or Methanol (switchable by driver)
Horsepower: 450 bhp
Transmission: BorgWarner 6-speed
Wheels: 16-inch forged aluminum
Body: One-piece molded carbon fiber

Mach III. Says Rinke today: "I can tell you a lot about the Mach III. The car had a tremendous impact on Mustang fans and there was such a big reaction to it when the Mach III went on display. A lot of people fell in love with that car."

What happened to the twin Mach III concepts? One supposedly caught fire while being transported and was severely damaged. There was some effort to repair the car but some say it was too far gone and was later scrapped. The remaining Mach III continued to be shown but was eventually retired. Somewhere along the way it acquired a green paint job and was ultimately sold off at auction.

The Creative Ship Finally Slips Beneath the Surface

Creative Industries as a name had disappeared. Meanwhile, a Detroit branch of a national housing organization eventually moved into the old, unoccupied Creative building on East Outer Drive and remained there for a few years. But things continued to change.

With Detroit's ever-slipping grip on the auto industry and the onslaught of foreign competition, the pace of things (or lack thereof) in the city suddenly began to accelerate downward. As a result, ever faster, more catastrophic changes began to take place, like falling dominoes. Even the housing organization people ended up moving to another location.

With no occupants and increasing amounts of maintenance needed, the old Outer Drive building quickly fell into disrepair. And being in the new piranha age of Detroit, with numbers of roving scrappers looking for empty structures to pilfer, the nail was in the coffin. Nothing was sacred.

Word soon spread that the yellow brick building on East Outer Drive was ripe for the pickings. The structure was quickly raped and pillaged of all its fittings. When last seen, the once-beautiful art deco building had been stripped of nearly anything with scrap value. Even the roof had collapsed. The heavy metal front doors disappeared and the once proud entryway was left gaping open, as if it were the mouth of a building in shock

Mustang Cobra "R"

As Creative Industries increasingly disappeared into Masco-Tech, there was one final gasp of a super car they helped to build in limited production. This was Ford's wing car, the latter of which was capable of speeds in excess of 170 miles per hour. Details of the Mustang Cobra R and Creative's involvement are in the chart.

MUSTANG COBRA "R" FACTS–THE OTHER WING CAR

Year	Production Total	Price	Engine	Horsepower	Transmission	Brakes	Performance	Model Name	Fuel Tank Size	Tires
1993	107	$25,217	5 Liter (302 cid)	235 @ 4,600 RPM	5-speed Borg-Warner T-5	Ventilated disc 13-inch front, 10.5 rear	0 - 60 = 5.7 seconds	SAT Cobra "OR"	15.4 Gallons	Good Year "Razorback" P245/45ZR-17
1994	none									
1995	250	$33,545	5.8 Liter (351 cid)	300@ 4,800 RPM	5-speed Tremec	Ventilated disc 13-inch front, 11.65 rear	0 - 60= 5.2 seconds	SAT Cobra "OR"	20 Gallons	B.F. Goodrich Competition T/A P255/45ZR-17
1996	none									
1997	none									
1998	none									
1999	none									
2000	300	$54,995	5.4 Liter (330 cid)	385@ 6,250 RPM	6-Speed	Ventilated disc 13-inch front, 11.65 rear	0 - 60= 4.4 seconds	SAT Cobra "OR"	21 Gallons	B.F Goodrich g-Force KD 265/40ZR-18

Note: Historians list "Maso-Tech" and "MSX" respectively for 1995 and 2000, but these are still Creative Industries in descendent form!

Creative Industries general offices at 3080 as the building appeared in late 1970s. Driveway paralleled across front and entry overhang was added, changed from 1950s–1960s. Note logo on building has deleted "of Detroit" from company name. Also note new decorative brick wall near sidewalk.

Right-hand view of Creative Industries general offices at 3080 as the building appeared in late 1970s. Roll-up door leads to main shop. Building extends to left. Former clock was removed when overhang was installed. (Photo Courtesy Edge Leasia)

The lower flag is for the State of Michigan. Remnants of driveway still exist today. (Photo Courtesy Edge Leasia)

Wheels	Color	Seats	Hood	Creative's Involvement*	Deleted Items
17-inch 5-lug	Red	Standard cloth		Wing fabrication, misc. parts fabrication, final trim assembly and graphics, hood paint.	Rear seat, sound insulation, radio, air conditioning, power windows, power door locks
17-inch 5 spoke, aluminum 5-lug	White	Standard cloth	Fiberglass	Hood and wing fabrication, misc. parts fabrication. Installation of cooling system and fuel cell.	Rear seat, sound insulation, radio, air conditioning, power windows, power door locks, fog lights
18-inch 5 Lug	Red	Recaro	Fiberglass	Hood and wing fabrication, misc. parts fabrication, final assembly including exhaust, brake ducts, oil cooler and graphics, hood paint,	Rear seat, sound insulation, radio, power door locks

Left-hand view of Creative Industries at intersection of East Outer Drive and Moenart Street. Front building with rounded corners was former office of Creative Universal division. Blue building behind and off Moenart was wood shop. Employees' entrance was farther down on right. Employee parking lot was on left across street. (Photo Courtesy Edge Leasia)

Left-hand view of Creative Industries at intersection of East Outer Drive and Moenart Street. Front building with rounded corners was former office of Creative Universal division. CU had already moved to Southfield, Michigan, by this time (note rectangular shadow over windows where sign was removed) but logo was still on awning over entrance. (Photo Courtesy Edge Leasia)

Left-hand view of Creative Industries at intersection of East Outer Drive and Moenart Street. Blue building was wood shop. Lot to left was employee parking lot. Note car transport carrier parked on street, either awaiting pickup or having just dropped off. (Photo Courtesy Edge Leasia)

Decades later, 3080 East Outer Drive's entrance was in ruins. Notice collapsed roof and missing front doors. Author's friends managed to save one of circular yellow concrete segments of wall here. Concrete segment now sits in author's office. (Photo Courtesy Detroit Yes!)

3050 East Outer Drive, entrance to Creative Universal office, corner of Moenart Street and East Outer Drive. CU sign over entrance was later moved above windows and awning was installed above door. Metal structure on Moenart side is sawdust collector from Creative wood shop. Farther down Moenart were two entrances to Creative.

Creative Universal, wood shop, etc., years later. Damage occurred after departure of housing organization. (Photo Courtesy Detroit Yes!)

Creative Industries general offices at 3080 as the building appeared in late 1970s. Note building to right and fireplug near curb.

Creative Industries general offices at 3080 are long gone as location appeared in 2015. Note building to right is gutted and strewn with graffiti but is still standing. Fireplug near curb still remains.

View in 2015 looking from Moenart toward Outer Drive. This was former location of Creative Industries' rear gate. Development Engineering Incorporated (DEI) once stood here to the left.

from betrayal. In the end, the five-acre site was leveled and soon overrun with weeds and discards of every size and shape.

The assets of Creative Group had been completely merged and morphed under Masco. Ironically, operations moved from the newer building on the boulevard named for the colorful man who had led Creative to such great success; 275 Rex Boulevard was now just another commercial address for sale or lease.

Creative Group eventually ended up as an ancestor to the company known today as MSX International. But the story continues.

Call it interesting. Call it coincidence. Or call it wishful thinking if you will. But after all of the years and changes, perhaps things have indeed gone full circle.

Minturn, the visionary CEO of MSX, was once the auditor of Creative Industries, having started with them back in the 1980s. Under his direction, the ancestral company has continued to prosper and expand. With employees numbering around 5,000, MSX currently has an annual growth rate reported at 15 percent and has offices as far away as Brazil and Thailand.

I have talked with Minturn and I can assure you, he knows the remarkable ancestry, and well remembers the name, Cre-

ative Industries of Detroit. As a further interesting sign, Minturn has only recently relocated MSX headquarters back to the City of Detroit, this time downtown in a high-rise on Woodward Avenue. And perhaps this is the final coincidence, or a hopeful sign, but the MSX CEO's first name is Fred.

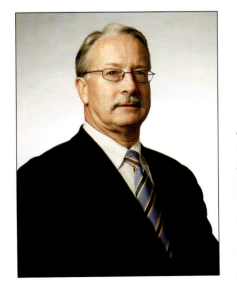

MSX International's CEO Fred Minturn. He originally started with Creative in the 1950s running the accounting division. (Photo Courtesy MSX International and Fred Minturn)

CHAPTER NINETEEN

THE CREATIVE LEGACY

I can tell you how to get to the original site of Creative Industries. It is on East Outer Drive in Detroit, Michigan. Of course, the site, the location, still exists. I've been there only recently. But the business, the buildings, and the people are all gone now. And there is no roadmap that can take you or me back to the way it once was, or back to the way the business or the city of those times worked.

For much of my life, I lived within the finest era of Detroit's automotive glory years on a daily basis. I saw it. I felt it. I breathed it. And I worked it. It says in my baby book that I could identify every car I saw on the streets of Detroit, including every Studebaker back to the early 1940s, and this was before I even started kindergarten. I worked for Ford on the original Mustang. I had a big-block Ford XL convertible. I bought a new GTO convertible and had it Bobcatted. And I bought a new big-block Dodge Challenger convertible. I hung out at iconic drive-in restaurants on North Woodward Avenue, including the Totem Pole, Big Boy, Big Town, and Ted's. My dad and I drove past the Packard plant almost daily on the way to and from commercial property he owned. In those days, gleaming new Packards jammed the storage lot on the corner of Mt. Elliot and Grand Blvd.

And I knew where every car plant was in and around the city, from De Soto to Hudson. I worked on the original Mustangs at Ford Rouge plant. I watched "submarine races" with girlfriends on Belle Isle and on the shoreline in Windsor, Canada. I also watched (this time for real) unlimited Gold Cup power-boat races on the Detroit River. I was there when Bob Hayworth lost his life as he flipped Miss Supertest going into a turn at the MacArthur Belle Isle Bridge. I went to the auto shows and stood in awe as gleaming dream cars with beautiful models spun slowly on turntables. I remember seeing the very first street version Ford GT being photographed and filmed late at night downtown at the modern Ponchartrain Hotel. I rubbed shoulders with car executives and real racecar drivers at a very cool restaurant and disco in the New Center area on Grand Boulevard, just steps from the GM building.

A few blocks away, I remember seeing Rex Terry's amazing Packard Panther often parked dead center in front of the doorway

Taken in 1978, front entrance of Creative Industries headquarters at 3080 East Outer Drive.

to the Brass Rail restaurant on Woodward Avenue near Grand Boulevard. A lot of important auto executives had lunch there.

Creative Industries of Detroit and the company that spawned it, Progressive Welder, were businesses founded and kept in operation by pure genius, passion, and dedication. The talent that operated throughout the company represented some of world's finest hands and brightest minds. Creative was a testament to the resourcefulness and genius that lived in Detroit's manufacturing and automotive industry during its heyday. It was also a big part of how Detroit once put the entire world on wheels. The city was truly a creative town (no pun intended).

Tool and die shops and fabricator businesses were squeezed into every nook and cranny of Detroit and the surrounding towns. People worked in those places and fed their families. Millions of people made their living, one way or the other, from the grand experience that was the American automotive industry in Detroit.

Taken in 1978, front entrance of Creative Industries headquarters at 3080 East Outer Drive. Parallel driveway here and covered entryway were added to original structure.

For many decades people made things there in factories. The smokestacks smoked and the machinery hummed. At night the intoxicating cocktail of fresh paint, new rubber, and welded steel hung heavy in the air, as if it were some kind of industrial perfume. You could also smell the money in the air, but it was more than mere money that drove the town.

Storage yards outside of the plants were stacked high with gleaming new automotive components. Employee parking lots were crammed with cars. At a huge complex like Ford Rouge, you'd better not be late at a shift change or you might end up driving in circles for half an hour, just to find a spot to park for work.

DSR buses and cars were filled with people on their way to and from work. Lunchboxes and thermos jugs were a staple in nearly every Detroit area household. Coffee shops pumped out gallons of the stuff. Donut shops started baking at 2:00 a.m. just to get ready for the day. Hamburger stands near plants were often choked with customers, and more waiting outside to get in.

Designers designed things that the factories made. Salesmen sold the things the factories produced, and people bought those things and used them happily, daily, proudly. And it was all in America, from the Motor City.

It certainly wasn't perfect. Nothing that big and complicated with so many people and so many ethnicities ever could be. But no single city, no country, no business had ever welcomed so many with open arms or showed such massive amounts of creativity. And no single place ever produced so many objects that fascinated and enhanced life throughout the entire world. But that was then and this is now.

Detroit as a city, even as an icon, has morphed from a teeming metropolis on top of a world industry to a struggling shadow of its former self. I also saw this happen in my lifetime. So what the future holds is anyone's guess.

But that era of wonder, at least in the way that I knew it, is gone. Many of the people are gone too. And perhaps worst of all, Creative Industries is gone. Even Creative's original buildings are gone, and there is nothing to take their place. If you never knew about the magic that was once there, you'd probably never know.

In my last conversation with the late and wonderful car designer Alex Tremulis, he praised Creative Industries and said it was one of the most remarkable companies he had ever known.

Not long before he died, Elwood Engle also praised Creative and told me (referring to concept car styles and the wild things Creative made over the years), "You'll never see anything like *that* again. It was one precious time when everything was just right for what happened." Indeed, Engle was right. We'll never see anything like that again.

Gary Hutchings, who had worked for Creative for so many years on so many projects, wrote me numerous times over the years. But the one letter I remember the most started out, "Well, I'm officially retired now, and I'm hating it!" Gary loved working in the car business and retirement was never on his bucket list. And most of all, he loved Creative Industries.

Rex Terry loved the business so much that he stayed on in an advisory role even after he retired. As one employee put it, "Rex just couldn't stay away!" He was a charismatic leader and dedicated to Creative and its employees.

I could go on with quotes, but David Margolis probably gave me some of the best advice and words about Creative Industries when I was in college. At the time, I was studying (unhappily) to become an attorney. One day I told him about an issue I had with a professor regarding client defenses and the attorney's responsibilities. Dave responded, "Well? Is that what you want? You're a car guy! Look at me, I come to work happy every day. Do you really want to spend the rest of your life in a courtroom with a bunch of angry people and an over-stressed judge glaring at you? Or would you rather come to work and play with cars every day?" Dave was right too.

But perhaps the most poignant thing ever said was in a note dated July 18, 2006, from the late Richard Leasia to his former business partner regarding Creative Industries and its people. It read, "Dear Verne and Miriam, Three days ago the attached photos arrived in the mail; no letter, no return address, no anything. On the possibility that these did not come from you I copied them for you both to bring back some great memories. After I looked them over for the fifth time I had an interesting thought; why not you locate Charly Shell and I know where to find Guy Tacconelli; then we can buy back Outer Drive and start all over again."

If only it were that simple, Mr. Leasia. If only it were that simple.

Souvenirs of Creative Industries and subsidiaries. Gold playing cards are from 1956, about the same time as the cigarette lighter on right was issued.

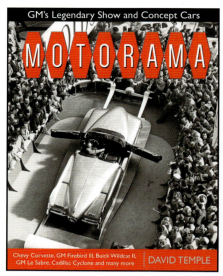
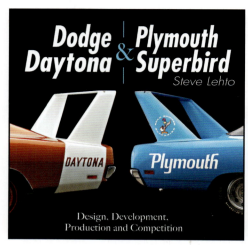
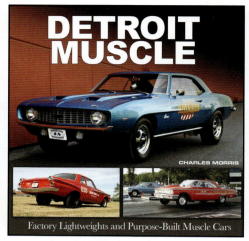
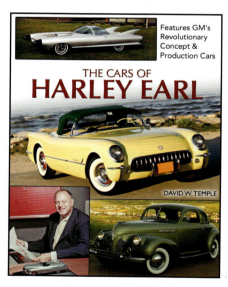